James Parton

Captains of Industry or Men of Business Who Did Something Besides Making Money

A book for young Americans

James Parton

Captains of Industry or Men of Business Who Did Something Besides Making Money
A book for young Americans

ISBN/EAN: 9783744797481

Printed in Europe, USA, Canada, Australia, Japan

Cover: Foto ©Suzi / pixelio.de

More available books at **www.hansebooks.com**

CAPTAINS OF INDUSTRY

SECOND SERIES

A BOOK FOR YOUNG AMERICANS

BY

JAMES PARTON

BOSTON AND NEW YORK
HOUGHTON, MIFFLIN AND COMPANY
The Riverside Press, Cambridge
1893

PREFACE.

THE friendly reception accorded to the volume published in 1884, containing sketches of business men noted for benevolence and public spirit, induces me to offer another of similar purport and tendency. From my youth, I have been powerfully attracted to such men, whom we may properly regard as the natural chiefs of industrial communities, and the rightful successors of the feudal lords of another time. Nothing seems more important than that those who perform labor and those who direct it should be justly related to one another, and so coöperate effectively against the sovereign evil of the world — poverty. This is my solution of the labor problem, and I believe in no other. For most of the persons described in this volume I have a personal affection, and this is the reason why I have included in it one or two individuals who are not exactly described by its title. Such as they are, I commend them to the consideration of readers, whether they are now, or only hope to become, Captains of Industry.

CONTENTS.

	PAGE
CHRISTOPHER LUDWICK, BAKER-GENERAL OF THE REVOLUTIONARY ARMY	1
GOVERNOR EDWARD WINSLOW, THE BUSINESS MAN OF THE PILGRIM FATHERS	9
SIR WILLIAM PHIPS, MARINER	18
DAVID RITTENHOUSE, CLOCKMAKER	27
COUNT RUMFORD, CITY RULER	35
GENERAL SETH POMROY, GUNMAKER	43
CAPTAIN MERIWETHER LEWIS, PRIVATE SECRETARY	51
ELEAZAR WHEELOCK, TEACHER	60
JOEL BARLOW, MERCHANT	67
NATHANIEL BOWDITCH, MARINER	74
MR. GEORGE B. EMERSON, BOSTON SCHOOLMASTER	81
JOSEPH LANCASTER, ENGLISH SCHOOLMASTER	89
ANDREW JACKSON, FARMER	98
GEORGE GUESS, JACK-OF-ALL-TRADES	111
WILLIAM MURDOCK, MACHINIST	119
EZRA CORNELL, MECHANIC	126
JAMES NASMYTH, INVENTOR	141
GABRIEL DANIEL FAHRENHEIT, INSTRUMENT-MAKER	148
JEAN BAPTISTE ANDRÉ GODIN, STOVE MANUFACTURER	155
JEAN LE CLAIRE, HOUSE-PAINTER	170
MARGUERITE BOUCICAUT, STOREKEEPER	177
MICHEL BRÉZIN, CANNON-FOUNDER	185

CONTENTS.

Louis Joliet, Fur-Trader	192
Bartholomew Thimonnier, Tailor	200
George Peabody, Banker	208
Abbott Lawrence, Merchant	216
Amos A. Lawrence, Solid Man of Boston	223
John Metcalf, Roadmaker	230
Thomas Brassey, Contractor	237
Thomas Telford, Engineer	244
Junius Smith, LL. D., Projector	251
Frederic Sauvage, Ship-Builder	259
William Ellis, Insurance Agent	274
Sir Joseph Whitworth, Tool-Maker	281
Charles Knight, Publisher	288
Philip Hone, Auctioneer	295
James Lenox, Book Collector	302
Alvan Clark, Telescope Maker	315
Jean Baptiste Colbert, Cabinet Minister	322
Erckmann and Chatrian, Lawyer and Railway Cashier	330
Sir Francis Crossley, Carpet Manufacturer	337
Elizabeth Fry, Wife and Mother	344
The Earl of Shaftesbury, Public Servant	353
Mrs. Coston, Ships' Signal Manufacturer	360
John Delafield, Merchant	368
Henry Fawcett, Public Man	373
Joseph Hugo, Master Carpenter	380
Baron von Stein, Prime Minister	387

CAPTAINS OF INDUSTRY.

SECOND SERIES.

CHRISTOPHER LUDWICK,

BAKER-GENERAL OF THE REVOLUTIONARY ARMY.

At the outbreak of the Revolutionary War in 1775, there was not in all the thirteen Colonies ammunition enough for one battle on the scale of the European wars. Arms, too, of the kind employed in military service were exceedingly scarce, and what few muskets there were commanded an extravagant price. Such a repairing of old guns, such a search for flints and accoutrements, such a furbishing of rusty swords and bayonets, such an inquiry into the ingredients of gunpowder, and such a hunting after deposits of saltpetre, were never seen before in any age or country.

Philadelphia being then the chief city of North America, and open to the enemy's fleet, was stirred to its depths on the question of defense. Dr. Franklin, old as he was, was out on the Delaware superintending the construction of *chevaux-de-frise* (huge beams sunk endwise in the river), to keep the British fleet from approaching the city; and the other members of the Philosophical Society were experimenting in the art of making powder. Militia were drilling in the public squares. Committees charged with various public duties were constantly in session. All was bustle, activity, excitement and preparation. But the grand difficulty remained. The government of the province had not arms to put into the thousands of willing hands stretched out to receive them; nor had it, at the moment, money in the treasury with which to buy the few that could have been obtained.

In these circumstances Governor Mifflin proposed to a committee of citizens to raise a sum of money by putting their hands into their own pockets, and expend the same in the purchase of arms. It was at once objected that the sum obtainable by private subscription would be a mere drop in the bucket, totally inadequate to the object. Upon this, a plain-looking, sturdy German rose and addressed the meeting in English that was not very well pronounced, but was very much to the point.

"Mr. President," said he, "I am but a poor gingerbread baker, but put my name down for two hundred pounds."

This masterly oration closed the debate. The motion was carried unanimously, and a sum was raised that far exceeded the governor's most sanguine hopes.

Every one in the assembly, and every one in Philadelphia, knew Christopher Ludwick, the baker of Letitia Court, who for many years had supplied the town with gingerbread of unequaled excellence, and had grown rich thereby. After a long period of wandering and adventure, he had settled in Philadelphia twenty years before, and had acquired universal good-will, as well by the sterling worth of his character as by a certain homely wit and wisdom that enlivened his conversation. He was one of the celebrities of the city, and his neighbors styled him the "Governor of Letitia Court."

In 1776, when General Washington, after the loss of New York and the action at White Plains, was in full retreat across New Jersey, Philadelphia was panic-stricken again.

"These are the times that try men's souls," wrote Thomas Paine in that famous tract which General Washington said was equal to a new regiment added to his flying and dissolving army. Among those who took a musket and volunteered to defend the city was the gingerbread baker, Christopher Ludwick, aged fifty-six. On one occasion during that season of alarm, when a number of the volunteers, tired of camp rations, threatened to abandon the service and go home, Christopher Ludwick ran up and dropped upon his knees before them.

"Brother soldiers," he cried, in a tone of passionate entreaty, "listen for a moment to Christopher Ludwick. When we hear the cry of fire in

Philadelphia, on the hill at a distance from us, we fly there with our buckets, to keep it from our houses. So let us keep the great fire of the British army from our town. In a few days you shall have good bread, and enough of it."

The men agreed to remain, and Ludwick soon had a bakery in order that supplied the camp with excellent bread.

General Washington held the enemy in check. In the autumn days of the campaign the Hessians began to desert, and occasionally small parties of them would make their way to an American camp. Eight of these discontented mercenaries were captured by Ludwick's comrades and brought to his commanding officer. A question arose as to where they could be safely confined.

"Let us," said the worthy Christopher, "take them to Philadelphia, and there show them our fine German churches. Let them see how our tradesmen eat good beef, drink out of silver cups every day, and ride out in chairs every afternoon; and then let us send them back to their countrymen, and they will all soon run away, and come and settle in our city, and be as good Whigs as any of us."

This was the beginning of a systematic attempt to lure the Hessians from the English service. Dr. Franklin caused printed papers to be folded inside of packets of tobacco, setting forth, in good German, the charms of America and the happiness of its inhabitants. These were sold and given away to the Hessians, until their officers discovered the trick. Ludwick risked his life in the attempt to increase the disaffection of the Hessian troops. Assuming the character of a deserter, he went to a camp of these soldiers on Staten Island, where he labored among them with such success that, in the course of the war, as opportunity favored, several hundreds deserted, and made their way, as Ludwick had advised, to the counties of Pennsylvania inhabited chiefly by Germans. Dr. Benjamin Rush records that, thirty years after, a large number of these soldiers were still living in Pennsylvania, settled on good farms of their own, with sons and daughters married and established near them.

But the great service rendered by Ludwick to the cause of his adopted country was in supplying her soldiers with good bread. In 1777, Congress gave him a regular commission as "Superintendent of Bakers and Director of Baking in the Army of the United States," at seventy-five dollars a month and two rations a day, with power to appoint his subordinates. When a Committee of Congress waited upon him to present him with this commission (a document preserved to this day in Philadelphia), they expressed the expectation of Congress that for every pound of flour he received he would furnish one pound of good bread. On these terms he would have made an enormous fortune.

"No, gentlemen," said he. "I will not accept your commission on any such terms. Christopher Ludwick does not want to get rich by the war. He has money enough. I will furnish one hundred and thirty-five pounds of bread for every hundredweight of flour you put into my hands."

From that time to the end of the war the soldiers were supplied with an abundance of good bread, except when Congress was unable to supply Christopher Ludwick with good flour. He generally lived near the headquarters of the army, where he often dined at the table of the commander-in-chief. General Washington not only valued his services and relished his bread, but enjoyed his humorous comments on men and things. "My honest friend, Ludwick," the general used to call him. It was a thing understood at headquarters, that old Christopher Ludwick was a privileged character, whose homely satire and pungent sense were to be taken in good part by high and low. From his voyages to the ends of the earth he had brought a rare stock of anecdotes and curious information, which proved highly entertaining to officers wearing out their time in winter-quarters. It was often remarked that wherever Christopher Ludwick was a guest, even in the gloomiest days of the war, there was mirth and good humor.

He was present at the surrender of Lord Cornwallis at Yorktown, and had the pleasure of baking six thousand pounds of good bread for the captured army the same day.

"Let the bread be good, old gentleman," said General Washington, when he gave the order, "and let there be enough of it, if I should come short myself."

After serving to the close of the war, he retired to his farm at Germantown, a few miles from Philadelphia. He found his house plundered of every article of value by the enemy, — plate, furniture, bedding, clothes, all were gone. Like the rest of the army, he had been paid in paper, which had become worthless; so that he was unable for several weeks to procure articles generally considered indispensable. Go in debt he would not. He sold part of his real estate to procure the means of refurnishing his house. But he used to point to a small object hanging in his parlor, and declare that it compensated him for all his losses. It was a certificate, neatly framed, written by the hand of General Washington, to the effect that Christopher Ludwick had been "a true and faithful servant of the public," had "detected impositions, and been the cause of much saving in his department," and "afforded unquestionable proofs of his integrity and worth."

He lived many years in retirement, enjoying universal esteem, and preserving his quaint humor to the last. Soon after the death of General Washington, the old man, then past eighty, was called upon to subscribe for a biography of the general.

"No," said he, "I will not. I am traveling fast

to meet him. I will then hear about it from his own lips."

During the last few years of his life he spent nearly all his time and a large part of his income in doing good, searching out deserving objects, and liberally responding to every proper application. During the prevalence of the yellow fever, in his seventy-seventh year, he volunteered to superintend the baking of the bread for the hospitals, and stood faithfully at his post through all the terrors of the time. His favorite mode of expending money was to send poor children to school. There were fifty persons at his funeral who owed to him the opportunity to acquire the rudiments of knowledge; and he left the greater part of his fortune to found and endow a free school in Philadelphia — the first of the kind established in the city.

He died in 1801, full of years and honors. A vast concourse of people followed his remains to their last resting-place in Germantown; and a memoir of his life was written by Dr. Rush. The free school which he founded was one of the most useful institutions in Philadelphia, until it was superseded by the public-school system.

GOVERNOR EDWARD WINSLOW,

THE BUSINESS MAN OF THE PILGRIM FATHERS.

We are not accustomed to think of the Pilgrim Fathers of New England as men of business; but when we look closely into their early history, we are struck with admiration at the boldness and wisdom of their business operations. If Edward Winslow was the leader and chief manager of their enterprises, he was well seconded by others of the colony. Governor Winslow was not a member of the congregation in England; but while making the tour of the Continent, he visited Leyden, in Holland, where he became acquainted with their pastor, Mr. Robinson, and others of the little band of Puritan exiles. He afterwards removed to Leyden, married a lady of the congregation, and emigrated with them to America. He belonged to a family of wealth and distinction in England, and it often happened in later times, when the Pilgrims were threatened with the hostility of the Government, that his influence with members of Parliament averted the evil. When he emigrated, he brought with him, besides his wife and an adopted child, two men-servants.

In order to understand how well the Pilgrims managed their affairs, it is necessary to know something of that part of the coast of Massachusetts where their lot was cast.

I suppose many people besides myself, after walking about the sandy old town of Plymouth, have thought what a pity it was the Pilgrim Fathers had not sailed a few miles further and discovered the deep, commodious, and beautiful harbor of Boston. Not that Plymouth and the waters about it are not most pleasant and inviting. If Mrs. Hemans had ever seen that coast, she would not have described it as "stern and rock-bound." There is not a rock anywhere about Plymouth Harbor, unless it be a few small boulders scattered at long intervals along the beach. The very rock upon which the Pilgrims are supposed first to have set foot, which is now covered by a granite monument, is a boulder — "an emigrant like themselves" — brought to that shore by floating ice. The harbor, however, is shallow, and becomes shallower every year, and the soil is so sandy that if the Indians had not taught them to plant a good fat fish in every hill of corn, they would have gone hungry longer than they did.

They were not ill-pleased with their new home, and they may well be excused for thinking that Providence had prepared it specially for them. I never saw so curious a harbor. It does not look like the work of nature, but seems as if it had been constructed by an engineer in pursuance of an Act of Congress. The harbor is formed by a natural breakwater — a long, narrow beach, eighty yards wide, and two miles long, running almost parallel with the shore, about half a mile from it. This thin strip of beach, within the memory of living men, was densely covered with trees, the roots of which protected it; but these have been cut down, and the ocean is making inroads in consequence. As you stand upon Forefathers' Rock, when an easterly wind has been blowing, you can hear the waves thundering and roaring on the other side of the beach, like ten thousand furious animals, eager to leap over the barrier and rush ravenous upon the town. The noise is the more impressive from the fact that the ocean is hidden from view by the long line of beach. As I stood there, during the gales of September, I could not but think how often the Pilgrims must have listened to the same sounds, and felt, as they listened, that Providence, ages before, had drawn that line of sandy barrier across the bay on purpose to protect his own.

Nevertheless, it must have been hard to row a mile and a half to the deep soundings where the Mayflower lay at anchor, near the end of this natural breakwater; and the soil of Plymouth is so little productive, that to this day a large portion of it is not cultivated, and furnishes only a crop of firewood every thirty years. The township is dotted all over with large ponds. When there are a great many islands in a lake, or ponds in a county, people usually say that there is one for every day of the year. Accordingly, when the reader gives himself the great pleasure of visiting the cradle of New England, he may expect to be informed that there are three hundred and sixty-five ponds in Plymouth; and he will be safe in believing one third of the story. Under the sand in all this region, there is a stratum of clay, which prevents the water from sinking into the earth, and in this way these numberless ponds are formed. On the highest ground of Plymouth, when the atmosphere is very clear, the entire outline of Cape Cod — a wave of sand curving sixty miles out into the sea — can be discerned; and the same movement of the waters which produced Cape Cod covered the original clay of Plymouth with sand.

There they were, then, in the spring of 1621, a little colony of fifty persons; some of them in debt for their passage, and the colony owing a considerable sum to the proprietors of the soil in London; for even this sand, thinly covered with soil and grass, was not their own. Let us see how Edward Winslow led them to swift and great prosperity.

Their sole capital to begin with, in the spring of 1621, besides their implements of husbandry, was a few bushels of Indian corn, obtained from an Indian depository on Cape Cod, several months before. This had been carefully saved to plant in the spring; but it would have availed them little if they had not from the first adopted the policy of strict honesty toward the Indians. Winslow and others had taken this corn with the intention of paying for it as soon as they should discover the owner, and this intention they carried out. Early in the spring they were visited by the Indian chiefs Samoset, Squanto, and Massasoit, to whom they gave liberal gifts; and they made with Massasoit, the principal chief of the country, a treaty of friendship, which was so faithfully kept on the part of the Pilgrims that they enjoyed unbroken peace with the Indians for twenty-four years. During all that period there was a continual interchange of good offices between the two races. If the Indians taught the white men to put a fish in every hill of corn, the whites supplied the Indians with hoes, which enabled them to raise twice as much corn as they had formerly done.

When the corn was planted and growing well, Edward Winslow and one of his friends, guided by a friendly Indian, made a journey, forty miles into the wilderness, to pay a visit to Massasoit, with a view to confirm him in his peaceful intentions. The chief received them well, and fed them upon corn bread and broiled shad roes — delicious fare in the woods to hungry men, if there had only been enough of it. The chief's larder, however, was but meagrely furnished. Winslow gave him a horseman's coat of red cloth and a suit of clothes, which the chief put on with great exultation, especially the flaming red coat.

When the harvest came in the fall they found that, by carefully attending to the directions of the Indians, they had raised corn enough to afford to each person through the winter a peck of meal a week. By the third harvest they began to have corn to spare; so that the more industrious sold of their abundance to the newcomers, to passing fishermen, and to the Indians.

There being few human inhabitants in New England then, the number of wild animals was marvelous. Through the firm friendship of the colonists with the Indians, they were able to procure wonderful supplies of beaver skins for exportation to England. They would send in one ship as much as three thousand pounds weight of beaver skins, the best of which was worth in England twenty shillings a pound. As many as three hundred otter skins were sometimes sent in a single vessel. This trade, conducted chiefly by Winslow, produced so large a revenue that when the colony was twenty-two years old it had paid its debts, bought its independence of the London Company, brought over a considerable number of poorer brethren from Holland, and possessed sufficient capital to carry on a vigorous commerce with the Dutch in New York, with friends at Boston, and with the fishing fleet off the coasts of Maine and Newfoundland. They went so far as to establish storehouses on the coast of Maine, well supplied with goods for trade with the fishermen and the French. One of these storehouses was captured by a party of Frenchmen, and the Plymouth plantation was strong enough to send a three hundred ton vessel to retake it. Thus began the contest between New England and Canada, which ended only with the conquest of Canada, a hundred and fifty years after.

The extensive commerce of the Plymouth people with the mother country compelled Governor Winslow to make frequent voyages thither. On his return from his first voyage, in 1624, he brought with him three heifers and a bull, the first cattle ever imported into New England. In three years, by the natural increase of these, and by fresh importations, there were cattle enough to supply the whole colony with a little milk and butter. They then divided themselves into twelve families, or companies of thirteen persons each, and to each company was assigned two goats, a milch cow, and two or three cattle not immediately productive, such as heifers, steers, and bulls. In this way everybody bore part of the burden, and enjoyed part of the benefit. Shares in the family herd or in single animals were bought and sold. Thus, for example, as I read in the records at Plymouth, under date of January 20, 1627 : —

" Edward Winslow hath sold unto Captain Myles Standish his six shares in the red cow, for and in consideration of five pounds ten shillings, to be paid in corn at the rate of six shillings per bushel."

Another entry begins thus: —

"Abraham Peirce hath sold unto Captain Myles Standish two shares in the red cow, for and in consideration of two ewe lambs, the one to be delivered at the time of weaning this present year, and the other at the same time anno 1628."

In this beautifully sensible and just manner the Pilgrim Fathers managed all their affairs, Edward Winslow being evidently the leading business man of the colony, which he served also for many years as governor. During one of his visits to England in 1635, he, as representing a Puritan colony, fell under the displeasure of the Archbishop of Canterbury. The archbishop arraigned him on the charge of preaching without ordination or license. He replied, very modestly, that in the infancy of the colony, when there was no minister in Plymouth, he did "exercise his gift to help the edification of his brethren." The archbishop also accused him of having performed the ceremony of marriage. He did not deny that in his character as magistrate he had married some couples, and maintained before the archbishop that marriage was a civil covenant, and added that he found no warrant in the Bible for the performance of the marriage ceremony by a clergyman.

"Besides," said he, "we were necessitated so to do, having for a long time together at first no minister. Besides, it is no new thing, for I was so married myself in Holland by the magistrates in their Stadt Haus."

This defense did not avail. He was committed to the Fleet prison, and remained in confinement for four months, to the great damage of the plantation, which had to pay his expenses and to suffer the loss of his services. At a later date, when the Puritans were in power in England, the Protector Cromwell gave him an honorable charge as one of three commissioners to estimate the value of some English ships destroyed by Danish forces in the West Indies. On the voyage, near Jamaica, he was taken sick and died, in the sixty-first year of his age. He was the first, and not the least able, of the many hundreds of bold, originating men of business that New England has nurtured or produced.

SIR WILLIAM PHIPS,

MARINER.

A VALIANT son of colonial New England was William Phips, born in 1650, at a little village on the banks of the Kennebec, in the province of Maine. He was one of the youngest in a family of twenty-six children, of whom twenty-one were sons, all the offspring of James Phips, once a gun-smith of English Bristol, and afterward a settler in the remote Maine wilderness. Until he was eighteen years of age he kept his widowed mother's sheep; and then, still unable to read and write, apprenticed himself to a ship-carpenter for four years. When he had served his time he removed to Boston, where, at twenty-two, he learned to read and write; and after following his trade for a year, married a widow of respectable family.

Even at that early day shipbuilding was carried on on the banks of the Kennebec, where then, as now, excellent ship timber was easily obtained. Soon after his marriage he took a contract from some Boston merchants to build them a ship, and he went home to Maine to execute it. His ship was launched and nearly finished, and he had prepared for her a cargo of timber, when the Indians broke upon the settlement, and all the people who escaped could find no refuge but the ship that lay in the harbor nearly ready for sea. Leaving his load of timber behind, he carried away to Boston his mother, brothers, and neighbors, and landed them all safe on the Long Wharf. This onslaught of the Indians robbed the young shipbuilder of all the profit which he had expected from his first undertaking, and he looked about him for a new venture.

In that age Spanish galleons were still going home from Hayti, Mexico, and Peru, laden deep with gold, silver, and precious things; not unfrequently striking upon rocks in the imperfectly known seas of the tropics, and bearing down to the bottom of the ocean tons of treasure. A famous wreck of this kind had taken place about fifty years before, in waters shallow enough to admit of the recovery of the treasure by Indian divers. William Phips, hearing of this, made a commercial voyage to those seas, during which he questioned the natives closely respecting the place where this richly freighted galleon had sunk. He felt a conviction that he was the man destined to discover the prize, and bent all his energies henceforth to the accomplishment of the object. Perceiving that his means were inadequate, he made the best of his way back to Boston, where he disposed of his cargo to some advantage, and sailed for England.

Laying his design before the British Admiralty, he convinced them at length of the feasibility of his scheme, and they assigned him a frigate of eighteen guns and a crew of ninety-five men, with which to prosecute the search. He had a terrible voyage of it. After many a week of weary sailing and searching under the burning sun of the tropics, his men sickened of the enterprise, and came aft one day, with drawn swords in their hands, demanding that he should join them and sail away upon a piratical cruise to the South Seas. Weaponless as he was, Captain Phips rushed into the midst of the mutineers, knocked down half a dozen of them with his tremendous fist, and quelled the mutiny on the instant.

Some time after, when the frigate lay careened near an uninhabited island, and the men were ashore, they entered into a conspiracy, more serious and better considered, to leave the captain and his friends on the island, take the ship, and go in quest of Spanish treasure vessels. One of their number betrayed them. The captain quietly made arrangements so efficient that, when they came to his tent to execute their purpose, they found the ship's great guns bearing upon them and the captain's friends ready to discharge them.

"We are betrayed!" they cried.

"Stand off, ye wretches, at your peril!" shouted the captain.

They took in the situation at a glance, and falling upon their knees, begged for mercy. Helpless and disarmed he received them on board ship, but only to convey them to Jamaica, where he turned them adrift. Here an old Spaniard gave him information of the wreck so clear and exact that he felt sure of getting some of the treasure. But alas! he had then scarcely men enough to sail his frigate, and he was obliged to return to England.

He was a man of inexhaustible patience, and so entirely certain was he of being able to find the treasure that he succeeded in convincing also a wealthy nobleman, the Duke of Albemarle. The duke and a few of his friends provided him with another ship, and Captain Phips was soon near the spot, off the coast of Hispaniola, which the old Spaniard had designated. Long he searched, peering into the green depths of the ocean from the side of his boat, sending out also his trusty men in every direction. The search was long fruitless. As a boat was on its way back to the ship, one afternoon, the crew fatigued and discouraged, one of them looking over the boat's side perceived, growing out of a rock, a peculiar kind of seaweed, called then the sea feather, and somewhat esteemed as a curiosity. He told one of the Indians to dive and bring it up, so that they might have *something* to carry with them back to the ship. When the diver emerged dripping from the deep with the feather in his hand, he began, as soon as he recovered his breath, to say that he had seen upon the bottom of the ocean a number of great guns scattered about.

Startled at this, they ordered other divers to descend, who made the same report, and one of them brought up what was then called a *sow* of silver, a lump of the precious metal worth as much as a thousand dollars. Carefully marking the place with a buoy, they hurried on board to tell the captain. But wishing to have a little sport at his expense, they pretended at first that they had found nothing, and spoke as discouragingly as they could. While they were talking they slyly laid the silver sow upon the floor of the cabin at the captain's side, and just as he was saying that he meant to persevere in the search until Providence guided him to the spot, he cast his eyes upon the rough and tarnished object. Recognizing what it was by its shape, he cried out, as if in agony : —

" Why, what is this ? Whence comes this ? "

The sailors told him where and how they had got it.

"Then," said he, "thanks be to God, we are made ! "

All hands went to work with such energy as we can imagine, and before many suns had set they had brought up thirty-two tons of solid silver, and as Cotton Mather records, " whole bushels of rusty pieces of eight." Some gold also, and pearls, and jewels were found, and they continued fishing in the sea until they had brought up treasure to the value of three hundred thousand pounds sterling. On the voyage home it required all the captain's tact and courage to keep the crew from rising upon him and seizing the ship. On arriving in London he delivered up the whole mass of treasure to the Duke of Albemarle and his friends, receiving back only his stipulated share, which amounted to sixteen thousand pounds. The duke was so much pleased with his honorable conduct that he had a golden cup made worth a thousand pounds, and presented it to Captain Phips' New England wife. James the Second, hearing the oft-told tale of his gallantry and honesty, made a knight of him; so that thenceforth he was styled Sir William Phips.

And this was but the beginning of his fortune. The king appointed him high sheriff of New England, and on his way home he made a second visit to the wreck, where he fished up a few more tons of silver. It was in 1688, when he was thirty-eight years old, that he returned to Boston, after five years' absence, and built for his wife a stately brick mansion. New England was in sore trouble then from the tyranny of James the Second, and Sir William Phips went again to England to "lobby," as we should say, for the restoration of the lost liberties of his country. In London the king offered him the governorship of New England. He declined it, because he thought that a government without an assembly of the people's own choosing was "treason in the very essence of it." After the flight of the king, he returned to Boston a private gentleman.

Then it was that the vigorous preaching of Mather touched his conscience and alarmed him for his spiritual state. The minister, I think, must have had Sir William Phips in his mind when he delivered the following passage of his sermon: —

" To make a public and an open profession of repentance," said he, " is a thing not misbecoming the greatest man alive. . . . A famous knight going with other Christians to be crowned with martyrdom, observed that his fellow-sufferers were in chains, from which the sacrificers had, because of his quality, excused him ; whereupon he demanded that he might wear the chains as well as they. 'For,' said he, ' I would be a Knight of that Order too.' There is among ourselves a repenting people of God. . . . But if any man count himself grown too big to be a Knight of that Order, the Lord Jesus Christ himself will one day be ashamed of that man."

Sir William heard, and was convinced. He joined the "Order," to which the preacher referred ; which led, ere long, to his being appointed through the influence of the Mathers, Governor-General of the province. He led a fleet and army against Nova Scotia, and made a conquest of it. In the same year he commanded the great expedition of thirty-two ships and two thousand men, prepared for the capture of Quebec. Adverse winds and other unfavorable circumstances caused the failure of this attempt, and he returned to Boston with that loss of prestige which invariably follows the most heroic endeavor, if it is not successful. It must be owned that he was not so well fitted to govern a province as to command a ship. He seems to have been as credulous as Cotton Mather himself with regard to witchcraft. He put an end, however, to the judicial murder of the supposed witches, on the ground that the detection of a witch was beyond the skill of man, and that it was better that innocent people should be bewitched than hanged.

If he was not equal to the difficulties of his high station, he appears to have been always an honest, worthy gentleman. After his return wealthy from the wreck of the Spanish ship, a knight and high sheriff, he gave a great feast to the ship-carpenters of Boston, in memory of the time when he had labored with them; and he used often to say to members of his council, when perplexed with public business: —

"Gentlemen, were it not that I do service for the public, I should be much easier in returning to my broad-axe again."

Sailing by the mouth of the Kennebec once, in command of an expedition against the French, he said to those about him on the quarter-deck: —

"Young men, it was upon that hill that I kept sheep a few years ago; and since you see that Almighty God has brought me to something, do you learn to fear God and be honest, and mind your business, and follow no bad courses, and you don't know what you may come to."

His enemies in Boston having complained of his conduct to the king, he was summoned to England to answer their charges. While in London, he was seized with a fever, of which, to the great surprise of all who knew the vigor of his constitution, he died, aged forty years.

DAVID RITTENHOUSE,

CLOCKMAKER.

Some readers may recollect that, when the Declaration of Independence was first read to the people near the State House in Philadelphia, the person who read it — a captain of a vessel, blessed with a stentorian voice — stood upon a platform which had been recently erected for the purpose of observing the transit of Mercury across the sun. I used to wonder in my youth what this meant; and it really is remarkable that in a colony like Pennsylvania, devoted of necessity to industrial pursuits, there should have been sufficient interest in science, and sufficient knowledge of science, for such minute observation of the heavenly bodies. This was chiefly owing to the fact that Pennsylvania had produced one mathematical and mechanical genius, David Rittenhouse.

His father was a farmer, who lived about twenty miles from Philadelphia, the descendant of a worthy German family, that first began the manufacture of paper in Pennsylvania. The father of David Rittenhouse had himself been a paper-maker, but had retired from that business to a farm, about the time of the birth of this son. What trifling circumstances give a bent to the mind of a susceptible boy! When David Rittenhouse was about ten years of age, he lost an uncle by death, who was serving an apprenticeship to the trade of carpenter. After the death of this youth, his chest of tools and other effects was brought to the farmhouse. It proved to contain a number of school-books, treating of arithmetic, geometry, and other branches, besides a number of manuscripts containing calculations and other evidences of the uncle's intelligence and research. It was the contents of this carpenter's chest which awoke and nourished the genius of David Rittenhouse. To the last of his life, he always spoke of this occurrence as a miser might speak of the early acquisition of a vast treasure; for while the books gave him the theory of mathematics and mechanics, the tools enabled him, while still little more than a child, to put theory into practice. He made ingenious waterwheels for his mother's churn, and many similar contrivances; spending all his leisure time in study. His brother used to relate that, when he would go to the field to call him to dinner, he would frequently find that not only the fences at the heads of many of the furrows, but also his plow and its handles, were covered with figures in chalk of geometry and arithmetical calculations.

At the present time we look upon a clock as rather a simple piece of mechanism. But in those old times a clock was not only a thing of great expense and huge dimensions, but it was considered almost the *ne plus ultra* of human ingenuity. Even in the great cities of the world, like Paris and London, the makers of watches and clocks ranked much above other mechanics, and occasionally received notice from nobles and kings. How little people then could have supposed that, within a hundred years, half a dozen men, with the assistance of machinery, would make the works of a thousand brass clocks in ten hours! When David Rittenhouse was seventeen years old, he astonished his neighborhood by making a clock out of wood. This event decided his career; for, previously, his father had lamented his devotion to study and mechanics, fearing that such tastes would interfere with his future prosperity. But the success of the clock seems to have reconciled him to his son's propensities. He gave him some money, and sent him to Philadelphia to buy a set of clockmaker's tools.

At the roadside on his father's farm, the lad, eighteen years of age, built with his own hands a small workshop, and regularly set up in the business of a clockmaker; which remained his chief occupation for many years. Unfortunately, much as he came to know of the heavenly bodies, he knew very little of those laws of nature which governed the body of David Rittenhouse. When his clockmaking was done for the day, he took up his books, and fell into the bad habit of studying far into the night. Astronomy was his favorite subject. While he was still a young man, he made himself master of the demonstrations in Newton's "Principia." Nothing could exceed his veneration for Newton, or the admiration he felt for his works. But no matter how exalted may be the object of our studies, the laws of nature are inexorable, and a sin against our bodies is never forgiven! During these ten years of incessant night study, Rittenhouse so injured his constitution that he never enjoyed comfortable health again as long as he lived.

Another accident — and this one more romantic than a carpenter's tool-chest — assisted his culture. A young clergyman of the Church of England, named Thomas Barton, two years older than David Rittenhouse, set up a school in the neighborhood, and fell in love with David's sister, whom he afterward married. The young schoolmaster, besides being himself an educated person, possessed a considerable number of books — then a very rare and costly commodity in a country place. The daily companionship of this young gentleman, and access to his books, contributed very much toward rendering Rittenhouse the man he afterward became. He was very far from thinking that his devotion to knowledge entitled him to any particular honor. He loved knowledge for its own sake, and he rather reproached himself for indulging so much in what he regarded as the greatest luxury of life. We find him writing thus at the beginning of the old French War: —

"I have not health for a soldier, and, as I have no expectation of serving my country in that way, I am spending my time in the old, trifling manner, and am so taken with Optics that I do not know whether, if the enemy should invade this part of the country, as Archimedes was slain while making geometrical figures on the sand, so I should die making a telescope."

Meanwhile his clockmaking business throve. He took a few apprentices, some of whom advanced in due time to be journeymen. He became a married man, and a happy father of children. Being now in circumstances of some ease, he projected the ORRERY, which was so famous in its day; although, in these modern times, we do not rank it much above an ingenious toy, useful to convey the rudiments of astronomy to children. It is difficult for us to realize the admiration, and, I may almost say, the *awe*, which the contemplation of this apparatus inspired a hundred years ago. When he had finished it, two colleges contended for the privilege of buying it — Princeton, in New Jersey, and the college of Philadelphia. Princeton won the prize; which so wounded the pride and feelings of the Philadelphians that, in order to pacify them, Rittenhouse said he would make a better one for them. But no; the honor of Philadelphia demanded that so sublime an invention should not be consigned to "a village," but should be exhibited first in the metropolis of the province that produced it. Rittenhouse contrived to accommodate this difficulty also. He kept the first orrery in his shop to serve as a pattern; and then, hurrying the second to completion, he was able to deliver both about the same time.

Both are still preserved in the institutions for which they were made. When one was exhibited in Philadelphia in 1771, the Assembly voted Mr. Rittenhouse a present of three hundred pounds, and requested him to make another for the use of the public, for an additional sum of four hundred pounds. When this was finished, he lectured upon it in a public hall of Philadelphia, to admiring crowds, day after day.

Meanwhile his business greatly increased. Several other colonies wanted orreries. Mr. Jefferson thought it a great triumph when he had secured from the philosopher only a *promise* to make one for Virginia. Many other pieces of fine mechanism, such as musical clocks (one of which was sold for six hundred and forty dollars), and fine mathematical instruments, were produced in his shop. In 1770 he removed to Philadelphia, where he continued to carry on a growing business until the War of the Revolution interrupted scientific pursuits. He was now gradually drawn into public life, his last scientific work being the observation of the transit of Mercury from the platform in Independence Square. During the whole war he was continually in the employment either of his native State or of Congress.

When the British evacuated Philadelphia, in 1778, one of the first questions asked by educated men all over the country was: "Is the orrery safe?" Yes, it was. Sir William Howe had caused the apartment containing it to be locked, and the key placed in charge of the provost of the college. Jefferson was disposed to censure the Pennsylvanians for permitting so rare a man as Rittenhouse to be employed in public office.

"Nobody," wrote Jefferson to him, in 1778, "can conceive that Nature ever intended to throw away a Newton upon the occupations of a crown. It would have been a prodigality for which even the conduct of Providence might have been arraigned, had he been by birth annexed to what was so far below him. Coöperating with Nature in her ordinary economy, we should dispose of and employ the geniuses of men according to their several orders and degrees. I doubt not there are in your country many persons equal to the task of conducting government; but you should consider that the world has but one Rittenhouse, and that it never had one before. The amazing mechanical representation of the solar system which you conceived and executed has never been surpassed by any but the work of which it is a copy."

After the war, he remained a public man. For many years he retained the office of Treasurer of Pennsylvania; and when General Washington came to the presidency, Mr. Jefferson, Secretary of State, procured his appointment as Director of the Mint, and prevailed upon him, after much entreaty, to accept it. He held this appointment for three years; after which, being advanced in age, he was glad enough to resign the burden to younger men. He was so scrupulously honest that, in several instances, Doctor Rush reports, he paid for work done at the Mint out of his salary, because he thought the people, ignorant of such things, would think the expenditure extravagant.

He died in 1797, aged sixty-five. He was succeeded in the presidency of the Philosophical Society by Mr. Jefferson, who said truly of his predecessor: "Genius, science, modesty, purity of morals, simplicity of manners, marked him as one of Nature's best samples of the perfection she can cover under the human form. Surely no society till ours, within the same compass of time, ever had to deplore the loss of two such members as FRANKLIN and RITTENHOUSE."

COUNT RUMFORD,

CITY RULER.

—•—

THE plain farmhouse is still standing at North Woburn, Massachusetts, in which the individual was born who is known as "Count Rumford." And Count Rumford really *was* a Count. In his native land he was called plain Benjamin Thompson; and of all the sons of Yankee-land who have roamed the earth, and pushed their way to its high places, this Benjamin Thompson of North Woburn had the strangest career.

First, he was a farmer's son, born in 1753, of a family perfectly respectable, but no richer than Yankee farmers usually were in the last century. Hard work, the year round, kept them out of debt — no more. This boy, from childhood, showed a singular aptitude for everything except the homely labors to which he was born. At fourteen he could calculate an eclipse, play the violin, repair a clock, engrave a name upon the handle of a knife, do all the hard sums in the arithmetic, make an electrical machine, churn by water power, and cut wonders with a penknife. A clergyman of the neighborhood, struck with his talent, gave him instruction in mathematics and astronomy; an opportunity which the boy improved to the utmost. He was a marvel of a boy in everything, except hoeing corn and doing chores.

Apprenticed to a storekeeper in Salem, he did everything better than serve the store. He drew capital caricature likenesses; he made fireworks; he experimented in chemistry; he collected plants; he observed closely the winds, the temperature, the weather; he reflected upon the mysteries of the universe, and mused respecting the origin of life. All this would have been admirable in a young gentleman of fortune, but it did not quite accord with the avocations of a storekeeper's apprentice.

At sixteen he determined to be a doctor, and to pay his way, while a student, by teaching school. He grew to be a remarkably handsome youth, tall, amply proportioned, graceful, with dark auburn hair, and blue eyes of the becoming shade — a really splendid young man, of manners most agreeable, and possessed of many unusual accomplishments. At nineteen, while teaching school at Concord, New Hampshire, a rich young widow fell in love with him. He married her. He was a made man. He lived in a fine, spacious mansion, had leisure to pursue his studies and exercise his many talents; became, in due time, a father; seemed settled for life as country gentleman and philosopher.

But by this time the storm of the Revolution was

impending, and Benjamin Thompson was constitutionally a Tory. He had great talent, and a truly benevolent heart, but a narrow, bigoted understanding, without faith in the people, a fanatical lover of order, rank, and subordination. He did not obtrude his sentiments, it is said; but at such a time no honest man can conceal his opinions, because mere silence betrays the secret of the soul. He became so obnoxious to his townsmen that his house was mobbed and his life threatened. He fled, sought refuge in Boston, and never again saw his home, his wife, or his native place.

With his winning manners, his commanding presence, his great knowledge, his indefatigable activity, his sincere zeal, he made himself so useful and agreeable to the British officers that when they were compelled to evacuate Boston, they sent him to England, to soften the news to the ministry, and give information respecting the state of things in America. No man could have been more welcome; for the ministry, stunned and confounded by this last disaster, wanted nothing so much as *information* respecting America. They were beginning to see how their tools and flatterers in America had deceived them, and they demanded the truth.

Information in great abundance Benjamin Thompson could give them, but not the truth. He did not know the truth. Such knowledge as he had, however, he imparted to them, and showed such ability that he was appointed to an honorable and lucrative office, which brought him into confidential relations with a minister. After two years' service, during which he gained much money, the minister was obliged to resign; but before doing so, he provided for his American protégé by getting him a commission in the regular army of lieutenant-colonel.

But there was no regiment for him in England. The understanding was that he was to go to America and raise a regiment there, of people of his own kind — disloyal Americans. He went. He raised the regiment, and led it in person against his countrymen who were faithful to their principles and to their rightful leaders. In one engagement, he met a portion of General Marion's command, and claimed to have killed several, taken sixteen, and put the rest to flight. He served in New York for a while, and commanded his regiment to the end of the war.

Returning to England, he was, as we should say, "mustered out." But he retained his title, his half-pay, and the considerable fortune made during his tenure of office. He made no attempt to induce his wife and daughter to join him; but set out, with an equipage of three horses and two servants, to make the grand tour of Europe. If he had gone to the bottom of the Channel on his voyage to the Continent, the world would never have heard of him; for all of his best work remained to be done.

He stopped at Strasburg on his tour. He appeared on the parade ground, on the day of a grand review, mounted upon a superb English horse, and dressed in his uniform. The commander of the garrison of Strasburg was Prince Maximilian, who, though then serving in the French army, was heir-apparent to the electoral throne of Bavaria. The prince rode up to this splendid English officer, talked with him, liked him, invited him to dinner; and in a few days became so attached to him that he offered him a high post in the Bavarian service, one that would give him a controlling influence. George III. consenting, and adding to his consent the honor of knighthood, he took up his abode in Munich, the capital of Bavaria, where he soon wielded all the power of a sovereign. The Elector created him Count Rumford, the title by which he has ever since been known.

Imagine a truly able and benevolent man suddenly placed in the New York City Hall armed with absolute power, and provided with enough millions a year to spend upon putting the city in order! What bridges he would build! What underground railroads he would excavate! What sinecures he would abolish! What tenement houses he would level with the ground they pollute! What wharves he would construct! How he would purify the islands! How he would reform the schools! How he would purge the public offices!

Benjamin Thompson, Count Rumford, did for Bavaria what such a mayor could do for New York. The country swarmed with beggars; he set them at work. There were too many priests; he reduced both their numbers and their power. An ugly fever-breeding swamp near Munich he converted into one of the most beautiful parks in Germany. He founded schools, established hospitals, invented kitchens, ovens, and laundries. He arranged an efficient system of draining and cleaning cities. He established national foundries and factories. For twenty years he labored, until Bavaria, from being one of the worst governed countries in Europe, became one of the best; and, what was strange, the people appreciated his services. To this day a handsome monument, surmounted by a statue of Count Rumford, adorns one of the public places of Munich.

The death of his great friend and patron, the Elector, set him free from these arduous toils, and he spent some years in England. Full of zeal for science, he founded in London the Royal Institution, an association of men interested in science, and willing to aid in promoting it. This was the institution that called from obscurity and set at work Sir Humphry Davy; and afterward enabled the great Faraday to spend his life in discovering scientific truth. It still exists and flourishes, and is doing a great work in the advancement and spread of scientific knowledge. Next to the Royal

Society which encouraged Newton, perhaps the Royal Institution founded by our Yankee count, has been the most useful society of modern times.

As he advanced in years, and saw the country he had abandoned rising in power and importance, his heart appears to have yearned toward his native soil. He gave five thousand dollars to the American Academy of Arts and Sciences. In making his will, he arranged his estate so that, after the death of his daughter, nearly the whole of his property should fall to Harvard College, which it has since done. He bequeathed to the United States, for the use of the Military Academy at West Point, all his books relating to military subjects, and all his maps and military designs. The Rumford Professorship of Science of Harvard is sustained by the property he left, as the gift of five thousand dollars to the Academy has increased to thirty thousand.

This singular man died at Paris in 1814, aged sixty-one years. He is buried at Paris, where a handsome monument covers his remains. His daughter, who joined him in Europe after her mother's death, but returned to New England again before his death, survived him many years and inherited his title. She was called Countess of Rumford, instead of Miss Thompson. One of his sons fell in the Crimean war, an officer in the French army, and a son of that son was living in Paris in 1870.

The American Academy of Sciences has published a splendid edition of his works in four volumes, and his life has been amply related by a distinguished member of the Academy, Rev. George E. Ellis, of Boston. His life was so crowded with events that I have only been able to give the merest outline, and have been obliged to omit mentioning many things of much interest.

GENERAL SETH POMROY,

GUNMAKER.

Seth Pomroy was the gunmaker of Northampton, in Massachusetts, from 1727 to the Revolutionary War. The gunsmith's trade was an exceedingly important one in the early days, and Seth Pomroy was renowned for his skill in it throughout New England, until his repute as a gunmaker was eclipsed by his fame as a gun user.

He came of age and was out of his time in 1727, the very year in which Jonathan Edwards was settled as minister over the church in Northampton. Seth Pomroy, descended from a line of deacons, had no difficulty in believing the terrific doctrines preached by this famous clergyman. One consequence was that, when war broke out between France and England, he felt perfectly sure that his province of Massachusetts, in waging war against the innocent and harmless Catholics of Canada, was waging war against the very powers of darkness. A braver man never carried a sword, nor a more disinterested one. Being a gunsmith, it was but natural that he should early learn to use a gun in military service. In 1745, when he was thirty-nine years old, he had got past carrying a gun, for he was a captain in the provincial army.

That was the memorable year when Governor Shirley, of Massachusetts, conceived the audacious scheme of sending an expedition to capture Louisburg on the island of Cape Breton, reputed to be the strongest fortress in North America. But the governor had discovered that the place was but carelessly guarded, and not near as strong as it was supposed to be. He proposed his plan to the legislature in secret session, and carried it only by a majority of one. But the people took it up with enthusiasm, and the solid men of Boston gave to it money and influence. It was, as a writer of the day remarked : —

"A marvelous thing to see so many likely men, and the most of them owners of lands and houses, and many religious, in all our towns readily listing even as private soldiers, with the small wages of twenty-five shillings a month, to leave their gainful farms and trades, as well as parents, wives, and children ; all as free volunteers in this hazardous enterprise."

Captain Seth Pomroy's company marched from Northampton to join the army, with their guns, doubtless, in excellent condition ; and away they sailed from Boston in a great fleet, March 24. 1745, the whole population gathered upon the shore to cheer their departure. The orders were for the fleet of a hundred vessels to enter the bay together at a given hour, land troops before daylight, and rush headlong upon the fortress.

Four weeks after leaving Boston the fleet entered the bay as directed, and saw the great fortress looming up in the dim light of the morning, surrounded by a ditch eighty feet wide, and defended with one hundred and one cannon, seventy-six swivels, and six mortars; the garrison more than sixteen hundred men. Other strong works defended the harbor. No sooner did the men of New England come within easy reach of the shore, and descry a party of French on the landing-place, than they lowered their boats, and rowed in all haste to attack them. The French were put to flight, and next day they abandoned one of the outlying batteries, spiked its guns, and sought refuge in the city.

Then to Major Seth Pomroy, gunmaker of Northampton, was assigned the duty of drilling out the touch-holes of the French cannon, aided by twenty blacksmiths from the ranks; and so from this battery the fire of the main fortress was promptly returned. The place being bravely defended, the siege was prolonged far beyond expectation. In the course of it Major Pomroy wrote a letter home to his wife, which has done more than anything else to rescue his name from oblivion. It fell into the possession of Mr. George Bancroft when he was living in Northampton fifty years ago. He gave a copy of it to Edward Everett, who inserted it as a note to one of his patriotic orations, and so passed it on to posterity. Major Pomroy related the events of the first few days of the siege, not forgetting to mention that the French "had stopt up ye Tutch hols of ye cannon," and that "General Peppril gave me ye charge and oversight of above twenty smiths in boaring of them out." He tells her, too, that "cannon boals & Boums hundred of them were fired at us from ye city and ye Island Fort." I add a few lines from this interesting epistle.

"My dear wife I expect to be longer gon from home then I did when I left it: but I desire not to think of returning Till Louisbourg is taken: & I hope God will inable you to submit quietly to his will whatever it may be: & inable you with courage & good conduct to go through ye grate business yt is now upon your hands & not think your time ill spent in teaching and governing your family according to ye word of God."

After sending messages of affection to various members of his family, he concludes his letter, thus: —

"My Dear wife If it be the will of God I hope to see your pleasant face again; But if God in his Holy and Sovereign Providence has ordered it others wise, I hope to have a glorious meeting with you in ye Kingdom of heaven where there is no wars nor Fatiguing marches, no roaring cannon nor cracking Boum shells, nor long campains; But an eternity to spend in Perfect harmony and undisturbed peace. This is ye hartty Desire & Prayer of him yt is your loving Husband

"SETH POMROY."

To this letter his wife made a reply worthy of it: —

"Suffer," she wrote, "no anxious thought to rest in your mind about me. The whole town is much engaged with concern for the expedition, how Providence will order the affair, for which religious meetings every week are maintained. I leave you in the hand of God."

The siege lasted more than ten weeks; but on the 17th of June the fortress and the city were surrendered, and Major Pomroy had the pleasure of hearing a New England minister preach in the French chapel.

The news reached Boston July 2, late at night. At the dawn of day, the soldiers of the garrison fired three volleys of musketry, which, as we are told, caused all the people to get up out of their beds with joy and thanksgiving, and to spend the whole day in rejoicing. The troops and the fleet on their return had an overwhelming reception; soon after which Seth Pomroy saw once more the pleasant face of his wife.

Ten years passed. Braddock was defeated, and dismay filled the colonies. Again Pomroy, promoted to the rank of colonel, was in the field about

Lake George, among the foremost of the valiant Puritans who defeated the French general, Dieskau. He was left almost alone unwounded among the commissioned officers. There was no doubt in his mind about this being a holy war. He wrote home after the great victory of Lake George: —

"Come to the help of the Lord against the mighty! You that value our holy religion and our liberties will spare nothing, even to the one half of your estate."

One of his brother officers on this gory field was Colonel Ephraim Williams, who paused on the march to make the will which founded Williams College.

Twenty years rolled away. The gunmaker of Northampton was then sixty-nine years of age, with five stalwart sons about him, named Quartus, Asahel, Lemuel, Seth, and Medad. He was fully entitled to rest upon his laurels. But the news of Lexington stirred his ancient blood. Some weeks later he was in camp at Cambridge, in time to hear of the movement of troops toward Bunker Hill. He asked General Artemas Ward, who was in chief command at Cambridge, to lend him a horse that he might ride to the front, about five miles distant, too long a tramp for an old soldier. On reaching Charlestown neck, he found it raked by a severe fire from one of the enemy's ships. The thought occurred to him that he was riding a borrowed horse, which he had no right to risk in such a fire. He dismounted, gave the horse in charge to a sentinel, shouldered a musket, and went on foot across the neck.

On reaching the summit of Bunker Hill, he entered the work, and was received with cheers by the soldiers, who recognized the veteran of former wars. He took his post at the rail-fence, and fired steadily as long as the ammunition held out. His musket was finally shattered by a ball; but he held on to it, brought it away with him, and did all that in him lay to prevent the retreat from becoming a rout. He thought it "strange" that General Warren, the young and generous soldier, the President of the Provincial Congress, should fall, and he, an old and useless man, escape unhurt.

Congress appointed him brigadier-general, but as younger men desired the appointment, he resigned in their favor. After the loss of New York in 1776, and the retreat from White Plains, hearing that Washington was pursued across New Jersey by the victorious British, he hurried to the scene with a handful of men and rendered such service as he could in circumstances so desperate. His exposure during that cold winter brought on an attack of pleurisy. He was conveyed to Peekskill, in New York, where he died February 19, 1777, cheered in his last days by the news that

General Washington, at Trenton and Princeton, had rescued the Revolution when it seemed about to perish.

I wish we knew more of this noble old hero and patriot.

CAPTAIN MERIWETHER LEWIS,

PRIVATE SECRETARY.

———•———

THE name, Meriwether Lewis, sounds strangely in our ears, familiar as it once was to the people of the United States. Meriwether was the name of his mother's family, an ancient and honored one in Virginia; and his father, William Lewis, of Albemarle County, sprang from a race that was identified with the early history of the colony. The Lewises were near neighbors of Thomas Jefferson. Indeed, I think their plantations touched, and to this fact Captain Lewis owed the opportunity of doing the one splendid thing which causes his name to be remembered. To Mr. Jefferson, also, we owe what little knowledge we possess of his early life, and of his tragic, melancholy death.

Even as a little boy, he was noted for the qualities that afterward distinguished him. When he was only eight years of age, Jefferson tells us, he habitually went out in the dead of night, alone with his dogs, into the primeval forests that then abounded in Albemarle, to hunt the raccoon and opossum; which, as they seek their food in the night, can only then be taken. No season or stress of weather could prevent his indulging this pursuit. He would plunge through the winter snows and frozen streams, and in this way early acquired that singular fortitude and that perfect familiarity with all the arts of frontier life which he afterward put to such excellent use. He also formed the habit of accurate observation of plants, animals, and natural phenomena, which fitted him to perform the task for which he was destined. From thirteen to eighteen he attended a Latin school near his home, and then, his father dying, he returned to assist his mother in the care of the family estate, which was considerable.

A planter's life could not content him. During the presidency of General Washington, he entered the army, and at twenty-three was promoted to a captaincy. When Mr. Jefferson came to the presidency in 1801, he selected this young officer as his private secretary, and Captain Lewis filled the post for two years.

In 1803, it became necessary for the United States to enlarge the scope of its Indian affairs, to establish posts further west, and to appoint more numerous Indian Agents. In order to prepare the way for these measures, the President proposed to Congress to send an exploring party to trace the Missouri to its source, to cross the Rocky Mountains, to find its way to the Pacific, to open communications with all the tribes of Indians on their way, and to endeavor to conciliate their good will. Congress voting an appropriation for the purpose, Mr. Jefferson eagerly set on foot the expedition proposed.

Captain Lewis, now twenty-nine years of age, applied for the command, which the President assigned him. The character which Mr. Jefferson gives of his secretary was amply borne out by his conduct: —

"Of courage undaunted, possessing a firmness and perseverance of purpose which nothing but impossibilities could divert from its direction; careful as a father of those committed to his charge, yet steady in the maintenance of order and discipline; intimate with the Indian character, customs, and principles; habituated to the hunting life; guarded by exact observation of the vegetables and animals of his own country against losing time in the description of objects already possessed; honest, disinterested, liberal, of sound understanding, and a fidelity to truth so scrupulous that whatever he should report would be as certain as if seen by ourselves, — with all these qualifications, as if selected and implanted by nature in one body for this express purpose, I could have no hesitation in confiding the enterprise to him."

To complete his preparation, he spent some weeks at Philadelphia, in order to acquire familiarity with the modes of taking observations, and to superintend the manufacture of the best arms and implements. He selected as his second in command Lieutenant William Clarke, of the army, a brother of that famous hero of the Revolution, General George Rogers Clarke. This officer, also, was a perfect woodsman, thoroughly acquainted with Indians, Indian life, and Indian arts.

Never was an expedition more thoroughly prepared, for Jefferson's whole heart was in the business, and every conceivable precaution was taken to insure success, and to prevent the total loss of the information gained, in case the party were defeated and scattered by the Indians. Beside the two officers, seven of the soldiers kept diaries; and Captain Lewis had a large number of tin cans made, each of which was designed to hold a small book containing a portion of his journal, and to be sealed water-tight. On the 5th of July, 1803, Captain Lewis left Washington for the West, but it was not until Monday, the 14th of May, 1804, that the expedition was ready to leave its encampment on the shore of the Mississippi, a mile below where the Missouri empties into it.

The party consisted of two officers and forty-three men. They sailed up the Missouri in three boats. The largest was fifty-five feet long, drew three feet of water, had ten feet of deck in the stern, and a ten-foot forecastle. It was propelled by twenty-two oars, beside being provided with a large square-sail, and it had movable sides that could be raised so as to protect the crew from the fire of an enemy. The other two boats, one of six and one of seven oars, were open. Beside the boats, they had two horses, designed to be led along the banks for occasional use in exploring and hunting. Their stores consisted of a great quantity of ammunition, a supply of concentrated food of various kinds, and fourteen bales of Indian presents, such as richly-laced coats, flags, medals, knives, tomahawks, beads, mirrors, handkerchiefs, ribbons, and paints.

Starting up the Missouri on that bright May morning in 1804, the whole party seemed to have been possessed with a quiet, modest confidence in the success of the expedition. In such an affair as this, imaginary perils usually far transcend the real dangers. The private soldiers, as we learn from the diary of a sergeant, expected to pass through a country "possessed by numerous powerful, and warlike nations of savages, of gigantic stature, fierce, treacherous, and cruel, and particularly hostile to white people." Rumor also had given out that the mountains that lay in their path were inaccessible to human effort. But they all seemed fully resolved to accomplish the purpose of the government and satisfy the high expectations of the people, unless prevented by absolute impossibilities. Sailing about twenty-five miles a day, never hasting, seldom resting, pausing now and then to hold talks with the Indians, or to secure supplies of game, they kept steadily on their way.

In a month they were past the Kansas River. They celebrated the Fourth of July by firing a swivel at sunrise and sunset, drinking a glass of grog all round, and naming a creek on which they encamped " INDEPENDENCE." August 2, 1804, they held a grand council on some high land adjoining the river, which, in consequence, has borne the name ever since of Council Bluffs.

Soon they came to their first buffalo, and discovered the prairie dog; and, at last, November the 2d, six months after starting, they went into winter-quarters among the Mandan Indians, sixteen hundred and ten miles above the mouth of the Missouri River. After a winter of no great hardship, during which they subsisted upon elk, buffalo, antelope, deer, porcupine, prairie dogs, and wild turkeys, they were ready, April 7, 1805, to resume the ascent of the river. The large boat, however, they sent back to St. Louis, with their diaries, bales of furs, horns of the antelope, and thirteen of their number; while thirty-one men and one squaw formed the party for further exploration.

May 3, 1805, they passed a stream to which they gave the name "Two Thousand Mile River." Then they came to the region of the grizzly bear, an animal none of them had either seen or heard of, but in hunting which they had remarkable success. Having arrived at the Forks of the Missouri, they tried their skill at bestowing suitable names upon the various branches and neighboring streams. The north branch they called Jefferson, the south, Gallatin, the middle, Madison. One small river above the forks they named "Philosophy," and another below they called "Maria," after the President's youngest daughter. Another branch was called "Wisdom," another, "Philanthropy." All of these names had but one object, which was to do honor to the President. August 11 they passed "Three Thousand Mile Island," and August 18 they left the Missouri; and after working their way across the mountains with exceeding difficulty, by a road which is still called "Lewis and Clarke's Pass," they bought twenty-seven horses and one mule of the Indians, which brought them in three weeks to the Columbia River. They buried their saddles upon its banks, intrusted their horses to the Indians, and having made canoes, they embarked, and floated down toward the ocean. In just a month they reached tidewater, and heard of ships. Eleven days more brought them to where huge waves came rolling in from the broad Pacific. November 15, 1805, one year and six months after leaving the Mississippi River, they saw the Pacific.

But now winter was upon them. They constructed huts, made salt, sent out hunting-parties, gained the friendship of the Indians, and made themselves comfortable until the 23d of March, 1806, when they started on their return. The last entry in Captain Lewis's journal, written on the 23d of September, 1806, was as follows: —

"*Tuesday*, 23*d*. — Descended to the Mississippi and round to St. Louis, where we arrived at twelve o'clock; and, having fired a salute, went on shore, and received the heartiest welcome from the whole village."

They had been gone two years, four months, and ten days. Long before, they had been generally given up as lost, and this unexpected return was the great sensation of that year.

"Never," says Mr. Jefferson, "did a similar event excite more joy through the United States. The humblest of its citizens had taken a lively interest in the issue of this journey, and looked forward with impatience for the information it would furnish."

Captain Lewis's diary was published in London in a costly, solid quarto, and in Philadelphia in two volumes octavo. The maps and charts, the observations and specimens, which were very numerous, and most accurately taken, were deposited among the archives of the government. Congress made a grant of land to all the members of the party, and the President appointed the two chiefs to important territorial governorships.

Unhappily, the sudden change from the intense and active life of the expedition to the sedentary occupations of Governor of Louisiana produced a habit of body in Governor Lewis which caused, finally, a mental derangement. While on a journey to Washington, in 1809, at a lonely farmhouse near Nashville, in the middle of the night, he died by his own hand. He had passed some days previous in the profoundest gloom, the causes of which were purely physical, for there was nothing in his circumstances or prospects that could have given a sane man apprehension or discontent. Mr. Jefferson mentions, also, that a tendency to hypochondria was hereditary in the Lewis family.

ELEAZAR WHEELOCK,

TEACHER.

THE reader remembers, probably, that affecting passage in the Autobiography of Daniel Webster where he describes his emotion upon learning that his father was going to send him to college.

"The very idea," he tells us, "thrilled my whole frame. My father said he then lived but for his children; and if I would do all I could for myself, he would do what he could for me. I remember that I was quite overcome, and my head grew dizzy. The thing appeared to me so high, and the expense and sacrifice it was to cost my father so great, I could only press his hands and shed tears."

The institution to which he was to be sent was Dartmouth College, away in the northern part of New Hampshire, near the Vermont line, and about thirty miles from the home of the Websters at Salisbury. It was the fact of there being a college so near that made it possible for a farmer and county judge to give his sons a college education; for, in those simple old days, a student would carry an important part of his provisions from home, or pay for his board in farm produce. If, therefore, the country owes anything to Daniel Webster and his brother Ezekiel, part of the credit of it is due to Eleazar Wheelock, the Puritan clergyman, who planted the institution in the woods when the Webster boys were in their cradles. The story of its origin is one of the most curious and interesting episodes of New England history.

In 1735, Eleazar Wheelock, a young man of twenty-four, recently graduated from Yale College, was ordained a Congregational minister, and settled at Lebanon, Connecticut. He was an exceedingly effective preacher, for he had that prime requisite of an orator, a very harmonious and penetrating voice. He was a handsome man, too, of an elegant figure, and he even enjoyed another external advantage: he was possessed of a considerable estate. Add to these qualities learning and zeal, and you have a combination sufficient to give a young minister in a country place brilliant *éclat*.

As usual with the more learned of the clergy at that day, Eleazar Wheelock received into his family for education a few boys, the sons of the wealthier people of Connecticut. Indeed, at that time, there was scarcely any other way to get a boy prepared for college, but to place him in the family of a clergyman. Dr. Wheelock's little school throve, and its fame extended to other colonies. In the winter of 1743, who should present himself as a pupil but an Indian youth named Samson Occom, aged about nineteen. Until recently this young man had lived with his parents the usual wandering life of the Indians, but having attended the preaching of one of the New London clergymen, he was so deeply impressed that he became desirous of spending his whole life in teaching his tribe the white man's arts and religion. Hence his application to Eleazar Wheelock.

He was received into the family. He soon learned to read, and his behavior was exemplary. He acquired other knowledge, and, after residing with Dr. Wheelock nearly five years, returned to New London, and opened a school for the education of Indian boys. Soon he removed to Montauk, on Long Island, where the Indians were more numerous, and there he taught and preached with much apparent success for eleven years, living in an Indian wigwam, and gaining his livelihood chiefly by the fish-hook and gun. He developed also some degree of the Yankee dexterity in the use of tools, and gained a little by binding books for the whites, and by making wooden spoons, gunstocks, pails, churns, and axe handles. Upon the whole, he was the most successful and satisfactory Indian convert of whom we have any credible account. If occasionally he yielded to the temptation of strong drink, it was a weakness to which few of his race have shown themselves superior.

The good conduct of Occom suggested to Dr.

Wheelock the idea of forming a school for the purpose of educating Indian missionaries. He carried out the scheme with such success that in a few years he had as many as twenty Indian young men under instruction, who were maintained in part by the governments of Connecticut and Massachusetts, and in part by private subscriptions. In order to interest the English people in the institution, Dr. Wheelock sent to England Samson Occom as a specimen of the results of his undertaking. The Indian preacher proved to be an immense sensation. The churches in which he preached were crowded to suffocation. He preached three hundred and sixty times in Great Britain, taking up a collection after each sermon, and raising in this way a considerable sum.

Among the contributors was the Earl of Dartmouth, a popular member of the British cabinet, Secretary of State for the colonies. He consented to serve as President of the Board of Trustees in whose hands the Occom funds were placed. Having now a considerable capital at command, and enjoying also the warm and active sympathy of the whole Protestant world, Dr. Wheelock took the bold resolution of removing the institution up into the northern wilderness, so as to be in the midst of Indian tribes, and to establish in connection with his Indian school a complete college, wherein young men, whether white or red, could obtain instruction in the usual college branches.

In 1770, when he was past sixty years of age, rich, honored, and beloved, with every inducement to remain at Lebanon at ease for the rest of his life, he resigned the pastorship of his church, which he had held for thirty-five years, and set out with his family and his pupils, seventy souls in all, for Hanover, in New Hampshire, one hundred and seventy miles north of Lebanon. He rode in his own coach, a present from a friend in London, but his pupils and their teachers of both colors went the whole distance on foot. Some slight preparations had been made to receive them on the chosen site of the college. A dense and lofty forest of pines had covered the plain. On an area of about six acres, the giants of the forest had been felled, and lay upon the ground, tangled together, an impenetrable mass of logs and branches. One of the fallen trees measured two hundred and seventy feet as it lay. On a patch of two or three acres the trees had been burned off, and two or three log huts had been constructed.

But the subduing of the wilderness was a familiar task to all the members of that band, and they went to work upon the college with surprising cheerfulness and energy. Paths were cut through the fallen trees. A little town of log huts quickly rose. A frame house for the doctor was begun. A college building, eighty feet long and two stories high, was soon under way. After making considerable progress, it was found that wells dug upon the spot would yield no water, and the settlement had to be removed to some distance, and all begun afresh. And yet, during the whole of that long and dreary winter — the snow four feet deep for more than four months — the young men pursued their studies in their log homes with enthusiasm, and the next summer a class of four graduated, one of whom was John Wheelock, son of the president, and destined to succeed his father at the head of the college.

Such was the romantic beginning of Dartmouth College, the institution which placed knowledge within the reach of Daniel Webster. The Revolutionary War made it difficult to keep alive the infant institution; but, owing in great part to the energy and talent, the tact and engaging power, of Eleazar Wheelock, the college was maintained. The Indian school, however, was less successful. Discovering that about one half of the Indian youth educated under his care relapsed into savage life, the president gradually changed his plan, and devoted his chief care to the education of white missionaries. Dr. Wheelock died in 1779, aged sixty-eight, leaving the college possessed of fifty thousand acres of land, and a sufficiency of whatever was most requisite for the education of the hardy students of that time.

His son John, who succeeded him in the presidency of the college, visited Europe as soon as the war was over, and procured a considerable addition to its endowment, as well as a number of books and philosophical instruments, returning to his native land to be wrecked upon Cape Cod, and escaping with life alone, to spend that life in the service of the college.

JOEL BARLOW,

MERCHANT.

Joel Barlow, born in Connecticut in 1754, was the first American who attained celebrity as a poet. He was the author of a long epic poem, the subject of which was Columbus and the Discovery of America, which was first published in 1787, and afterwards in a sumptuous, illustrated volume, of which copies are to be found in most of the old libraries of the United States. He also wrote some occasional and humorous poems which were admired in their day.

His poetry, written in the swelling diction of the last century, though not wanting in merit, is now obsolete, and almost forgotten. But in the course of his long and interesting life he performed acts which give him a place in the history of his country, and entitle him to our respect and grateful remembrance. He was chiefly instrumental in delivering from slavery in Algiers more than a hundred American captains, sailors, and merchants, whom the piratical Algerines had captured on the high seas; and this he did at the imminent risk of his own life.

The Algerines began to prey upon the commerce of the United States as soon as its flag was known upon the ocean. A month after Thomas Jefferson reached Paris in 1785, he was alarmed by a rumor which ran over Europe that Dr. Franklin, his predecessor in the French mission, had been captured by these pirates on his voyage home, and was held by them for ransom in Algiers. Nor was there anything improbable in the report, as Mr. Jefferson very soon discovered when he received a sorrowful letter from three American captains in Algiers who had incurred the disaster.

They told him they had been captured off the coast of Portugal, and having been carried into Algiers were reduced to slavery. They were deprived of their clothes, furnished with two small rolls of bread per day, and subjected to hard labor. This was only the beginning of trouble. All the powers of Europe had been long accustomed to negotiate with these pirates, to buy treaties of them, and pay enormous ransoms for their subjects in captivity among them. Hence Mr. Jefferson could not induce Congress, and Congress had not the means, to vote the vast sums of money which the Dey of Algiers demanded. The ransom of a captain was six thousand dollars in hard cash; mates, four thousand; cabin passengers, four thousand; sailors, fourteen hundred. For a treaty of peace with the four piratical powers — Tripoli, Tunis, Algiers, and Morocco — Mr. Jefferson was asked six hundred and sixty thousand dollars ; and this at a time when it was with the utmost difficulty that Congress could pay the interest on its European debt.

For years Mr. Jefferson's chief employment at Paris was to negotiate and strive for the deliverance of the American captives. He strove in vain, because it was never in his power to offer the requisite amount of money. When he returned home, and served as Secretary of State in the cabinet of General Washington, he was still employed in the same negotiation. He went out of office ; General Washington retired ; Mr. Adams became President, and yet nothing had been done for the release of the captives. Even the three captains who wrote so dolefully to Mr. Jefferson in 1785 were still in Algiers, though maintained there and their lot mitigated at the expense of the government.

The number of captives continually increased. In 1786, Mr. Jefferson ascertained that the Dey held in slavery twenty-two hundred Christians. In a single autumn, that of 1793, ten American vessels were taken by the corsairs of Barbary, to the grief and consternation of the whole country, but especially of New England, where on Thanksgiving Day of that year a collection was made in every church for the ransom of American slaves in Barbary.

At length, in 1795, Congress put its pride in its pocket and authorized an adequate expenditure for the ransom of American captives, which amounted finally to more than a million dollars. One item was a thirty-six gun frigate for the Dey, which cost a hundred thousand dollars, and was loaded with another hundred thousand dollars worth of naval supplies, including powder, lead, shells, rope, sailcloth, and timber.

But the demands of the Dey, a savage, sensual, mindless brute, rose as Congress became more liberal, and still he haggled over the ransom offered. The American sailors were treated with extreme cruelty. Some were performing menial service in the Dey's palace, others were toiling in the quarries, chained together; and some were employed in loading and unloading their own captured vessels.

In these circumstances, Joel Barlow, who was then living in Paris and engaged in commerce, was entreated to go to Algiers and negotiate with the Dey for the ransom of the prisoners. He had large interests in France, and was most tenderly attached to his wife. The plague was devastating Algiers. He had every reason for declining the perilous mission, except his remarkable fitness for conducting it to success. He accepted, and spent several months of a burning summer in Algiers. The plague decimated the population. Every kind of hindrance arose, and there were long delays in the arrival of the money, causing extreme distrust on the part of the Dey.

In discharging this mission Joel Barlow employed

tact, knowledge, patience, and good nature, and his final success was owing directly to his personal qualities. Before the year ended, one hundred and twenty-two captives came home, among whom were ten who had been in slavery for eleven years.

While Joel Barlow was in Algiers that summer, he wrote a letter to his wife which is one of the most singular and beautiful letters ever written by a husband to a wife. Many people were dying of the plague all around him, and he wrote this letter in view of his own probable death; but it was not to be delivered to his wife unless he should die. With it he inclosed his will, leaving her all he possessed, and intrusting to her judgment and generosity the care of all who had claims upon him. The letter is full of curious things, but the most peculiar passage is one in which he urges her to marry again : —

"Let your tenderness for me soon cease to agitate that lovely bosom, and transfer your affections to some worthy person who shall supply my place in the relation I have borne to you. It is for the living, not the dead, to be rendered happy by the sweetness of your temper, the purity of your heart, your exalted sentiments, your cultivated spirit, your undivided love. Happy man of your choice, should he know and prize the treasure of such a wife! Oh, treat her tenderly, my dear sir; she is used to nothing but kindness, unbounded love, and confidence. She is all that any reasonable man can desire. She is more than I have merited, or perhaps than you can merit. My resigning her to your charge, though but the result of uncontrollable necessity, is done with a degree of cheerfulness — a cheerfulness inspired by the hope that her happiness will be the object of your care and the long-continued fruit of your affection."

This letter, happily, was never sent to its address, for he rejoined his wife in excellent health a few months later. A few years after, they returned to the United States, bought a handsome place in Washington, and made it the seat of an elegant hospitality.

In recognition of his services in Algiers, President Madison appointed him Minister to France, trusting that his skill would heal the growing irritation between Bonaparte and the government of the United States.

He found Napoleon in the midst of his Russian campaign. Full of zeal to serve his country, he made an arduous winter journey to meet the emperor, and during it he was met by the ghastly torrent of the perishing French army. He witnessed and felt the horrors of the retreat from Moscow.

The biting frost of that terrible winter, which destroyed Napoleon's power, caused Barlow's death near Warsaw. A severe cold developed into the disease which we now call pneumonia, of which he died. During some of his last days he had not even a hut to shelter him at night, and was obliged, sick as he was, to eat frozen bread and drink frozen wine. He was truly a martyr to his zeal for his country's service. A marble slab, set into the brickwork of his house near Washington, bears to the present hour this inscription : —

"Sacred to the repose of the dead, and the meditation of the living. Joel Barlow, Patriot, Poet, Statesman, and Philosopher, lies buried in Zarniwica, in Poland, where he died 24th December, 1812, æt. 58 years and 9 months. Ruth Baldwin Barlow, his wife, died 29th May, 1818, æt. 62 years."

NATHANIEL BOWDITCH,

MARINER.

One of the most remarkable traits in the character of this eminent mathematician was the power he possessed to interest other men in his favorite subject. When he was captain of a ship sailing out of Salem to the East Indies, almost all his crew became ardent mathematicians, and even the ship's cook made such progress as to be able to work out a lunar observation. The secret of it was his own intense and passionate love of the science. In one of his early voyages, when he was little more than a boy, the ship was chased by a privateer; and the captain making up his mind to fight, assigned to young Bowditch the duty of handing up the powder. In the midst of the hurly-burly of preparing the ship for action, he was observed seated by a keg of powder, wholly absorbed in his slate and pencil. Such love as that is very contagious.

This interesting man, born at Salem in 1773, came of a long line of tough and valiant Yankee sea-captains; but his father, after going to sea for several years, came ashore, and settled at Salem in the business of a cooper, and reared a family of seven children. He had a hard time of it during the Revolutionary War to support so large a family; so that when his son Nathaniel was a boy of ten, he was obliged to take him from the town-school and put him to work in his cooper shop. Soon after, the boy was regularly apprenticed to a ship-chandler, and served out his time of seven years.

From an early age, even while still at school, he had shown a strange aptitude for arithmetic, being one of those boys who learn to do all the hard sums, and help their companions out of their arithmetical difficulties. During his apprenticeship, such was his love of calculation that, in the long and frequent intervals when there were no customers to serve, he still assiduously employed himself with slate and pencil. I have never heard of such devotion to knowledge, such energy, zeal, and indefatigable industry in acquiring it. Hearing one day that there was a way of doing sums by letters instead of figures, he pursued his inquiries until he had found an algebra. Upon looking over it, he was so fascinated and so agitated that he could not sleep during the next night, and he gave himself no rest until he had mastered its contents. Getting access to an Encyclopedia, he read it all through, article after article, in their alphabetical order. An old sailor settled in Salem gave him some notion of navigation, and he pursued the science until he could work out all the problems.

At seventeen, while still an apprentice, he obtained a copy of Newton's "Principia," the most abstruse mathematical work then existing, in which the great philosopher develops in mathematical form his theory of gravitation. The curiosity of the boy was instantly roused; but, alas! the work was written in Latin, of which he knew scarcely a word. Nothing daunted, he began to learn the language, and continued until, by the aid of the diagrams given in the work, he could read and understand Newton's demonstrations. Early in life he also acquired the French language, in order to read the many excellent mathematical works written in it; as later he learned German, Italian, and Spanish, to get possession of their treasures of literature and science.

It was fortunate, perhaps, for this energetic genius that no wealthy patron released him from the necessity of daily toil; for if the gift of leisure had made him a greater mathematician, it might have rendered him a less admirable man. With all his talent, he was left to pursue precisely the same course as the most ordinary youth in Salem. After his apprenticeship, he was a ship-chandler's clerk for a few years. At twenty-two, he sailed as captain's clerk in an East India ship, and was promoted, in due time, first to be supercargo, and afterward captain; in the course of his sea-service, visiting most of the important ports of the world. It could not be said of him that he was merely a book mathematician, for he was one of the best and safest practical navigators that ever lived. His son relates that, coming on the coast of Massachusetts in winter, after a long voyage, he arrived off Salem harbor by night, in a tempest of wind and snow. Besides his reckoning, he had no help except one momentary glimpse of the light on Baker's Island; but he stood by the helm, and steered the ship safely in. He was not yet thirty years of age when he published his " Practical Navigator," which was so exactly what navigators wanted that it found its way speedily into the cabin of almost every American and English ship.

A pleasing incident of his seafaring life occurred soon after the publication of this work. While his ship lay in Boston harbor, one day, waiting for a fair wind, the young captain (he was then but twenty-nine) went on shore to attend the Commencement of Harvard College at Cambridge, near by. When the president read the names of the men upon whom the college had conferred honorary degrees, Captain Bowditch was thrilled with delight to have his own name among those who had received the degree of Master of Arts. This was a great honor in those honest old days, and would have remained such to this hour if colleges had been chary and conscientious in the bestowal of degrees. In after years, when he had received many such distinctions and was a member of most of the learned societies in the world, he always looked back upon that day as the proudest of his life.

Yankee sailors of any force and sense are not apt to be sailors long after middle life. When Captain Bowditch had followed the sea for about fifteen years, he settled in Salem as president of an insurance company, an employment which gave him as much leisure as he could profitably employ. He was still an ardent and constant student, and contributed frequently scientific papers to "The North American Review," and other works; these, however, were but trifles compared with the great task upon which he entered soon after settling at Salem. There had been coming out for many years the volumes of the extensive work of the French mathematician, Laplace, entitled, "La Mécanique Céleste," or, as we should say, "The Mechanism of the Heavens." This work, divided into sixteen books, was designed to embody the entire science of astronomy, mathematically treated. It embraces such topics as the Laws of Motion, the Attraction of Gravitation, the Form of the Heavenly Bodies, the Revolutions of the Heavenly Bodies, the Moons of Jupiter and Saturn, the Theory of the Comets; all illustrated with diagrams, and treated in such a way that only a very accomplished mathematician can read it. As Bowditch says himself: —

"I never come across one of Laplace's 'Thus it plainly appears,' without feeling sure that I have got hours of hard study before me to fill up the chasm, and find out and show *how* it plainly appears."

So abstruse was this work, that it was supposed at the time that not more than three persons in the United States, nor more than twelve in Great Britain, could read it. Bowditch formed the design, not merely to translate the whole into English, but to elucidate it with notes, and to add to it such discoveries in astronomical science as had been made since its completion. The execution of this task occupied the remainder of his life. When he had made considerable progress in it, the important question arose, how he should bear the expense of publishing five quarto volumes of a thousand pages each. The plan of subscription was suggested; but with a sturdy and perhaps excessive independence, he declined to avail himself of that method, and determined to wait until he could afford to publish it at his own expense, leaving it to the public to buy the volumes, or let them alone, as they should see fit. Fortunately he was invited, in his fiftieth year, to accept the post, at a liberal salary, of actuary of a Boston life insurance company, which soon put him in circumstances to begin the publication.

"I would rather," he used to say, "put by a thousand dollars a year for my book than spend it in keeping a carriage."

The volumes, as they appeared, met with a better sale than he had expected; but of course they did not pay the great expense of publication. While he was correcting the proof-sheets of the fourth volume, he was seized with a mortal disease, which ended his life at the age of sixty-five. The fifth volume has since been added to the series by Professor Peirce.

Bowditch accomplished the great labors of his life as much by the regularity as by the ardor of his industry. In winter he was up two hours before daylight, and spent the day in labor, happy at its close to receive his friends in the midst of his family, and pass the evening in cheerful conversation. It appears, too, that he was an extremely able and sagacious man of business, and conducted the affairs of the companies intrusted to his charge in such a way as to place them upon the most solid basis of prosperity. A statue was erected in his honor at the cemetery of Mount Auburn, where his remains repose.

MR. GEORGE B. EMERSON,

BOSTON SCHOOLMASTER.

THE name at the head of this article is that of one of the most celebrated and successful teachers of New England, who, in honorable retirement, after half a century of faithful and skillful labor, was happy to communicate to others the results of his observation and experience. He was born as long ago as 1797, in Maine, then a district of Massachusetts. George B. Emerson and Horace Mann had, perhaps, more influence upon the educational system of the United States than any other two men: one by his example as a teacher, the other by his energy and enthusiasm as superintendent of education. Both may have committed errors; Mr. Mann may have overvalued an education chiefly intellectual; but both were valuable citizens, worthy of the universal esteem in which they are held.

Mr. Emerson was fortunate in his own education, because it was *not* purely intellectual. His father was a physician in large practice, who had a farm, and kept his boys out of school in the summer to work upon it. They thus became acquainted, not only with all the operations of farming, but with the natural objects amidst which they labored, the trees, the plants, the weeds, and their modes of growth. They learned to use the spade, shovel, hoe, rake, sickle, and scythe, and, what is still better, *liked* to use them. Neither then nor ever was labor irksome to George Emerson; and in taking care of his father's animals he learned a secret which was useful to him in the school-room. He discovered that to make the horses and the cattle safe and kind to him, it was only necessary to be kind to them.

"For many years," he says, in his Reminiscences, "I have had no doubt that it would be far better for all the boys in the country towns not to be allowed to go to school in the summer, but to educate their muscles, and form habits of occupation and industry, by pursuits similar to those which it was my privilege and happiness to be engaged in."

Every one who has observed the blighting effects of six hours' school a day ten months in a year, and seen how children are frequently educated by it into helpless ignorance, will assent to Mr. Emerson's remark. He speaks, too, of the immense advantage it was for the girls of his day to assist their parents by superintending large flocks of hens, turkeys, and ducks, assisting in the garden and the kitchen, using the spinning-wheel, and thus gaining a bodily development which enabled them to bear with ease and pleasure the burdens that awaited them in maturity.

Entering Harvard College during the War of 1812, he found Edward Everett the Latin tutor. Among his classmates were Caleb Cushing and George Bancroft. Like most of the boys of that day, he had to work his way through college by teaching, and when he was only sixteen years of age he found himself at the head of a school in which several of the pupils were some years older than himself. He quickly gained an ascendancy over them. In the course of his first week, a young fellow of nineteen or twenty brought him an exceedingly hard sum in arithmetic by way of putting his knowledge to the test. This was a custom in the schools of the olden time, and woe be to the master who failed! Luckily, the young teacher had learned a little geometry, and he recalled a proposition which made this arithmetical puzzle very easy. He not only mastered the problem, but explained it, and showed how several other of the noted difficult questions could be solved by the same method. He had borne the test, and from that moment the boy teacher governed his school without difficulty.

Like most young men, he entered college totally ignorant of the physical laws governing his own constitution, and thus presumed upon his strength, endeavoring to do with only four hours' sleep. The consequence was that his health gave way, and he injured his eyesight so much that it was some years before he recovered it. On Commencement day he was almost prostrated, and it was some time before he was well enough to go home. He had lived with much economy in college, but on reaching his father's house after graduation he was considerably in debt. Country doctors, in those simple days, performed a great deal of gratuitous labor, and, in some instances, scarcely ever presented a bill. His father was one such, and when he was urged to collect some of his oldest debts, he always said: —

"These people are poor; when they can afford it they will pay. Meanwhile, they will bring us wood and hay, and other products of their farm or their fishing."

The young graduate, therefore, had to pay his own college debts, and he was wondering how he should do it, not without anxiety. Two days after reaching home from college he received a letter from the president, offering him the place of master of a private school, at a salary of five hundred dollars, then unusually large. With this school he had great success. His income was soon doubled, and his college debts ceased to trouble him. He was, however, very far yet from having mastered his profession, and he fell into some errors which troubled his conscience long.

"I kept," he says, "a switch and a ferule, and used them both, often feeling, as I did so, like a malignant spirit, and sometimes acted in an evil spirit. I have many times wished that I could ask the pardon of one boy whom I had punished unjustly and in passion. But he never came to see me, and I have no doubt he retained, perhaps always, a righteous grudge against me."

Another of his errors, as he thought, was in employing the motive of emulation. He had a head to every class, and urged his pupils by medals, commendation, and other rewards, to surpass their fellows. No one objected either to the rewards or the punishments, and his school was universally approved. He was a gay lad out of school, and was so fond of dancing that on one occasion he rode and danced all night.

From this school he was summoned to be tutor at Harvard College, where he fell in with Professor Norton, of the theological department, whose conversations led him to question the methods which he had pursued in training the young. He concluded, at last, that to excite the emulation of children was unchristian and wrong; pardonable in a pagan like Cicero, but not to be tolerated in a teacher who accepted the Christian principle, "in honor preferring one another." He also came to the conclusion that "inflicting cruel bodily pain on a child was savage and almost brutal." He made up his mind that, if ever again he should be a teacher of children, he would faithfully try the experiment of doing without emulation and bodily torture. The opportunity soon occurred. Having been elected to the mastership of an important school in Boston of seventy-five boys, he began by explaining to them the principles upon which he should endeavor to govern. He made a little speech to them, which I present here in full.

"I do not believe in the necessity of corporal punishment, and I shall never strike a blow unless you compel me. I want you to learn to govern yourselves. I shall regard you and treat you all as young gentlemen, and expect you to consider me a gentleman and treat me accordingly.

"I shall always believe every word you say, until I find you guilty of lying, and then I cannot; nobody believes a liar, if he has any temptation to lie.

"Never tell me anything to the disadvantage of any fellow-student. I mean to have strict rules, and to have them strictly obeyed; but I shall never make a rule which I would not more willingly see broken than I would have any one of you violate what ought to be his feeling of honor toward a fellow-student. It is the meanest thing that any boy can do.

"I have examined you very carefully, as you all know, and have taken every means of finding out your character and capacities, and your opportunities. Some of you have enjoyed every advantage. You have lived in pleasant homes, with intelligent and well-informed parents and friends, and you have formed habits of reading good books, and being otherwise pleasantly and well employed. Others of you have been blessed with none of these privileges, and have had no opportunities of forming good habits. Now I am going to examine you, for some weeks, carefully and severely, in a considerable variety of studies. I shall do this that I may arrange you according to your attainments and capacities, so that no one may be kept back from doing what he is capable of, and that the slow and ill-prepared may be fairly tried.

"After I shall have ascertained, in this way, of what each of you is capable, in all the studies, I shall, when I find that a dull boy has done his best, feel for him the same respect, and give him the same mark, that I shall to the brightest boy in school who has only done *his* best.

"I beg of you, boys, never to try to surpass each other. Help each other in every way you can. Try to surpass *yourselves*. Say, 'I will do better to-day than I did yesterday, and I resolve to do better to-morrow than I can do to-day.' In this way, you who are highest and most capable will always through life be friends, and the best friends. But if you try to surpass each other, some of you will inevitably be enemies."

This system, as worked by an exceptionably able teacher, upon the pick of Boston school-boys, answered well. In the school-room scarcely any offenses were committed, and if anything went wrong in the play-ground he made the boys form a court, in which the culprit was tried. Whether this system would succeed with rough boys gathered from the streets of a large city, unaccustomed to discipline and self-control, may well be doubted.

Mr. Emerson spent the greater part of his life as the master of a young ladies' school in Boston, which for many years enjoyed great celebrity, and in which a large number of the most estimable ladies in New England were educated. All his life long he preserved his love of natural objects, and he probably knew more of the trees and shrubs of New England than any individual then living. He was one of the first to welcome to the United States the late Professor Agassiz, with whom he coöperated in many practical schemes for the promotion of science in the United States. Ralph Waldo Emerson, writing to this aged instructor, begins his letter thus : —

"MY DEAR GEORGE: If there be one person whom I have from my first acquaintance with him held in unbroken honor, it is yourself."

Sixty years had passed since these two Emersons met — George just leaving college, Ralph Waldo just entering.

"All the years since," added the philosopher, "have not quite availed to span that gulf to my imagination. But I know not the person who has more invariably been to me the object of respect and love."

JOSEPH LANCASTER,

ENGLISH SCHOOLMASTER.

When I was eight years of age, I attended for a short time, in the city of New York, a large public school, on what was called the Lancasterian plan. Most of our public schools, I believe, were arranged upon that system; the author of which, Joseph Lancaster, was then a resident of New York. The chief peculiarity of the system was that the boys taught one another. The elder pupils, or those most advanced in their studies, were instructed during part of the day by the principal and his assistant, and during the rest of the time each of them taught a class of younger boys sitting at a semicircular desk in front of the monitor.

Of this school I have a very lively recollection, for it was the worst one I ever attended, or even heard of. The monitors, according to the best of my recollection, were not only most inefficient and neglectful teachers, but they corrupted their classes by indecent stories, and by putting them up to mischief out of doors. Some of them exacted contributions from their classes. At a certain time in the morning, when the principal and his assistant were busy at the other end of the room, and when there was a steady roar of voices all over the school, the monitor of my class would remove the inkstand from its hole in the top of his desk, and we would see two or three of his dirty fingers thrust up in its place. This was the signal that the time had come for taking up the collection. One boy would put in a piece of candy, another a handful of chestnuts, another a skate strap, another a white marble, and occasionally one would go so far as to drop in a cent.

The inducement to contribute was indeed irresistible, for these monitors were intrusted with fearful power. For any offense, real or imaginary, a monitor could send a member of his class to stand along one of the walls, or at the teacher's desk. If he sent him to one wall, he was liable to receive two blows on the hand with a rattan; if he sent him to another, four; but if he sent him to the desk, he had a regular trouncing. Who can wonder that the despot received plenty of good things from his subjects? On rainy days, and in the depth of winter, the boys used to take their dinners to school, and many a cold sausage and long doughnut and bunch of raisins I have seen pass through that hole in the monitor's desk.

Such was the Lancasterian system of education, as I remember it. It was worse than a failure; for it not only did no good, but great harm.

Joseph Lancaster, born and reared in one of the worst districts of London, was the son of a mechanic who had served out his time as a private soldier in the king's footguards. His father, being a zealous dissenter, intended to bring up his boy as a Calvinist minister; but when Joseph was eighteen years of age he turned Quaker, which frustrated his father's scheme. Finding mechanical labor disagreeable, and pitying the condition of the swarms of neglected children about his home, he determined to set up a school for their benefit. His father lent him the use of a room, and for twenty shillings he bought a quantity of old flooring boards, which, with his own hands, he made into desks and benches. When all was ready, he threw open his school to boys and girls at four pence a week each, payable every Monday morning.

The low price was the first attraction, because there lived in the neighborhood a large number of persons who had seen better days, and many mechanics who were working at reduced wages. But Joseph Lancaster must have had a particular talent for winning and governing children. The school rapidly filled up. It was removed to a larger apartment, which also soon began to overflow; and it was then removed to one still larger. At that period, the hand of Napoleon was heavy upon mankind, and almost every family in Europe was oppressed directly or indirectly by him. A large number of Lancaster's pupils, impoverished by the war, failed to bring their weekly four pence; but he could not find it in his heart to let them go, and he told their parents to pay when they could, and, in the mean time, he would never solicit them for payment. This was very good of him; but it lessened his income, and increased his expenses to such a degree that he was obliged to send away an assistant whom he had lately employed.

It was this unavoidable dismissal of his assistant teacher, he says, which "*compelled* him," to use his own language, "to make use of the services of his pupils to teach each other as monitors; and finally, this practice, the sheer offspring of necessity, ended in the demonstration of the power of one master to teach hundreds by means of juvenile and economical auxiliaries." Henceforth he devoted his chief care to training his class of monitors; and such was his power to mould and influence the minds of the young, that so long as the system was worked by him and the teachers whom he had personally trained, it produced good results.

But, in truth, almost any system of education worked by an able, sympathetic, and laborious teacher will answer its purpose; while the best system, in incompetent or negligent hands, will fail. To make the Lancasterian system succeed, there must be a Lancaster in every school. The only system which will yield tolerable results is one that can be worked by persons of average ability and average virtue. Lancaster took extraordinary pains to win the hearts of his pupils, and this he did by taking an interest in their pleasures, as well as in their duties. On Sunday evenings he used to have an immense tea-party of his scholars — they bringing their own bread and butter, and he providing the tea and sugar. The tea was made in an enormous copper, and the elder pupils served the younger; while Lancaster himself moved about among them, the happy father of the whole company.

On holiday afternoons he used to make excursions to villages about London with large parties of the pupils. Each monitor was converted, for the occasion, into the captain of his class, marching at its head, and keeping it in soldierly order until they had got out of town, when all were allowed unbounded liberty. Nothing that a teacher can do gives such intense happiness to his school as well-arranged excursions of this kind. I can speak from experience; for, in my own teaching days, I have rambled many a mile in the country with a troop of noisy boys at my heels.

In another way also Joseph Lancaster endeared himself to his pupils and their parents. Those winters, during the early Napoleon wars, were periods of ever increasing suffering among the London poor. In the early part of 1800 the price of food rose to such a point that, as Lancaster's eye surveyed his school of a morning, he could see many children who had come to school without having tasted food, some of whom were almost ready to fall off their seats from exhaustion. By this time his fame had spread over the city, and people came from distant points to visit his school. In this period of distress he availed himself of his celebrity to make collections for the poor of his neighborhood, and went about among the rich Quakers, personally soliciting subscriptions. Such success had he that, during the worst of the winter, he was enabled to provide a good substantial dinner of soup and potatoes for sixty or eighty persons every day.

His school increased to three hundred, and then, in a larger room, to five hundred; and, finally, to seven hundred. Those who could pay, paid for their children; but for those who could not, he received subscriptions from the nobility and others, undertaking to educate a pupil one year for every guinea subscribed. He actually performed more than his promise, for he educated three pupils for every guinea.

A peculiarity of his school was the oddity of the punishments he inflicted; his great object being to do away with all violent corporal punishment. For persistent idleness, he made a boy carry a wooden yoke upon his neck, weighing five or six pounds. He would shackle the legs of two offenders together, and oblige them to walk around the school-room until they were tired.

"Occasionally," he says, " boys are put in a sack or basket suspended to the roof of the school, in the sight of all the pupils, who frequently smile at *the birds in the cage*. This punishment is one of the most terrible that can be inflicted upon boys of sense and abilities."

So I should think. Old offenders were sometimes yoked together like a pair of oxen, and made to walk backward up and down the school-room. In some instances a culprit was dressed up with labels describing his offense; and while thus decorated, he was marched up and down the schoolroom preceded by two boys, who proclaimed aloud the offense of which he had been guilty. If a boy had a dirty face or hands, a girl was appointed to wash him in the sight of the whole school. When he kept in boys after school, and could not conveniently stay with them himself, he used to tie each of them to his desk, to keep them from running away. Such punishments as these seem to me far more degrading than the simple, old-fashioned one with which we are all familiar. Coleridge, who was delivering his lectures upon Shakespeare at the time in London, was so indignant at them that, in the course of a lecture upon Romeo and Juliet, when he came to speak of the Nurse, he digressed into a warm denunciation of Lancaster's punishments. Charles Lamb whispered to a friend sitting next to him that Coleridge ought to have saved this passage for his lecture upon Henry the Sixth, which bore hardly upon the House of *Lancaster*.

After teaching a few years, the fame of Joseph Lancaster was spread all over the world. George the Third received him at his palace, and was so delighted with his system, as expounded by himself, that he sent him a message, assuring him that if he could conform to the Church of England conscientiously, there was nothing he might ask for, within the bounds of reason, which should not be granted him. Lancaster replied that he could not conform, and kept on his way as a Quaker.

All went well with him until his excellent wife lost her reason in 1805. She became at last raving mad, and he was obliged to place her in confinement. For seventeen years he was tormented with anxiety on her account, since she had intervals of reason, during which she came home, and then her madness would return, and she would grow worse until he was compelled to place her again in the asylum. His domestic misery injured his health so much that his friends advised him at length to go into the country for a few weeks. While he was staying near Bristol, he was invited to deliver a public discourse explaining his system, which he did to a large and deeply attentive audience. This event changed the course of his life. After lecturing in every part of England with great success, he crossed to America, introduced his system here, went to South America, where Bolivar patronized, flattered, and deceived him. Returning to New York, utterly impoverished, old, and infirm, he was for a considerable time so poor as sometimes to be in want of the necessaries of life. A few wealthy gentlemen at length subscribed, and purchased him a small annuity, upon which he lived for the rest of his life. He died in New York in 1838, aged sixty-seven. With all his errors and the errors of his system, he doubtless gave an impetus to popular education, and suggested some valuable improvements in the art of instructing great numbers at small expense.

ANDREW JACKSON,

FARMER.

General Jackson never showed more wisdom than in selecting a tract of land on the banks of the Cumberland River for his farm. His estate there consisted originally of two thousand acres, as fertile and as convenient for cultivation as any tract in the United States. At the time of his death the farm was reduced to a thousand acres, of which he then cultivated about four hundred. The Hermitage Farm was a hundred miles above the line of safe cotton culture, and, although some cotton was still raised in that region, it was liable to be nipped by frost about one year in three.

The consequence was that the planters there chiefly raised such crops as we are accustomed to see growing in the best portions of the Northern States — corn, wheat, potatoes, fruits, and some tobacco. I do not think there can be better farming land anywhere in the world than in that portion of western Tennessee through which the Cumberland winds its tortuous way to the Ohio. It is a hard wood country, and the annual overflowing of the

Cumberland renews the fertility of much of the soil with almost the unfailing regularity with which the Connecticut enriches the flat country along its banks near Northampton.

The Hermitage is between eleven and twelve miles from the beautiful and pleasant city of Nashville. The country between the city and the Jackson farm is not striking to the lover of the picturesque, but pleasing in the highest degree to the agriculturist. There is something about it that reminds us of the farming regions of Pennsylvania, between Philadelphia and Harrisburg, except that the fields are a great deal larger and the houses much more spacious. The Cumberland, flowing noiselessly in its deep bed, is not visible, though its course is indicated by the line of bluffs, and the road crosses several creeks which flow into it. Before the war there were several extensive groves of excellent wood on the way. Major William B. Lewis, I remember, had a tract of six hundred acres of magnificent primeval forest, then worth six dollars a cord. During one of the winters of the war many thousand cavalry were encamped on his plantation, and before the spring opened, as he told me, you could not pick up a piece of wood as large as a man's hand on his whole estate. Even the stumps and roots had been consumed, to say nothing of the fences and outhouses. But when I saw the country, in 1859, the woods were still there in all their original density and luxuriance.

On the way, an old gentleman, who had spent his life in that country, pointed out a tract of land which, to his knowledge, had been sixty years in culture with scarcely any rotation of crops. The land of that region made such an impression on my mind that I have ever since been in the habit of saying that, if I were to live my life over again, I would plant myself on a tract of land in western Tennessee, and establish there my right to exist by cultivating it. True, I was but a visitor and knew no more of land and farming than others of my craft. The Cumberland River, too, may be an inconvenient neighbor, for it rises sometimes forty feet in a day or two, and pours itself over the land in a tumultuous flood. There are drawbacks, no doubt, there as everywhere; still, I remain under a strong impression that the place for Mr. Hughes to have founded his American Rugby was somewhere within fifty miles of Nashville, in the valley of the Cumberland.

All the road between Nashville and the Hermitage speaks of Jackson. After passing the roomy old mansion of Major William B. Lewis, his stanchest political friend and ally, who made him President and lived with him in the White House, we come soon to where Andrew Jackson once kept a country store, having as partner General Coffee, of warlike renown. The old blockhouse, long uninhabited, the mortar crumbling out of the chinks, the windows broken, and protected by no fence, stood there, a manifest proof that a pile without inhabitant to ruin runs. But in that old blockhouse, it seems, General Jackson entertained Aaron Burr for several days, while his partner, Coffee, built the boats in which Burr descended the river. Near by is Clover Bottom, where Colonel John Donaldson, the pioneer of this region, first encamped. Here, too, was the race-course, much loved by Jackson, where he ran his famous horses and made liberal bets upon their success. Clover Bottom was, in 1859, a great, broad, level, superb cornfield of unsurpassed fertility.

Upon reaching the Hermitage Farm we observe the same characteristics: forests of hard wood, broad, rolling sweeps of land, level, large, magnificent fields, the ideal land of an agriculturist, and so favored by climate that it can be plowed on every fine day of nearly every year. There is just frost enough there to assist the disintegration of the clods, and the fields are so large that it is common to see a dozen plows moving up and down within the same inclosure.

On the way, the visitor passes, at a distance of a quarter of a mile from the mansion, a small building which looks like a miniature brick barn, and he is much surprised to be told that this is the Presbyterian church which General Jackson built for his wife. It is impossible to imagine a plainer edifice; for if we except the grove of trees in front of it, which dignify the scene, it is destitute of any kind of decoration. It has no steeple, no portico, and not even a double door. Within, we see forty unpainted pews, a brick floor, a plain, low pulpit. When I saw it, it had not been used for some years, and there were no books or other signs of occupancy. Within this little building, however, General Jackson, at the age of seventy-six years, joined the church and received his first communion, the little audience all in tears, and the windows filled with black faces showing deep emotion.

I need not describe the mansion itself, the home of General Jackson during the last twenty years of his life. No doubt it was a grand edifice for its day. It appeared a plain, shabby, two-storied brick house, with white piazzas and tall white pillars, with a garden of an acre and a half behind it, then much neglected. After walking in this garden awhile, I said to my companion, Major Lewis, "Let us go and see the general's summer-house before we leave." I pointed to a circular, high structure with a round metal roof, sustained by white stone pillars, in a distant corner of the garden. "Summer-house," said the major, "that's the general's tomb."

I regret to be obliged to state that the structure, although the heir of the general's estate was still living, was much dilapidated and very shabby. The slab which covered Mrs. Jackson's grave rocked under my foot. There were gaps in the pavement, as though the foundation had sunk; the roof leaked badly, and the plaster ceiling was peeling off and was much discolored. Five dollars a year would have kept this tomb in order, but nothing probably had ever been done to it since the general's interment. The inscription on General Jackson's stone contains merely the dates of his birth and death, but that which records the character of his wife is of some length, and expressed, though imperfectly, the general's sense of her merits.

Of all the objects then standing upon the Hermitage estate, the most interesting were the two log-cabins (once joined by a passage, but then separated) in which General Jackson lived, and had lived for several years, when he went to the Creek War in 1812, and which were still his home when he fought the battle of New Orleans. They stood two hundred yards behind the Hermitage, and were quite in the old backwoods style — log-houses, pure and simple, a story and a half high, and unceiled. When I saw them, the larger one was occupied as a negro cabin, and was neither better nor worse than the average cabins of the place. The other was used as an old storehouse, or, as my good informant, Hannah, expressed it, "There's nothing but plunder in it." The interior of the principal cabin was as black as ebony with the smoke of fifty years. According to my notes, the windows were too small to light it perfectly; there was no cellar, but only a trapdoor in the floor with a small excavation under it in which to stow away things. Near by there is a fine and very noted spring of water with a stone house over it, highly prized by Mrs. Jackson. All about these houses, in the same field, twenty or thirty negro cabins, some log, some block, some brick, some frame, were scattered in various irregular groups.

In the carriage-house near the mansion, there was then preserved the buggy made of the wood of the ship Constitution, in which Jackson and Van Buren rode to the capital on the day of Van Buren's inauguration. There was also the huge, heavy family coach, as large as a stage-coach, in which the general made his last journey from Washington. I believe, too, I saw there the remains of the wagon composed of hickory sticks, unpainted, which was one of the odd presents General Jackson received during his presidency.

But all the curiosities of the place were as nothing compared with those two blackened log-cabins, in which the hero of New Orleans lived during the heroic period of his life, and from which he went to the defense of his invaded country. Whatever may be thought of General Jackson's methods as a statesman, no one will now deny that his defense of the Southwest, take it for all in all, considering the means at his disposal and the power of the enemy, red and white, has not been surpassed as a piece of defensive warfare on the continent of America. I could not but feel a peculiar pleasure in thinking that the hero of those campaigns had gone from this humble home, like another Cincinnatus. If I were the State of Tennessee, I would not permit those log-cabins to fall into further decay.

All accounts agree that General Jackson was a vigorous, vigilant, and always successful farmer. To use the language of the country, he "made good crops." The extraordinary fertility of the soil rendered this a comparatively easy task; but the crops on the Jackson estate were exceptionally large, even for that productive land. In middle life he was a man of noticeable activity, of brisk, quick movement, and capable of long-continued exertion. He "looked after everything," as old Hannah remarked. He was also a man of forethought, and laid out the work of the plantation with care and skill. One of his neighbors said: "If Andrew Jackson heard a lamb bleating in the night, he would get up and see to it." His strong point as a planter was, however, the constant care he took of his slaves. He was a thoughtful and wise master, although one of his overseers complained that he was too indulgent, which made discipline difficult when he was at home. On retiring from mercantile business in somewhat embarrassed circumstances, he had but about twenty slaves, but these increased in number, until at the time of his death he possessed more than a hundred, and could put into the field a working force of forty hands. They were like so many children under a liberal and patient father. "Yes," said one of his overseers, "he half spoiled some of his negroes, and if they got into trouble, right or wrong, they flew to him, and he would get them off, if it were possible to do it."

We think of General Jackson as a passionate and fiery man. To his enemies he usually appeared such, although he was prudent in his anger, and often was much cooler than he appeared. But to his servants, to children, and to all dependent persons and creatures he was one of the most gentle and considerate persons that ever lived. His tenderness towards children was extraordinary. The late Mr. F. P. Blair, editor of the "Globe," related to me an incident which he himself witnessed at the Hermitage, when the general was suffering from an acute attack of the disease which he acquired in the Creek War, and from which he never fully recovered. One of his little nephews, Johnny Donaldson, a boisterous, noisy boy, was playing about the room. The general was sitting in his armchair, suffering the tortures of one of his nervous headaches, his temples visibly throbbing, his head bowed upon one of his hands. The boy, playing goat, butted his head plump into the general's stomach, who fell back in his chair breathless and in agony. On recovering his power of utterance, he said with peculiar fondness, as though pitying the boy for a mishap, "Oh, my dear, you don't know how much pain you have given me!" Another anecdote, also related to me by Mr. Blair, who witnessed the occurrence, exhibits the same trait of character. During his presidency, the general's favorite servant, George, got drunk on duty and let the President's four horses run away with his best carriage, for which he had recently paid a thousand dollars. The carriage was completely broken to pieces, quite beyond repair. George had nothing to do but to return to his master and report the damage. "How was it, George?" asked the President. George replied: "It was so cold, master, I could n't stand it, and I had to go in just one minute to get warm, and while I was gone the horses started." "Well," said General Jackson, "it was cruel to you and cruel to the horses to keep you waiting in the cold. Go along, George."

His neighbors told me, and many of his old slaves also, that he was as familiar and respectful in speaking to negroes as to white people, and in all his intercourse with his neighbors exemplified the democratic and Christian doctrine of human equality. A lady who was much in the family assured me that Mrs. Jackson was in full sympathy with her husband in this particular. My informant described a scene at family prayers, for during the last period of his life the general had prayers every morning, often reading them himself from the Episcopal prayer-book. The overseer's wife entered the room somewhat late to attend prayers.

Mrs. Jackson rose from her chair and gave her a place by her side. A clergyman's wife who was present expressed great astonishment at an attention so marked to the wife of an overseer. "Oh, it's the way here," was my informant's reply; "and if she hadn't risen and given her a seat, the general would." To the Northern mind this does not seem anything in particular, but it was related to me by a Tennessee lady as a very uncommon concession.

The same lady described the general and his wife as the most devoted of couples. He was always somewhat deferential in his manner to her, and she to him. As my informant remarked, it was a marriage of the old school, and a certain etiquette was observed even at familiar moments, when they sat in opposite corners of the fireplace, each smoking a corn-cob pipe. He has been frequently known both to fill and light her pipe for her, as she would his for him. Mrs. Jackson, in her best days, was overflowing with humor and anecdote. If she had a company of good country neighbors, she would keep them in roars of laughter for a whole evening, her husband listening to the old stories with evident enjoyment. When he heard something that pleased him he would straighten up and laugh most heartily. It must be owned, however, that her conversation was much better adapted to the fireside in the old log-cabin than it was to the elegant dining-rooms of Nashville. The general perceived this much more readily than his wife, and his friends often admired the adroit manner in which he would take one of her long-winded stories out of her mouth, and bring it to a happy and speedy conclusion.

The general was exceedingly fond of a good song, and the reader is perhaps aware that in the early time every one was expected to sing a song on a festive occasion. He had two favorites above all others, both by Burns — "Auld Lang Syne" and "Scots Wha Hae." Every lady who came was asked to play them, and he would join in the chorus with great fervor. My informant remembers his glowing face and blazing eyes when he came in with " *Chains and Slavery!* "

In going about among General Jackson's old friends, I was struck with the deep impression which he had made upon their affections. I will copy from my notes two estimates of his character, the first by old Mr. Blair, the intimate companion of his friend during his Presidential terms. And I may mention that Mr. Blair could not speak of Andrew Jackson ten minutes without emotion bordering upon tears.

"Jackson," said he, "was a man of absolute sincerity. There was no guile in him. He loved the masses of the people with deep and constant love. He would have laid his white head on the block for them. He was a man without fear and without secrets — open as the day. He never locked a door nor concealed a paper. He was never puffed up and never depressed. He was sufficient for himself at all times. Fighting men loved him and cowards loved him. He was the most eloquent of men. When excited, his old bristles shook, and he thrilled the nerves as no other man did. In the bank affair, as in other measures, he was alone, against friends and against foes. Members of his cabinet wanted to back out, but were appeased by Jackson's habitual remark, 'I take the responsibility.' Andrew Jackson was, in my opinion, the greatest man that ever lived."

Such were very nearly the words of the editor of the "Globe," whose business was for years to put General Jackson's thoughts into the form of editorial articles. The other estimate which I will quote was that of old Hannah, the faithful and favorite servant of the Hermitage all her days. She fancied that some one in the company smiled derisively at an anecdote which she related of General Jackson. She fired up and spoke thus: —

"We black folks is bound to speak high for old mawster. He was good to *us*. You know what he was to you and must speak accordin'. But *we* is bound to speak high for him."

GEORGE GUESS,

JACK-OF-ALL-TRADES.

About the year 1769, a disreputable German peddler, with two packhorses laden with merchandise, made the tour of the Cherokee villages in Georgia, selling to the Indians such articles as suited them. In the course of his round, his fancy was attracted by a maiden of the Cherokee tribe, whom he wooed in the usual way by making presents to her father. He married her, and remained in her village.

She could not speak a word of his language, and he could talk but imperfectly in hers. But they built their wigwam, and set up housekeeping on the well-known Indian system, the squaw doing all the work, and the husband having all the pleasure. If he hunted the deer or caught fish in the stream, it was she who prepared the game for food, planted the corn, gathered the firewood, took care of the horses, and made the moccasins, priding herself, as Indian wives do, upon leaving her husband nothing to do but hunt and fight.

The disreputable peddler soon tired of this way

of life. One night he disappeared, and his wife never saw nor heard of him again. The tribe who had adopted him, although the Indians are keen news-gatherers, never received tidings of him. The name of this scurvy adventurer was George Gist, afterwards corrupted into Guest and Guess. Some time after his departure, the deserted wife gave birth to a son, whom she named, without any reference to his father, Se-quo-yah, which is said to mean in Cherokee, *He guessed it*, though for what reason she named him so is not known. Among the Cherokees he was and is called Se-quo-yah. Among white men, and in white men's books, he is now invariably called George Guess.

Here was a German boy in an Indian village, with no white men near, born a member of the Cherokee tribe. He was reared wholly in the Indian manner, trained as an Indian, taught only the Indian arts and the ancient Indian beliefs and traditions. He never learned a word of the German language, and never became at all proficient in the English. During his early years, he was completely severed from all the influences to which a white boy is usually subject. Those who believe in the power of what is called "environment" would naturally expect him to grow up an Indian.

But he did not. In the heart of the Cherokee country, associating only with Indians, and having for his mother a woman of pronounced Indian character, he was little more of an Indian than if he had been reared in Germany. He was German in the cast of his mind, German in his beliefs and unbeliefs, German in the industries he followed, German in his capacity for dogged perseverance, and peculiarly German in the invention which made him famous. As a mere boy, he showed a particular skill in the use of his knife, the same kind of skill that one or two white boys out of a hundred exhibit at school. As his mother kept cows, he exercised his ingenuity in cutting out for her milk-pans and skimmers of wood. He built her a milk-house over one of the mountain springs. Still more un-Indian-like, he helped his mother milk the cows, added to her clearing, and worked in the cornfield by her side. When he grew older, he took entire care of the cattle and horses, and broke the colts to the saddle. It requires but little knowledge of Indian life to be aware that such things as these, except the breaking of the colts, are not done by young Indians, who from boyhood despise the ordinary useful employments.

Upon reaching maturity, he entered into his father's trade of peddler. He went round the country buying furs, which he exchanged for powder, lead, guns, paints, blankets, cloth, a kind of trade which then yielded large profits, and he soon had an abundant supply of Spanish dollars, English crowns, and French five-franc pieces. He had indeed more of this kind of money than he could spend to advantage, and he became in consequence a silversmith, making rings, silver bands for the head, breastplates, necklaces, anklets. A good many of these articles are still in existence, and are described as being of very good workmanship.

By and by, when the white settlements were less distant, he had the opportunity to observe the working of a blacksmith. He appeared to understand at once the whole art of the smith. He made a bellows and blacksmith's tools with his own hands, set up a forge, and added blacksmithing to his other occupations. And now, though unable to read or write, he perceived the necessity of putting a stamp upon his work, such as white men call a trademark. He asked a white man to write for him his father's name in English letters, and the man wrote it as it was usually pronounced in the tribe, "George Guess." He made in his blacksmith's shop a steel die, which was a facsimile of the name so written, and with this he stamped all his silverware. In the Cherokee nation many specimens of his work bearing the trademark are shown to visitors.

With the white man came the blasting vices of the white man. Se-quo-yah was one of those who acquired the love of strong drink, which he bought by the keg, and treated all his customers, according to the bad custom of that time. He became a drunkard. Fortunately the temperance movement had gained some force at this period. One of the

Cherokee chiefs expostulated with the artificer, and strongly urged him to take the pledge. At length he did so, and became a strict teetotaller to the end of his life. About the same time he listened attentively to what the missionaries had to say concerning the Christian religion. After meditating long upon the subject in the patient, German manner, he arrived at conclusions from which he never could be moved. The old Indian beliefs, which he had derived from his mother and the medicine men, he rejected as false and superstitious. But he never could be brought to accept the supernatural claims of the Christian religion. This was, perhaps, the most German of all his traits, and the least like the conduct of a Cherokee, who usually embraces with ardor the teachings of the missionaries when once he has abandoned his native creeds.

While he was still a young man, this German Cherokee began to brood over the mystery of written words. The Cherokees took a white prisoner, in whose pocket was found a crumpled piece of paper with writing upon it, and they brought it to Se-quo-yah for explanation. Already he had some idea of what it was.

"Much that red men know," said he to the chiefs, "they forget; they have no way to preserve it. White men make what they know fast on paper, like catching a wild animal and taming it."

From that day onward for twenty years, he pondered this problem, and when the Moravian mission schools were set up in the tribe he got possession of an English spelling-book, which increased his zeal and gave him important aid, though he never learned to read it.

During the last three years of his inventive period, he passed most of his time in the seclusion of his cabin. At length he completed an alphabet of the Cherokee language, which consisted of eighty-five letters, each of which represented the sound of one Cherokee syllable, and the whole eighty-five represented all the distinct sounds used in speaking Cherokee. His system was so simple that a Cherokee boy could learn to read and write with it in a few weeks, or even in a few days. The pupil had indeed to learn and remember eighty-five letters; but as soon as this was thoroughly done, he could read his native language. Albert Gallatin, of President Jefferson's cabinet, when a copy of the alphabet was submitted to him, gave it very high praise, not merely for its ingenuity, but for its practical utility.

One of the first of the inventor's pupils was his own daughter, a child six years of age, who was soon able both to read and write Cherokee with considerable ease. Some of the Cherokee boys learned to write sentences in three days, and very soon a passion arose in the tribe for learning it. The inventor lived to see three printing-presses in the Cherokee country printing the Cherokee language in his alphabet. Four million pages of Cherokee were printed in it before he died. He saw school-houses all over the territory, in which his system was taught, and churches in which his alphabet was the medium of communication employed. He himself traveled extensively in the Cherokee nation teaching his alphabet. It has had a most important influence in promoting the civilization and prosperity of the tribe. Congress gave him five hundred dollars in recognition of its value, and the Cherokees voted his family a pension of three hundred dollars a year. His portrait adorns the Indian collection at Washington, and a marble bust of him stands in the Cherokee Council House. One of the counties of their nation and one of their seminaries bear his Indian name, Se-quo-yah.

When he was past seventy (about the year 1840), he started in an ox-cart, as it is said, in pursuit of knowledge, and he reached, after two years' journeying, a ridge of the Rocky Mountains. Thence descending to the valleys of California, near San Bernardino, he halted his cart, worn out with the toils of his long journey. A few hours after, he died, aged seventy-two years. He is still greatly honored by the Cherokees, who are to-day maintaining more than one hundred schools, besides an asylum for orphans, and almost every other institution of civilization. His history furnishes a curious example of the force of hereditary tendencies, which made this child of an Indian mother, living in an Indian land, a thoughtful, dreamy, brooding, industrial, inventive, skeptical German — almost as German as the other inventor of printing who lived and died in Germany.

WILLIAM MURDOCK,

MACHINIST.

———

I HAVE observed that the reputations which dazzle mankind were taken excellent care of by their proprietors. Julius Cæsar wrote his Commentaries, and Bonaparte his bulletins. General Washington requested his intimate friends to let him know if any public act of his excited disapproval. A certain New Yorker, noted for his colossal wealth, entertained at one time a project of building in the Central Park the highest tower in the world, to perpetuate his name. He did not carry out this notable scheme, but his inclination to do it was characteristic of the class of men who strongly attract the public gaze.

On the other hand, men of merit who neglect their reputations are apt to be overlooked by the world, if not totally forgotten. I think it highly probable that some of the greatest men and some of the greatest benefactors of our race have passed into oblivion, their names not even mentioned in the most voluminous biographical dictionaries.

A meeting was held some time ago in London

for the purpose of recovering, as well as honoring, the memory of a man who rendered his country services which were both important and striking, one of which was the invention of the machinery for producing illuminating gas. This was the most remarkable of his inventions. He was one of the most ingenious and successful mechanics of modern days; and yet, chiefly owing to his modesty, his generosity, and his indifference to fame, his name occurs in only one of the noted cyclopædias and dictionaries within my reach, and then not in a way to confer distinction.

This injustice, however, will probably be rectified ere long. It is now proposed to place a statue of Murdock in a public place in the city of London. When he died, in 1839, no leading journal in the world noticed the occurrence, and it is a matter of difficulty now to get particulars of his career.

He was a Scotchman, born in 1754, in Ayrshire, the native county of Dr. Johnson's Boswell and the poet Burns. Mechanical talent had been in the family for some generations. His father, John Murdock, a miller, made, it is said, one capital invention, that of the iron-toothed gearing, now an important device in almost all large machinery, without which power could scarcely be distributed from a central engine.

William Murdock, until he was twenty-three years of age, worked under his father. At that time another great Scotchman, James Watt, the improver of the steam-engine, had become famous, and he had lately formed his celebrated partnership with Boulton, a manufacturer of Birmingham. William Murdock came to Birmingham in 1777, and sought employment of the firm of Boulton & Watt. A trifling accident proved to be the turning-point of his destiny. Boulton, the capitalist of the concern, chanced to observe that the young applicant was twirling in his hands a hat of unusual appearance. Upon examining the hat and questioning its owner, Boulton discovered that Murdock himself had made it. It was of wood, and had been turned by the young man upon a lathe invented by himself. It occurred to the manufacturer that a young man living in a remote Scotch county who had invented without assistance the process of turning an oval would be a valuable acquisition to an establishment like his own. He engaged him on the spot, at a salary about equivalent to four dollars a week.

Murdock at once proved himself a useful hand, and a still more useful head. The steam-engine, as the reader is aware, was first employed in pumping the water from the deep mines in Cornwall and elsewhere. Hence the proprietors of the Cornish mines were the first to avail themselves of Watt's improved engine. William Murdock displayed so marked an intelligence in this branch of the business that the firm posted him in Cornwall to direct the putting up of the engines, and to set them going when the local foremen were baffled. In this business he showed extraordinary zeal and ability, and contributed greatly to the prompt success of the new engine.

And here we have another proof that if a man does not look after his own interest no one else is likely to do it for him. He continued in the service of Boulton & Watt for twenty-one years without having his wages increased beyond five dollars a week; and this while he was giving every year the most decisive proofs of possessing a mechanical genius not inferior to that of Watt himself. He did not demand an increase till he was forty-four years of age, and that was the reason why he did not get it.

He was an inventor, and his mind was absorbed in perfecting the devices of his brain. One of his early inventions was a steam carriage, which at first seemed to promise success. He made a working model about a foot high, the boiler of which was heated by a spirit lamp. Wishing to keep his invention secret, he chose a dark night for the trial of his machine, which he placed upon a path leading to the parsonage just out of town, the path running between high hedges.

When all was ready, the inventor lighted his lamp, which proved to be more powerful than he had calculated. Before he could suppose steam was generated, the carriage started down the narrow path, the steam hissing, the lamp blazing. The clergyman of the village, returning home late in the evening, saw this hideous thing approaching him at a frightful pace, and he rushed out of its way, screaming for help.

Probably the engine was as much damaged as the parson's nerves, for at this point, notwithstanding Boulton's earnest encouragement, the young man discontinued the experiment.

At the age of forty-four, then, this great mechanical genius was still working in Cornwall in the service of Boulton & Watt at five dollars a week. He then asked for an increase of salary. Strange to relate, the firm hesitated to grant it; whereupon he resolved to leave them and return to Birmingham. Then, for the first time, the people he had served seemed to become aware of the pecuniary value of his services. The mining companies of Cornwall offered him five thousand dollars a year if he would remain and continue to do what he had done for twenty years at four or five dollars a week.

He declined this invitation, and his old employers offered him the same sum to superintend their works. He accepted the offer. He was soon after admitted a member of the firm, and proceeded to fill the establishment with ingenious devices. The mere catalogue of these would occupy too much space. He made many improvements in Watt's steam engine. He invented an engine propelled by compressed air. He invented a steam gun, and several excellent machines for boring metallic cylinders. He long endeavored to utilize the power generated by the tread of men and horses on the streets. He invented the atmospheric railway, and suggested the pneumatic tube for sending parcels.

Without dwelling upon these, let us come at once to the invention of the gas machinery. The Chinese, our forerunners in everything, used illuminating gas centuries and centuries ago, obtaining their gas from crevices in salt mines. It was an English clergyman, Dr. Hales, who appears to have first procured illuminating gas from coal. This was in 1727. Several persons had observed that gas issuing from coal mines afforded an excellent light, and it was frequently collected in bladders and conveyed short distances in tubes for the purpose.

Until Murdock turned his attention to the subject, these things were done merely by way of experiment, and the gas-light was sometimes exhibited at popular lectures for the amusement of the audience. But in 1792 Murdock invented the apparatus which is now usually employed for extracting gas from coal by raising it to a high temperature without permitting combustion. He first used coal gas for lighting his workshop and office in Cornwall. Then he lighted portions of the manufactory of Boulton & Watt at Birmingham.

Soon after, he lighted some large cotton mills at Manchester. He made a grand exhibition of it in Birmingham in 1802, when, to celebrate the peace of Amiens, he illuminated the whole front of his manufactory in the most brilliant manner with gaslights. In 1813, London Bridge was lighted with gas. Paris adopted the new light in 1820, but as late as 1822 New York was still lighted with oil, and the city was not generally lighted with gas until some years later.

Murdock did not patent his invention, and the consequence was, the name of the inventor was not connected with it in the public mind, and was not recorded in connection with it in any way. His firm did not think it worth while to spend five hundred pounds for a patent, which was then the fee charged by the British government. It is pleasing, however, to know that the inventor had no need of any profit from this invention.

He spent the latter half of his life in developing and perfecting other devices, and died at the age of eighty-five years, after having added essentially and in many ways to the resources of civilization. Next summer's crowd of American travelers in London will have the satisfaction of seeing his statue on the bank of the Thames.

EZRA CORNELL,

MECHANIC.

On the Hudson River, above Weehawken, there is a pleasant region which is still called "English Neighborhood," because it was originally settled by a few English families. Here, in 1819, lived Elijah Cornell, a Yankee Quaker, who had been trying for a few years to establish a pottery, aided by his eldest son Ezra, a strong, handy boy, twelve years of age. Elijah did not succeed with his pottery. He could not compete in quality and price with earthenware imported from Europe.

So he made up his mind to remove with his wife and six children (the youngest a baby) to what was then spoken of as the Great West. He meant to settle in Madison County, in the State of New York, at the village of De Ruyter, about a hundred and fifty miles west of Albany. He intended to establish a pottery there, and he supposed that at such an immense distance from a seaport, — two hundred and fifty miles, at least, — he would be free from competition with foreign manufacturers. His idea was to cultivate a farm with the assist ance of his sons, and to add to his income by making as much pottery as he could sell in Madison County.

It was in 1819 that Elijah Cornell moved westward, but as yet there was no Erie Canal, and no public conveyance of any kind to the place of his destination. The family, with all their goods and chattels, were conveyed in two wagons, each drawn by two horses. They went by way of Goshen, through Orange County, and so reached the line of the present Erie Railroad, traversing the almost unbroken wilderness of Sullivan and Delaware counties, and the desolate hills of Chenango.

During the first half of the journey, they could usually reach some kind of shelter at night, either at a tavern or a farmhouse; but they were soon obliged to content themselves with sleeping in their own covered wagons, cheered and protected by a bright camp-fire. It was the winter season; the days were short and cold, and they were more than two weeks in accomplishing their migration.

Elijah Cornell found life easier in his new home. Assisted by his sons, he succeeded in his objects, and passed the rest of his active life in that region, enjoying a moderate but sufficient prosperity. The pottery established by him at Ithaca, to which place he afterwards removed, remains to this day one of the industries of the village, and gives good employment to many persons. Both he and his wife were exemplary members of the Society of

Friends. In the western country they lived in cheerful abundance, the centre of a large and virtuous circle.

Their eldest son, Ezra, had every kind of advantage in his youth for free and manly development except one, which he intensely craved — schooling. He soon outgrew the common schools of the region, and at that period there were no others. He exhibited a trait of character in his youth which is the mark of a superior intelligence, namely, a strong desire for knowledge. He studied a good deal at home, deriving some assistance from his father. At the age of sixteen, he undertook, with his brother's aid, who was one year younger than himself, to clear four acres of heavy woodland, as well as plow and plant it, on condition of being permitted to attend school during one more winter term.

That was the last of his schooling. But he learned two trades in his youth — those of farmer and potter — to which he at length added a third. Before he was eighteen his father found it desirable to build a larger shop for his pottery, and he employed his two sons in the work, under a hired carpenter. Ezra worked on this building from the beginning to the end, observing closely every process; so that he seemed to become all at once a competent builder. So confident was he in his powers that he and his younger brother undertook the building of a new house for the family, and accomplished the work without making a mistake, to the admiration of the neighborhood. In truth, besides having been handling tools ever since he was six years of age, he had inherited mechanical skill from a long line of industrious ancestors, and he seemed to be a mechanic by nature. But there is no such thing as a mechanic by nature. He had been brought up to use his hands, his eyes, and his head in conjunction, with care and diligence, from his earliest years.

When the family had removed into the new house, which was much the best in the village, and the architect had enjoyed for a short time the applause bestowed upon his work by his relations and friends, he found that the farm and the pottery were rather dull work compared with building, and therefore, at the age of eighteen, with his parents' consent, he left his home, hoping to find some congenial work at his new trade.

He was a splendid young fellow for vigor and strength, and he was particularly fond of walking. Up to an advanced age he could do his forty miles a day with ease and pleasure, and keep it up for a month at a time. He liked nothing better than to take a thousand-mile walk in a new and interesting country, and during his early rambles in search of work he almost always preferred to take his bundle in his hands and go on foot.

He made his way to what is now the beautiful city of Syracuse, then a mere cluster of shanties on he canal, and there he worked for nearly two years in felling the magnificent trees of the primeval forest for transportation to the city of New York by the Erie Canal. Then he worked for a while in a machine shop at a village which had indulged itself with the classic name of Homer, about twenty miles from his father's house. It cost him no self-sacrifice to trudge the twenty miles on Saturday evening, and back to work on Monday morning.

In the mean time, the Erie Canal having been brought into connection with Cayuga Lake, the little village of Ithaca suddenly became an important place, the centre of a thriving trade. Its fame having reached the ears of Ezra Cornell, he determined to seek his fortune there. His son, ex-Governor Cornell, tells us that, with one extra suit of clothes, and a small sum of money in his pocket, he walked from De Ruyter to Ithaca, a distance of forty miles, and much enjoyed the trip. He had no acquaintance in the village, and brought no letter of introduction; but he had the qualities which originate and carry on the world's business. He was the kind of man who is wanted everywhere.

He obtained work at Ithaca as a journeyman carpenter, and the first work he did there was to aid in building a dwelling-house, which is still standing, and which is pointed out to strangers. In a few weeks he was offered a better situation by a cotton manufacturer, who employed him to keep his mill and machinery in order; and a little later, he entered the service of a capitalist who carried on mills of various kinds near the village, and who wanted a good mechanic to oversee and perfect his machinery.

For twelve years, during which he remained in this employment, he had to do almost all kinds of work done by practical men. He became gradually the indispensable factotum of his employer, his inventor, general manager, and confidential agent, directing the expenditure of several hundred thousand dollars every year. He planned mills, invented labor-saving devices, constructed tunnels, built dams, and did everything else required by an extensive manufacturing and milling business.

The panic of 1837, which ruined so many men and prostrated so many enterprises, deprived Ezra Cornell of employment, and made him once more a wanderer in search of business. It was while traveling in Maine, introducing an improved plow, that he was drawn into connection with the new telegraphic enterprise in which he made a fortune of some millions in about twelve years.

There is no instance on record, I believe, of a great invention completed by the efforts of one man. Usually an invention of first-rate importance is originated in one age and brought to perfection in another; and we can sometimes trace its progress for thousands of years. Probably so simple a matter as a pair of scissors — one of the oldest of inventions — was the result of the cogitations of many ingenious minds, and has undergone improvement from the days of Pharaoh to those of Rogers & Sons. The most remarkable case of rapid invention with which I am acquainted is that of the sewing-machine, which in twenty-five years has been brought to a point not distant from perfection. But then *thousands* of ingenious minds have exerted themselves upon it! In the Patent Office at Washington, not less than two thousand devices and improvements have been patented relating to this beautiful contrivance.

The electric telegraph is an instance of the slow growth of a great invention. The first step was taken toward it thousands of years ago, when some one observed that if a piece of amber was rubbed against cloth, it attracted small objects, and emitted a spark. In Greek the word *electron* signifies amber; and hence the name which has been given to the mysterious and wonderful fluid that pervades the universe. The second step toward the telegraph was not made until the middle of the last century, when a Dutch professor invented the Leyden jar, by which electricity can be accumulated, and from which it can be suddenly discharged in an electric shock.

From that time electricity became, in all civilized countries, the favorite branch of science. Franklin's discoveries quickly followed. Galvani led the way to electro-magnetism, which Volta pursued with striking success. The galvanic battery was speedily added to the resources of science. The electro-magnet followed; and in 1819 Professor Oersted of Denmark so increased our knowledge of these instruments, that little remained except for ingenious inventors to devise the mechanical apparatus of the telegraph.

Ezra Cornell has a place in the history of the telegraph, which would have caused his name to be remembered if he had never founded a university. At a critical moment his ingenuity came to the rescue of Morse's enterprise, and saved it, perhaps, from premature extinction. The telegraph, in return for this service, has since given him a large fortune, part of which he has expended in a manner with which the world is acquainted.

On a certain day in 1842, when he was a traveling agent for a patent plow, he arrived at Portland, in Maine, and, naturally enough, called at the office of an agricultural journal, edited by Mr. F. O. J. Smith, with whom he was well acquainted. This visit proved to be the turning-point in the plow agent's career. Horace Greeley often said that every man has one chance in his life to make a fortune, and Disraeli has informed mankind that the secret of success is to be ready for your opportunity when it comes. Mr. Cornell's opportunity was now coming, and he was ready for it. On entering the office, he found the editor on his knees with parts of a plow by his side, drawing on the floor with a piece of chalk, and trying to explain his drawing to a plow-maker named Robinson, who was standing near.

"Cornell," said the editor, with animation, and as if much relieved, "you are the very man I want to see. I want a scraper made, and I can't make Robinson understand exactly what I want. But you can understand it, and make it for me too."

"What do you want your scraper to do?" asked Cornell.

Mr. Smith explained. Congress had made an appropriation to build a line of telegraph between Washington and Baltimore, and Mr. Smith had taken the contract from Professor Morse to lay down the pipe in which the wire was to be inclosed. Finding that it would cost a great deal more to do the work than he had calculated upon, he was trying to invent something which would dig the ditch, and fill it with dirt again, after the pipe was laid at the bottom. Cornell asked various questions concerning the size of the pipe and the depth of the ditch, and after thinking awhile, said : —

"You don't want either a ditch or a scraper."

Mr. Cornell now took the chalk, drew his plan, and explained it to the contractor, who could not be convinced that it would answer the purpose. The whole day was spent in discussion and explanation, which had the effect of confirming both gentlemen in their opinions. The next morning Mr. Smith was still more an unbeliever, while Cornell's confidence in his machine had greatly increased. At length the contractor proposed to put the idea to the test of experiment.

"I will pay the expense," said he, "whether the machine is successful or not, and if successful, I will pay you fifty dollars, or a hundred dollars, or any other price you may name. The price is a matter of no consequence, if the machine is successful."

In a machine shop of Portland, Cornell began forthwith to construct his pipe-laying plow. As the work went on the contractor's confidence in it greatly increased, and at his invitation Professor Morse came from New York to witness its trial, which was made on the 17th of August, 1843, on Mr. Smith's own farm near Portland. Ezra Cornell once described the particulars of the experiment.

"The trial," he said, "was made with a team consisting of four yoke of oxen, quite unused to work together. They were under the direction of a son of sweet Erin, whose lingo was Greek to their ears. He flourished the gad vigorously, and soon produced the most violent disorder with the cattle. Soon, however, the oxen started with a rush for a distance greater than the length of pipe we had on the drum of the machine. The consequence was that, when the driver brought his team to a halt, the pipe had disappeared."

In the confusion of the moment the contractor and Professor Morse were utterly bewildered, and could not imagine what had become of the pipe. Mr. Smith asked if they had forgotten to put the pipe in the machine, and the professor in his turn anxiously inquired what had become of it.

"The pipe," said Cornell, "is where we intended it should be — about eighteen inches beneath the surface of the ground."

So it proved. The driver got a spade and dug for the pipe, and, after working an hour, uncovered the whole of it. It was again coiled on the drum of the machine, and a second time buried in the earth at the required depth. The great problem of laying the pipe within the appropriation was solved. Professor Morse returned to New York in the highest spirits.

The striking success of so complicated a machine, invented on the spur of the moment, made such an impression upon the mind of Mr. F. O. J. Smith that he induced Ezra Cornell to go to Baltimore and superintend the working of his own invention. It was with much hesitation that Cornell abandoned his patent plow and embarked in this new enterprise. But he was satisfied from the start that the electric telegraph was going to become an important and indispensable addition to the resources of man.

He went to Baltimore, and entered soon upon the business of laying the pipe, which was done by his machine at the average rate of three quarters of a mile a day. Another difficulty arose. The pipe contained two wires, which had to be kept apart and perfectly insulated. If at any part of the forty-mile line the two wires came in contact, all their labors were in vain, and it would be a matter of immense difficulty in the infancy of the art to discover the point of contact. Mr. Cornell soon became satisfied that the insulation was imperfect, and by secret midnight experiment he was enabled to demonstrate the fact. He caused it to be communicated to Professor Morse, who reached the scene of operations when all the pipe was laid except about ten miles.

"Mr. Cornell," said he, "can you not contrive to stop this work for a few days in some manner so that the papers will not know that it has been purposely interrupted?"

Cornell had been expecting something of the kind and was at no loss what to do. He stepped back to the machine, and said to his drivers: —

"Hurrah, boys! Whip up your mules! We must lay another length of pipe before we quit for the night."

The teamsters cracked their whips; the mules started on; Cornell grasped the handles of the plow, and, canting it over so as to catch a point of rock, broke it all to pieces. The event made a sensational incident for the next morning's Baltimore papers; which also stated that the work would be interrupted for a week or two while the machine was undergoing repairs.

The situation was really critical. The appropriation was spent except seven thousand dollars, and there were large claims upon that. Professor Morse, Mr. Smith, and their scientific friends consulted anxiously how to insulate the wires. There were many suggestions; and it was finally concluded that to reinsulate the wires effectually and complete the work would cost twenty-five thousand dollars. Hence they made up their minds to suspend the enterprise until another appropriation could be obtained from Congress.

During the discussion, no one thought of consulting Ezra Cornell, who was still regarded merely as a very ingenious mechanic. But this mechanic had an excellent head upon his shoulders, and he utilized his unwelcome leisure by getting a number of electrical books out of the library, and making a thorough study of the subject. He read that similar pipe-laying had been attempted in England without success, and that at length the English projectors had adopted the plan of placing their wires upon poles.

The mechanic soon received orders to adopt the English plan. The whole line was promptly placed upon poles, and at so slight an expense as to leave on hand a large portion of the seven thousand dollars to continue the salaries of Professor Morse and his assistant. The line was soon in a condition to transmit from Baltimore to Washington the truly *electric* intelligence that Polk and Dallas had been nominated for President and Vice-President.

It was thus that Ezra Cornell began his connection with the electric telegraph. He took the lead in the construction of the first lines. He organized many of the early companies. He shared in all the early struggles and disappointments, to be rewarded at length with such success that, at the age of fifty, he was enabled to withdraw from active business, worth millions of dollars, and to spend the rest of his life in rendering services to his village, to his State, and to his country. He was an enthusiastic farmer and improver of the breeds of cattle. He established a free library at Ithaca, and finally gave the bulk of his estate toward founding Cornell University, in establishing which he personally labored for many years with equal diligence and tact. In one particular he was powerfully influenced by the example of Peter Cooper. He said, in presenting the public library to the citizens of Tompkin's County : —

"The result of the noble and wise example of Peter Cooper, as contrasted with the equally well-meaning but less successful example of Stephen Girard, led me to decide in favor of the policy of executing the scheme during my lifetime."

Both the library and the university have taken root, and promise to convey the name of Cornell to the latest posterity. The university is situated on a plateau, elevated nearly five hundred feet above the village of Ithaca, and commanding an enchanting view of the whole of Cayuga Lake and of the country beyond it as far as the eye can reach.

He was a man of sterling worth and inexhaustible generosity, simple in his demeanor, and blameless in every relation of life. He died in 1874, aged sixty-seven years, revered and lamented by every one who knew him. His son, the late governor of the State of New York, has given the public a too brief but deeply interesting memoir of his career, which will aid to perpetuate his name and extend the influence of his example.

JAMES NASMYTH,
INVENTOR.

"Is life worth living?" a noted author recently asked.

Such a victorious and cheerful life as that of James Nasmyth, the inventor of the steam-hammer, answers the question. The answer is, Yes; most decidedly! Fortunate in his ancestors, blest in his parents, successful in his business, and happy in the tastes and pursuits of his declining years, he enjoyed uninterrupted welfare, and diffused happiness around him, from childhood to old age.

Born in Edinburgh in 1808, he inherited from a line of excellent Scotch workmen a *love* of thorough and highly-finished workmanship. His grandfather, Michael Nasmyth, a carpenter and builder, was particularly noted for the high quality of his work. He took pride in selecting just the right kind of wood for every purpose, and all his joints fitted to a nicety.

"The hanging of his doors," says James Nasmyth, "was a matter that he took great pride in. His own chamber doors were so well hung that they were capable of being opened and closed by the slight puff of a hand-bellows."

The attention of the future machinist was frequently called to the excellence of his grandfather's workmanship, as a great number of houses of his building were, and are still, in perfect preservation in Edinburgh. The house of David Hume, the historian, was built by Michael Nasmyth, and the one in which Sir Walter Scott passed his boyhood and youth. The inspection of these well-built houses stimulated in the lad the desire to aim at excellence in everything that he undertook; and, indeed, this was the rule of his whole life.

His father, who was an artist, besides inheriting this love of thoroughness, possessed also a good deal of an inventor's ingenuity. For example, when he was a young man he invited his sweetheart one day to go with him to a fashionable public garden, where every one was required to appear in full dress, which then included striped silk stockings, visible to the knee. On going to his room to dress he found that his only pair of stripes had been singed and spoiled; upon which he opened his box of water colors and painted his bare legs in black and white stripes. No one observed the difference, except that one of his friends complimented him on the perfection of the fit, and asked him where he bought his stockings.

Again: when the Duke of Athol wished to plant with trees a rocky crag which no one could climb, this ingenious artist, father of a great inventor, procured a number of tin canisters, filled them with tree seeds, and fired them against the crag with a cannon. The canisters burst, and scattered the seed all over the craggy height. Some years after, when his father visited the place, he was delighted to find that vigorous young trees were growing from all the recesses of the cliff. This ingenious father imparted to all his children much of his own skill with the pencil, and brought them all up to be cheerful, industrious, and efficient persons.

James Nasmyth was one of those boys who do everything well except their school lessons. Latin and Greek were always to him — Latin and Greek. He did his duties at school in a respectable, routine fashion, and no doubt derived from them a considerable advantage. His heart, however, was not in his books. As a boy, he was a great collector of coins; he learned to make excellent spinning-tops on his father's foot-lathe; he made the best kites in the school, and admirable paper balloons. As he grew older, he learned how to make small brass cannon from large keys, and turned old files into little steels for sharpening knives. He early learned the art of hardening and tempering steel; an art which he considers the most important of the mechanical secrets. He was a frequenter of shops, factories, and chemical laboratories, as the fathers of many of his school-fellows were engaged in manufacturing. Soon he began to make the acids, the alcohol, and the phosphorus which he used in his experiments. All these things required money, and this he obtained by selling various articles of his own manufacture.

He declares with great emphasis that this is the only kind of education that will fit a boy to take a leading part in mechanical business.

"The eyes and the fingers," he remarks, — "*the bare fingers*, — are the two principal inlets to sound practical instruction. No *book* knowledge can avail for that purpose. The nature and properties of the materials must come in through the finger ends; hence I have no faith in young engineers who are addicted to wearing gloves. Kid gloves are perfect non-conductors of technical knowledge."

By the time he was twenty years of age, he had made several small steam-engines, besides turning-lathes and a great deal of other mechanical apparatus. But he was as modest and reasonable as he was skillful, and his great ambition was to get a place ever so humble in the famous machine works of Henry Maudsley, one of the best mechanics then living. His father took him to London and presented him to the great man and stated his desire.

"Well," replied Maudsley, "I must frankly confess to you that my experience of pupil apprentices has been so unsatisfactory that my partner and myself have determined to discontinue to receive them, no matter at what premium."

The poor lad was wofully disappointed. Maudsley, however, showed them over his place, and noticed the young man's intense interest in the machinery. They came at last to the engine-room, where the attendant happened to be shoveling out the ashes from under the furnace into a wheelbarrow. The youth, in a transport of enthusiasm, said : —

"If you would only permit me to do such a job as that in your service, I should consider myself most fortunate."

"So," said the master, with a keen and kindly glance at the lad's glowing face, "you are one of that sort, are you?"

When they had finished their round, the youth mustered up courage to say : —

"I have brought up with me from Edinburgh some working models of steam-engines and mechanical drawings, and I should feel truly obliged if you would allow me to show them to you."

"By all means," said Maudsley, "bring them to me to-morrow, at twelve o'clock."

The business was done. After inspecting the young man's work, Maudsley came to him, showed him into his own beautiful private workshop, and said to him, with a beaming friendliness of expression : —

"This is where I wish you to work, beside me, as my assistant workman. From what I have seen, there is no need of an apprenticeship in your case."

The young man fixed his own rate of wages, in obedience to the cashier's request.

"If you do not think ten shillings a week too much," said he, "I could do well enough with that."

"Very well," said the cashier, "let it be so."

This was equivalent to two dollars and a half of our money, upon which he not only lived very well, but saved. After a few years of working side by side with Maudsley, having accumulated a little capital, much credit, and more skill, he set up in the business of a machinist at Manchester, and prospered from the start. In a very few years he had a large manufactory, and supplied a vast number of labor-saving machines to the manufacturers of that part of England. He married happily, and lived in a pretty little country cottage near his works.

The way he came to invent the steam-hammer was this: he had been known as an inventor all his life, and in 1839 the contractor for building the engines of the Great Britain, the largest steamer that had yet been undertaken, consulted him. A difficulty had arisen.

"I find," said the contractor, "that there is not a forge-hammer in England or Scotland powerful enough to forge the paddle-shaft of the engines for the Great Britain. What am I to do? Do you think I might dare to use cast iron?"

This set him thinking, and the result was that wonderful steam-hammer of his, which can give so gentle a blow as to crack the end of an egg placed in a wine-glass on the anvil, while the next blow may shake the teacups in a cupboard a quarter of a mile away. The same principle he applied to the steam pile-driver. It cost five hundred pounds sterling to patent an invention, and business being then depressed, he had to borrow the money for the purpose.

Upon the return of better times the steam-hammer, with his other business, made money for him so fast that when he was forty-eight years of age, which was in the year 1856, he retired from business. He has spent the evening of his days in various noble and useful studies. He has published a superb volume on the Moon, illustrated by exquisite photographs taken by himself. In addition to his other good qualities, this admirable man was so fortunate as to have an amiable vanity which enabled him to enjoy his own achievements, and to take pleasure in relating them, as he has done in his autobiography.

GABRIEL DANIEL FAHRENHEIT,
INSTRUMENT-MAKER.

Under the bronze statue of Dr. Franklin, which stands opposite the "Tribune" office in New York, I saw a boy the other day selling thermometers at ten cents each. I looked up, almost expecting to see the eyebrows of the philosopher rise in astonishment, and a smile of approbation brightening his metallic countenance. He used to say that he would like to return to the earth at the end of every hundred years, to see how we were getting on; and if his wish could be gratified this year, I am sure that, among the minor street sights of New York, nothing would amuse or surprise him more than this small dealer in card thermometers.

When Dr. Franklin first had a thermometer, about a hundred and fifty years ago, few persons in America had ever seen one, and there were probably not more than six on the continent. There may have been one at Harvard, one at Yale, one at New York, and two or three at Philadelphia. After Franklin obtained his thermometer, he was never weary of experimenting with it; and for many years the laws of heat and cold, the varying temperature of the body, and the effects of heat upon the air currents, both in doors and out, were objects of his vigilant investigation. It was he who discovered the effect of color upon temperature, and first established that dark clothes warm us best in cold weather, and that white clothes are most suitable for hot. It was he who suggested the white cap covering, now called the Havelock, used by the English soldiers in the East Indies, and by travelers in the desert. All this, and much more, from the use of Fahrenheit's thermometer.

And who was Fahrenheit, whose name is usually printed on our thermometers to this day? He was a Prussian merchant of Dantzic, a very ancient, narrow-streeted, gloomy seaport on the Baltic coast, from which, in barbarous ages, the Danish freebooters set forth to ravage the English shores. Interested from his youth in the study of nature, he made a small discovery when he was nineteen years of age, one effect of which still appears on the face of all our common thermometers. The winter of 1709 was remarkably cold, the temperature falling lower at Dantzic than the oldest inhabitant could remember it; and young Fahrenheit observed that by mixing salt and snow he could produce a degree of cold equal to that which prevailed on the coldest day of that winter. He concluded that that was the lowest degree of cold known in the world, and the lowest also that could be produced artificially. It was an unfortunate error; for when, at a later day, he arranged the scale of his improved thermometer, he called that degree of cold *zero*, and fixed the boiling point at two hundred and twelve degrees above it, a scale which is both arbitrary and inconvenient. Zero should have been the freezing point, and then the boiling point might have been indicated either by one hundred or two hundred, which would have made calculation easy. Such a scale the whole world would have finally adopted, and we should have had one scale in use instead of four.

While still a young man, Fahrenheit became so interested in natural science that he gave up his business in Dantzic, and went abroad in search of knowledge; for, in those days, if a man wanted knowledge of that kind, he had to go and place himself under the personal instruction of the few men who possessed it. After residing for a while in various parts of Germany, France, and England, he settled at Amsterdam, then one of the most renowned capitals of Europe, where he established himself as a maker of philosophical instruments.

But he was not content to follow the established patterns. The instrument which we now call a "thermometer" was an improvement upon a rude contrivance, invented about the year 1600, styled a weather-glass. This was merely a glass bulb and tube, from which the air had been partly expelled, inserted in a vessel of colored liquid. When the air in the bulb was rarefied by heat, the liquid rose; but when it was condensed by cold, the liquid fell. This was the beginning of it. The next improvement was to fill the bulb with spirits of wine, expel the air from the tube, and seal it. This was a real thermometer; which was further improved by coloring the spirits of wine, and fastening the instrument to a piece of wood or metal marked with a scale of degrees. This was the point of development which the thermometer had reached in 1720, when Fahrenheit directed his attention to it in Amsterdam.

Two changes are attributed to him: first, he substituted mercury for spirits of wine; and, secondly, he constructed the scale which still passes by his name. Whether he originated the substitution of mercury, or whether he derived the idea from some of the learned men with whom he associated, is not certainly known. The Royal Society at London, at the time, evidently regarded him as the originator; for in 1724, two or three years after the introduction of his thermometer into England, he was elected a member of the Society. In the Philosophical Transactions for 1724 are several papers by Fahrenheit, which show him to have been a man capable of improving the instrument without assistance.

The Fahrenheit scale has only been adopted by

three countries, Holland, Great Britain, and the United States. Various other scales have been introduced, but the thermometer of the future has yet to be made — the freezing point at zero, and the boiling point fixed at the figure best adapted to decimal subdivision and calculation. In the mean time, as Dr. Ure suggests, a portion of Fahrenheit's antiquated nonsense might at least be omitted; such as the unmeaning words, *summer heat, blood heat, fever heat, temperate, spirits boil*, and others. Real information, Dr. Ure thinks, could well be substituted for such words as these. The average temperature of winter, of summer, and of the year, in the country where the thermometer is to be used, might be given.

The use of the thermometer has added greatly to our knowledge, and is doubtless destined to play a still more important part in the future. The following facts the reader may find interesting. The lowest degree of artificial cold that has yet been produced is one hundred and eighty-seven below zero. The hardest thing to freeze is carbonic acid, which requires a temperature of one hundred and forty-eight below zero. At forty below zero mercury freezes; and this is also the average winter temperature at Nova Zembla. The average temperature of the year round at the North Pole is thirteen below zero. Salt water freezes at fourteen above; wine, at twenty above; blood, at twenty-five; vinegar, at twenty-seven; milk, at thirty; water, at thirty-two. Alcohol boils at a hundred and seventy-three. On the summit of Mt. Blanc, water boils at one hundred and eighty-two; on the summit of Etna, at one hundred and ninety-two; at the Catskill Mountain House, at two hundred and six; on the surface of the earth, at two hundred and twelve. At two hundred and thirty-two sulphur melts, and at three hundred and twenty-two petroleum boils. The temperature of the ocean, at a few hundred feet below the surface, never changes, but stands at about forty-five the year round. The interior of the earth, however, grows warm as we descend. The temperature at the bottom of an artesian well, one thousand three hundred feet deep, is seventy-three; but there are some mines, not more than one thousand feet deep, where the temperature begins to be oppressive, and the thermometer marks seventy-five. The animal heat of various creatures varies remarkably. The maximum heat of man's blood is one hundred and two; but of ducks and guinea-fowls, one hundred and nine; and if you wish to hatch hens' eggs in an oven, the proper temperature is one hundred and five. The highest point which the mercury reaches in an ordinary situation, in the hottest part of the East Indies, is one hundred and fifty-four; at which point also the mercury occasionally stands in the engine room of a steamship.

Such are a few of the facts which the thermometer reveals. It has become one of the most indispensable and universal of all instruments. There are even pocket thermometers, as well as a thousand curious varieties of mantel ornaments, for which a thermometer furnishes the excuse.

Fahrenheit, besides improving the thermometer, was a universal improver and inventor, as every man of his vocation must be who has an intelligent mind. He died in the midst of his career, when he was but fifty years of age, leaving some important projects incomplete.

JEAN BAPTISTE ANDRÉ GODIN,
STOVE MANUFACTURER.

A BOY nine years old sat on a bench in the school of a French village. He was the son of a worker in sheet iron, and his school was such as was provided in France seventy years ago for the children of workingmen. A hundred and forty-one children were crowded together in this school, the atmosphere of which was stifling, the benches hard and without backs. The teacher, having so many pupils to serve, had but one means of fighting disorder and getting a chance to be heard, namely, the stick. What other instrument of repression could be wielded by a schoolmaster with a hundred and forty-one boys breathing poison, and suffering from hard seats and nothing to do?

And yet one of these boys, Jean Godin, was of high and rare quality. He had thoughts in his little mind. He often reflected upon the badness of his school, and upon the insufficiency of one teacher to benefit so large a number. He thought also that the plans pursued by the unhappy teacher were unwise, and he often said to himself: —

"If I were a teacher, I would teach my pupils better than they are taught in this school."

It was natural that this poor boy should think that the chaos and misery around him were due to the modes of teaching; but in truth the wisest and ablest man could do little for a hundred and forty boys in a close room, except to let in upon them some fresh air, and give them as long periods of recess as his employers would permit.

This boy was so impressed with the imperfections of the school that, even before he left it, he was strongly inclined to be a teacher, for the sole purpose of trying better ways of teaching. He might have done this if another thought had not taken possession of his mind.

"No," said he, still talking to himself on the school benches, "I will learn a trade. I will become skillful in manual arts, for in these I have an example to set the world."

That such a boy as this, of delicate constitution, timid, poor, untaught, should have had such thoughts as these is so extraordinary that we should be pardoned for not believing the story but for the subsequent history of the child. It is himself who relates these events in a printed book, in which he shows how this dream of a child became the serious and successful project of the man. He admits himself the improbability of the tale.

"This persistent idea," he remarks, "at so early an age, is at least a singular fact, especially considering the excessive timidity which I then showed in all my actions, and my frail and delicate temperament."

At the age of eleven and a half years he left his wretched school, and took his place as apprentice in his father's shop. He says again that at that tender age, while hammering away upon his iron, he had a distinct idea that the trade he was learning would lead him to play an important part in the industrial world. He worked beyond his strength, for he occasionally lent a helping hand in the fields and gardens cultivated by his relations.

Having finished his apprenticeship, he complied with the custom of France and Germany in making a tour for improvement in his trade. Young French journeymen, with a knapsack on their backs, go on a kind of tramp, and work for a while in shops supposed to excel in some particular branch of their trade. He carried with him on this tour his thoughtful, benevolent mind. He observed the injustice with which many workingmen were then treated, the smallness of their wages, and the bad feeling between employer and employed. Workingmen were beginning to reflect. Fourier's writings were circulating among them, and at length Jean Godin began to read Fourier. The works of this philosopher were like a revelation from heaven to the untaught philanthropist, and in carrying out the scheme of his youth, he was greatly aided by them.

Having returned to the vicinity of Guise, his native land, he was soon established in business for himself, and laid the foundation of a brilliant prosperity by introducing a capital improvement. He made stoves of cast iron instead of sheet iron, and gave to his new product something of the variety, the cheapness, and the convenience with which we have been familiar ever since Benjamin Franklin invented the Franklin stove. In the course of a few years he found himself at the head of iron works employing from twelve to fifteen hundred persons.

During the creation of this business, though obliged to devote nearly the whole of his time and his strength to its management, he behaved to his men with so much consideration that he never had a dispute with them. If there was any difference of opinion between himself and any portion of his workmen, he invited them to a conference on the subject, stated his case, patiently heard every one in reply, and never once failed to come to a friendly understanding with them.

In considering the lot of the workingman, he came to the conclusion that the real pinch and hardship of French poverty was in its mean, small, dirty, and insalubrious habitations. A good mechanic with a family, earning the wages paid in France to mechanics, could afford to live only in two or three inferior rooms of a crowded house, in a disagreeable street. Upon this point M. Godin fixed his attention. It was not, he thought, the toil of the workingman which took the heart out of him, nor the food which he was obliged to eat, nor the company he had to keep. The toil was often excessive, but not generally injurious; the workman's food could be tolerably nourishing and savory, and he could find good society among his brother mechanics. But the house, the *home*, its mean and hateful surroundings, the noise, the dirt, the bad air, the forlorn appearance of every object — here was an assemblage of evils of the most blighting and lowering character, against which the individual workingman could not contend. It was beyond his reach, and beyond his means. He could decorate his own little parlor, but he could not let the sun into it, nor the good country air, nor keep out horrid smells and discordant sounds. Unaided, he could not place his children in comfortable circumstances.

At the same time M. Godin, by a very simple process of arithmetic, discovered that it was not in the least necessary for French workingmen to live as they did. He discovered that the sum total of the rents they were actually paying was sufficient to procure for each and all of them a proper home, provided the capital which those rents represented was judiciously expended on a concerted system. The result was that he built for the habitation of his men and their families a great cluster of buildings, which he called the *Familistère*, in which every family had its suite of convenient and well-ventilated apartments, while all of them enjoyed in common spacious parlors, meeting-rooms, halls, school-rooms, gardens, gymnasiums, covered walks, and even shops for the sale of the most essential articles of daily use. These suites of rooms he rented at rates which his men could afford to pay; at rates somewhat lower than they had previously paid for their inferior and demoralizing tenements. He went farther. He arranged a system by which a man, out of his savings, could acquire stock in the *Familistère*, and thus obtain for his family a permanent right to the rooms they occupied in case he should be disabled.

The experiment appears to have been gloriously successful. The *Familistère* afforded an attractive, commodious, and delightful home to eighteen hundred persons, of whom five hundred and twelve were children, most of them going to school under the same roof. On a stormy day in winter the children could go to school in the morning without being exposed to the weather; the mother of a family could buy the daily supply of provisions, and do a little domestic shopping besides, without needing even the protection of an umbrella. As only a narrow river separated this great family home from the shops and factories where the money was earned which supported it, the fathers and brothers, by a short walk over an elegant bridge, transported themselves to the scene of their daily labors.

The founder of this admirable establishment and the lady who had from the beginning assisted him in its management by her intelligent zeal were united in marriage. The happy event occurred on the 14th of July, which is to the people of the French republic what the Fourth of July is to us.

A French marriage is peculiar. To us it seems rather cold-blooded and business-like. At nine o'clock in the morning the Executive Committee of the *Familistère*, ten in number, a delegate representing the workmen, the bride and bridegroom and their relatives, assembled at the office of a notary to sign the marriage contract, which consisted of a preamble and four articles, drawn up in legal form. The preamble set forth that, in marrying, they desired to reaffirm their interest in the success of the *Familistère*, and in the publications on social subjects written and to be written by Monsieur Godin.

"Their desire is to render their collaboration more efficient by giving this consecration to the bond which has constantly associated them in labors inspired by their love of humanity, no thought of personal interest mingling with that pure sentiment."

The four articles of the marriage contract expressed the intention of the married pair that each should retain and enjoy the property which they already had. Whatever Monsieur Godin possessed before marriage should remain his own after marriage, and whatever Mademoiselle Moret possessed should remain legally hers. But each was to enjoy all the good of the other's possessions. No accounts were to be kept between them. They were practically to have all things in common, and in case of the death of one of them the survivor should continue to possess all that they had used in common, such as their furniture, clothing, carriages, horses, and the apartments they had inhabited in the *Familistère*.

When this contract had been duly signed by all the persons present, the company proceeded to the office of the Mayor of Guise, by whom the marriage ceremony was performed, according to the laws of the republic. The married pair, their relations and witnesses, then returned to the *Familistère*, where they held a reception. The band of the institution received them with a burst of joyous melody. First, the little children of the infant school presented their bouquets. After them, the primary scholars made their bows and courtesies. Then the boys and girls of the higher schools offered their respects. Two ladies, attached to the institution, presented bouquets in the name of the numerous corps of persons employed in the *Familistère*.

Next, the legal adviser of the association presented, on behalf of some workmen of Belgium, a beautiful bronze, representing a blacksmith seated upon his anvil in deep thought, his eyes fixed upon a book lying open in his lap. This present was singularly appropriate, since Godin had himself once been a blacksmith, and the father of the bride was also a blacksmith. Then Godin's own workmen presented an exquisite bronze, representing a girl at the spinning-wheel, accompanying the gift with a brief and appropriate speech. Monsieur Godin then came forward and returned thanks for himself and his wife for the sympathy which had been shown to them on the happy occasion. He declared that the members of the association over which he presided had rightly interpreted the motives which had governed him in founding, extending, and improving the *Familistère*. His object had been to provide for all the men who assisted him, as well as their wives and children, as good, as secure, and as elegant a home as he desired for himself. This, too, had been the desire and aim of the beloved woman who had labored at his side for twenty-five years.

"Our marriage to-day," said he, "is only the consecration of the past. Its object is to establish, if possible, our institution on a still firmer foundation. But to this you must give your assistance, for upon you will depend, when we are gone, the prosperity of the association, and the happiness of your families. Through your fraternal and cordial union you will demonstrate to the world that Capital and Labor, by *uniting* their efforts, can solve all those great problems which in the immediate future will embarrass every government."

The whole company, including the workmen, their families, Monsieur and Madame Godin, and the invited guests, partook of an elegant and abundant repast, with which the ceremonies of the day appropriately concluded.

I do not claim that Monsieur Godin has solved "the labor problem," as it is now called. I fear that he has not. Much of the success of the *Familistère* is due to him personally — to his tact, benevolence, knowledge of the world, and inexhaustible patience. I regard his establishment merely as one experiment looking to a better life for the men who labor, and to a more cordial cooperation between employers and employed. If it should fail, I should find consolation in the fact that it is better to fail in an attempt to serve mankind than to succeed without serving them.

There are various organizations in the *Familistère*, one of which is a Society for the Promotion of Peace and Arbitration — peace among the nations, and arbitration between employers and employed. This society, which has existed for some years, has become of more importance than before, owing to the great number of strikes which have occurred in France and in the adjacent country of Belgium, where industry was for a time almost paralyzed, and the people lived in hourly fear of destructive revolution.

The society meets every month in one of the large rooms of the *Familistère*. The meeting for

October a few years ago was of particular interest, and was largely attended both by the male and female members; for this society does not exclude from membership the sex which has the deepest interest in the peaceful and rational termination of labor disputes. When men go out on strike, the women do not go out, but toil on at home, sorrowful and anxious. Our workingmen might take a hint from this French society, and admit to all their labor societies the membership of women.

At this October meeting, Monsieur Godin, the president of the society, made an address, in the course of which he unfolded a scheme for putting a check upon the decline of wages in the branch of industry in which the society was particularly interested. He began by glancing back to the period when the industrious people of France had no rights and no liberty, when chief warred against chief, and forced his vassals to fight and die in petty and fruitless warfare. Then came the period when France was one nation, and kings warred only against kings. But still it was from the industrious people of the country that their armies were recruited, and it was their fields and cottages which were ravaged and destroyed. From childhood to hoary age the working people of France toiled and saved to make good the waste of unnecessary wars.

The speaker reminded his hearers of the recent war with Germany, a wanton, needless war, without cause or pretext, which had cost the country a million lives, two beautiful provinces, and twenty-five hundred wagon-loads of silver. All this treasure and most of this blood belonged to the workingmen of France.

So much for the past. How is it now?

"To-day," said Monsieur Godin, "industrial warfare has taken the place of the tribal and national warfare of other times. A new aristocracy has replaced the ancient feudal aristocracy, and the workman continues to be oppressed. His bread of to-morrow is not assured to him; his work, no more. The lords of to-day wield another weapon. It is by *cutting rates* that they do battle with one another, and he is the victor who can cut them down so low as to ruin his rivals. But now, as always, it is the unfortunate workman who furnishes the means for such struggles. Wages are reduced. But in their turn other employers reduce wages, and at last we all find ourselves in a narrow way without outlet. We are under a necessity to find a remedy, for this industrial war can no more give prosperity to a people than the feudal warfare of other days."

In making these remarks, Monsieur Godin was relating in part his own experience as an employer of labor. As a maker of stoves, grates, and the utensils thereunto belonging, he had many rivals in France. He had to sell at the market price or not sell at all, and he had a difficult task during his last three years in resisting the tendency to a reduction of wages. It is said, indeed, that the task would have been impossible if he had not been protected by some valuable patents, as well as by having had possession of some markets for almost thirty years.

He next brought forward a scheme for remedying the evil which he had so eloquently described. He said he meant to address a circular letter to all French employers in their trade, proposing to them to form a union, and to agree upon rates of wages for the different departments of labor in their shops. This he intended to propose at once on his own responsibility, but at the same time he advised the workmen also to "syndicate themselves." He urged them to meet frequently, to understand their needs and rights, and thus to be able, if necessary, to act as one man in self-defense.

The speech of Monsieur Godin was heard with the deepest attention, and frequently interrupted with the warmest applause. A few days after, Monsieur Godin sent out his circular letter to all the competing manufacturers of stoves and stove ware in that part of France. He asked each to join the proposed syndicate of manufacturers, with a view to agree upon the following objects: First, to establish uniform rates of wages for the same number of hours of labor. Secondly, to fix upon the same graduation of wages, so that the same degree of skill and experience should receive the same amount of compensation in every establishment. Thirdly, to agree upon the number of hours that should everywhere constitute a day's work.

Here would be two societies, both powerful and both necessary. If the syndicate of employers abused their power, there would be the syndicate of workingmen to object and resist. If the syndicate of workingmen made unreasonable demands, there would be the society of employers capable of uniting to resist them.

But these two powerful bodies could come into painful conflict!

In that case, the committee representing the syndicate of workingmen should confer with the committee representing the syndicate of manufacturers, and if each cherished the right spirit they would at length come to an agreement. In the absence of legal provision, these two syndicates seemed to offer the best remedy for the grievances under which both workmen and employers suffered.

"It is of the greatest urgency," said Monsieur Godin, "to put a stop to the reduction of wages, for when they are reduced in one establishment, other employers are fatally condemned to do the same, although it affords relief but for a moment, and that relief is purchased by the deprivation and misery of workingmen and their families."

It remains to be seen what effect this scheme

will have in France and Belgium. All power is abused, but in this project there are two powers. Power will negotiate with power, and, we may hope, with salutary results.

Godin and his wife have both passed away, but their House remains, the many excellent works which he wrote remain, and the memory of his noble example remains, and will remain as long as man concerns himself with the welfare of his fellow.

JEAN LE CLAIRE,

HOUSE-PAINTER.

During the volcanic rule of the first Bonaparte there was a shepherd-boy in France named Jean Le Claire, who will probably be remembered with honor when there is not a well-informed man in the world who will pronounce the name of Napoleon with respect. He was the son of a very poor village shoemaker, of old Burgundy; a lively, vigorous little fellow, well-disposed, but somewhat less tractable and orderly than French boys usually are. He attended the village school long enough to learn how to read and write—a fact often mentioned in France to prove the advantage of universal education. What would Le Claire have been, said the free school advocates, if he had never learned to read?— Le Claire, to whom France owes one of the most pleasing and useful lives lived within her borders during the last hundred years.

From his tenth year this boy earned his own subsistence; first, as shepherd-boy, pig-tender, and cow-driver; then, as mason's assistant, harvester, and thresher of grain; noted in all for his spirit, courage, and resolution. He even had his fights with the village boys, for he was not disposed to receive an injury without seeking redress.

One day, when he was seventeen years of age, seeing a number of harvesters getting upon the Paris coach for a ride to the next county, the idea seized him to ride away with them, and he kept on all the way to Paris, a hundred miles distant from his native place. And there he was, in the year 1818, a perfect stranger, a country youth acquainted only with country things and employments.

By a mere chance he obtained work with a house-painter in grinding and mixing colors, carrying the pots and brushes, drawing the ladder-cart, and running of errands. He received, by way of compensation, a chunk of bread for breakfast, his supper in the evening, a corner in an attic for a sleeping-place, two cents every day, and an extra franc every other week. He worked hard, lived hard, and suffered much from short allowance, fatigue, and loneliness.

But he worked with such intelligence, skill, and fidelity that, in three years, he asked and received the full wages of a journeyman house-painter, equal in our money to sixty-five cents a day. His fellows laughed at him for working so hard and so carefully avoiding waste. They would talk to him in this way, as he afterwards reported : —

"Ah, you wish, then, to enable your employer to wear silk stockings! You wish to enrich him! Believe me, you will get no thanks from him. Don't you see that it is your labor which provides him with a carriage? True, he has a daughter. Do you wish him to give her to you in marriage? He may do so. We have seen kings marrying shepherdesses. Very well, my boy, try and get it into your head that she is not for you. Work as you will, as soon as work is slack you will be discharged like another, and then, when you are out of work, your old comrades will not employ you, but let you alone as a simpleton."

House-painters then were noted as being among the most dissolute of the workmen of Paris; partly from the fitful nature of their employment, but chiefly because wine and brandy were supposed to be antidotes to the poison of the white lead in their paint. There was a place in Paris where they stood to be hired, and where they had to wait long in wet and cold. The wine-shops of the vicinity offered shelter and temptation.

There was something in this young Burgundian which kept him from going their way and living their poor life. He worked on with such assiduity that he saved enough in his first year of journeyman's wages to buy himself free of the conscription, which then cost $120. He never had to join the waiters for work. Intelligent, prompt, ambitious, he was always in demand at the highest wages. At twenty-two, when he was earning seven francs a day, he married; at twenty-six, upon a capital of two hundred dollars, he hired a paint shop at sixty dollars a year, and set up in business for himself.

His success was immediate and very great, for he was gifted with abundant confidence in himself, and he executed every contract in the best manner. Every day at twelve his excellent wife brought him his dinner in a neat basket, and he ate it with his men around him. He had the art of inspiring all who worked for him with something of his own energy; and so, before he was thirty-five years of age, he was the leading man in his vocation in Paris, boldly undertaking the most extensive contracts, and executing them with notable promptitude and skill. He kept eighty-five men at work, and he had at once the pick of the best workmen and the confidence of the largest landlords and architects.

The personal victory being won when he was still a young man, he had an overplus of energy, and this he employed in improving the trade which had enriched him, and the workmen who had rendered him such loyal and efficient aid. He did not do this as a conscious philanthropist. He did it as a man of business, for business reasons, by business methods; although, no doubt, there was a large ingredient of generosity in his motive. But he did not say to himself: "Now I will benefit my fellow-men." He said, more modestly: "I will bring my great business still nearer perfection."

One immense service which he rendered to his trade was to deliver it from the necessity of mixing paints with white lead, the poison which entailed upon house-painters several painful and dangerous diseases. After a long course of experiments and the expenditure of a great deal of money, he produced a white zinc which was a good substitute for white lead, and not poisonous. He bought zinc mines, and opened a manufactory of the zinc basis, which is now frequently employed in the trade, both in Europe and America. This service was good business, as well as good benevolence.

Like every able commander of men, he reflected much upon the best way of dealing with those who assisted him in his business. A man who employs a hundred house-painters, working in all parts of a large city, is obliged to put great trust in them, and especially in the men who direct the separate companies. He reflected continually upon the best mode of supplying them with adequate motive for doing their very best. He paid the best wages, but this was not sufficient, because most French workmen are so burdened with the support of relations and families that they cannot rationally expect to make adequate provision for sickness and old age. They cannot ordinarily have the motive of ambition which originally actuated Le Claire. He kept thinking, too: —

"What will become of these excellent men whom I have trained, who are attached to me, to whom I am attached, and to whom I am, in part, indebted for my success? How unworthy in me to abandon them, and leave them to the tender mercies of another proprietor, who may not value them!"

After much reasoning on such problems as these, and conversation with political economists, he seized the idea that a remedy for most of the difficulties between employer and employed would be a just system of profit sharing. Pencil in hand, he " figured on " this idea, and found that the difference between a tolerable workman and an excellent workman might be represented by a sum of money, say, in the house-painting trade, twenty-five cents a day. He perceived that if all his men worked as earnestly and carefully as he himself had worked, the profits of the year's business would be so increased that he could give them a liberal share of those profits, and yet be himself a gainer.

After thinking and figuring, reading and consulting, for five years, he announced his intention of trying the experiment. His own workmen distrusted and discountenanced the movement. The government of Louis Philippe opposed it as a scheme that savored of revolution. At length, however, he got his men together and began the exercises of the meeting by placing upon the table before them a bag of gold coin, containing 11,886 francs, which he said was the portion of the year's profits to be divided among them. He proceeded to make the division in accordance with the plan previously announced.

From this time there was no distrust on the

part of his men, and he continued every year, as long as he was in business, to make an annual division among all his workmen, finally extending the benefit even to men who had worked for him only a few days or hours. The second year more than twelve thousand francs were divided, and the sum increased every year, not only to the advantage of the employed, but to the still more signal advantage of the employer. He retired from business in 1865, a millionaire, went into the country, where he became mayor of his village, and took the lead in all kinds of good works to the last days of his life.

He did still better than that. Before withdrawing from his business, he arranged it on a plan so wise, just, and simple that nobody was disturbed in his employment, and the establishment has continued prosperous and famous to the present day. The House did an important part in the decoration of the Exposition buildings in 1889, in which there was a pavilion consecrated to the Le Claire establishment. Every man employed in it who does his best has a sure place as long as his strength holds out, and a pension (earned by himself) sufficient for his comfort in sickness and old age.

MARGUERITE BOUCICAUT,

STOREKEEPER.

Visitors to Paris find the huge, miscellaneous bazaar founded by the Boucicauts as flourishing and attractive as ever. It resembles the establishment created in New York by the late A. T. Stewart, who in fact copied from the Boucicauts the general scheme of his uptown store. Stewart, however, omitted to make any adequate provision for the continuance of the business after his own withdrawal from it, and therefore soon after his decease the vast fabric fell to pieces, and many hundreds of faithful and well-skilled men and women, some of whom had grown gray in the service, were deprived of their accustomed employment. The enormous capital involved in the business has proved of little real advantage to any one except the lawyers.

It was far otherwise with the Bon Marché of that noble and well-mated pair, Aristide and Marguerite Boucicaut. Their business flourishes after their death, and their faithful employees still enjoy the fruits of the founders' admirable management.

No litigation followed their decease, and their example has become an inspiration and an admonition to the whole business world of Europe and America.

Their personal story is full of beauty and romance. She, a lowly village maiden, stout of limb and strong of heart, a very poor man's daughter, earning her livelihood by washing clothes in the river Sâone; her mind intelligent, but almost wholly uncultivated. He, a young peddler of linens, owning his horse and cart, the result of long and severe economy. At the annual fair and festival of her village, in the flower of their age, they met. He cast a favorable eye upon the cheerful, vigorous, and good-looking girl. He proposed to her parents for her hand. The horse and cart won their consent; the attractive personality of the young man gained hers; and so they rode away together on the peddler's cart, an original kind of wedding journey. Besides being husband and wife, they were now fellow-laborers and partners in business.

Even after their boy was born, she still rode in the cart, their object being distinct before them, to save money enough to try their fortune in Paris. After some years this object was accomplished. They went to Paris, sold their horse and cart, and lived in one room, in a very cheap street. But the smart and active young ex-peddler obtained employment as clerk in a dry-goods store near the fashionable quarter of Paris, and at wages which enabled his wife to stay at home and keep house for the little family.

By this time they had both discovered the absolute necessity of knowledge for any kind of desirable success in modern business, and the young husband engaged a teacher at a few francs a week to instruct himself and his wife in arithmetic, book-keeping, geography, and other elementary branches; also, in English and German.

And still they saved the surplus of their income, practicing an ingenious economy not yet known to the people of the United States; and at last, in 1848, when Aristide Boucicaut was thirty-nine years of age, they bought a small store on part of the site of their present establishment. They furnished their little shop with every kind of household merchandise which they could buy extremely cheap. They called their place GOOD-BARGAIN STORE, which in French is *Bon Marché*. When they had bought articles very cheap at auction, they sold them at a fixed price, a little beyond cost, thus giving the customers the advantage of their experience and tact. They placed upon every object a ticket plainly stating the price, and from this they never departed.

Husband and wife again labored together, she occupying the cashier's desk in the daytime, and posting the books in the evening. All storekeepers in Paris are polite, but the Boucicauts were something more than that to their customers. They adopted the principle of trying to satisfy them, to serve them in such a way that they would remember their visit to the Bon Marché with pleasure. For the first year or two their progress was slow, but when once they began to prosper their success was rapid and remarkable. Store was added to store, and clerk to clerk. In a few years they had absorbed a whole block, and occupied an edifice five stories high. During their first year the whole sum taken over the counter was nine thousand dollars; in their seventeenth year their receipts were more than four millions of dollars; and still the business grew, until it was the talk of the city, and one of the wonders of France.

So far, they had won a kind of success common to many energetic and skillful men of business. Now begins the grand part of the story, which will cause the lives of these two Paris shopkeepers to be remembered with honor when cannon-balls and swords, as Victor Hugo predicted, will be seen in museums side by side with the rack and the thumbscrew, curious relics of the barbaric period.

Boucicaut's early lot had been hard. As soon as he began to feel himself a victor, he made up his mind that no apprentice or clerk of *his* should suffer from the abuses which had embittered and shamed his own young life. He was a good master from the first, and he was continually revolving in his mind larger plans for the benefit of those who served him. He founded a library for their use; he opened classes in the evening for their free instruction in the languages most required in the business of the store — English and German. To these he added classes in fencing and music. He adopted as much of the early-closing principle as was possible in Paris at that time, and he tried various schemes of making the salary of the clerk bear a certain proportion to the average amount of his sales.

There is a great deal of trouble in city dry-goods stores about giving the clerks a chance to take nourishment, because the natural dinner time occurs when business is most active. To meet this difficulty, they finally converted their uppermost story into a complete restaurant, where dinners and lunches were furnished to the whole body at cost, in the best manner, and without loss of time. They established also among them a Mutual Benefit Society, to the funds of which they made a large donation of money, the object being to provide a resource for all employees in sickness and old age.

It had long been the intention of M. Boucicaut to convert his business into some kind of joint-stock or profit-sharing enterprise, in which every person in his employment would enjoy the advantage and security of ownership. But he was a very prudent man — one of those who are unwilling to take a step until they feel sure of the consequences. Hence it came to pass that, while he was still meditating his plans, and had only partly carried them out, he died, aged sixty-eight years. A few months after, his only son died, leaving Madame Boucicaut the head of one of the largest businesses in Europe. This was in the year 1877, when she herself was well stricken in years. She approved herself more than equal to the opportunity.

Her first and last thought was the permanent welfare of the great multitude of clerks, apprentices, and girls who were in her service. She appears to have had toward them the provident feeling of a mother, as if she had transferred the affection for the son she had lost to the children with whom she labored day by day. Three years after her husband's death, she executed his plan of forming a joint-stock company by admitting to partnership about one hundred of the upper clerks, whom she enabled to buy shares in the business, while retaining herself a little more than one half the capital.

It is not possible here to give the details of her scheme. Her great object was to make every person who was permanently attached to the business an equitable sharer in its profits, and to secure to all faithful employees a sufficient pension when they were disabled by sickness or old age. She was extremely solicitous to make herself of less and less necessity to the concern, so that her death would cause no interruption of the business, and reduce no deserving families from abundance to poverty.

As she lived, so she died. Her death occurred in December, 1887, just ten years after that of her husband, when she was seventy-two years of age. Besides having given large sums for benevolent purposes in her lifetime, she still remembered such objects in her will. To every person in her establishment who had worked less than six months, even including those who had served her but one day, she left twenty dollars. To those who had worked ten years or more, including several hundreds of persons, she bequeathed two thousand dollars each. She also gave her favorite country house as a resting-place for those in her employment who needed change and recreation. In many other ways she showed that, in disposing of her immense property, her only thought was to do with it the greatest amount of good to the greatest number of people who had claims upon her attention.

The bequests to her employees amounted to about four millions of dollars, and she also gave large sums to societies of artists, musicians, dramatists, inventors, teachers, and others. Her pictures she bequeathed to her country; her linen and silverware to a school for poor girls. She left to M. Pasteur, who invented the process of inoculating for hydrophobia, a parting gift of twenty thousand dollars.

We cannot wonder that when this glorious woman was borne to her grave in Paris, she was followed by representatives of almost every benevolent organization in the republic, who overflowed the church, and filled the cemetery itself with a mourning crowd.

MICHEL BRÉZIN,

CANNON-FOUNDER.

THERE was a pretty festival lately at the French village of Garches. The French excel all nations in the art of graceful festivity, particularly when the object is to honor the memory of a departed benefactor.

In Garches there is an asylum for aged mechanics called *Hospice de la Reconnaissance,* wherein three hundred workmen find a peaceful shelter in their old age and abundant supplies of the necessaries of life. This asylum does not consist of one huge, splendid, fever-breeding edifice, a monument to the vanity of the founder. It is a village, rather, in the midst of a pleasant park, where the old men live in companies, according to their trade, choice, and disposition, each house having not many more inmates than the number composing a large family.

Besides food and clothing, they are allowed a few sous per week for tobacco and other cheap luxuries. Recently it occurred to the old men to ornament their village with a bust of their founder, Michel Brézin, and they raised the greater part of the money by economizing their tobacco fund, the rest being added by benevolent persons living in the neighborhood. The bust was executed by one of the first artists in France. It was unveiled lately in the presence of all the inmates and a numerous company of invited guests. A distinguished public man pronounced the oration, in which he related the history of the founder and the circumstances attending the establishment of the institution. He read the will of Michel Brézin, dated in 1829. I will translate the material part of this remarkable document, which we may call a model will, although written by a man who never went to school: —

"As, unhappily, I have neither father, mother, wife, nor children, and as the law permits me to dispose of the whole of my property according to my desire, I believe I cannot make a better disposition of it than in accomplishing a scheme long since meditated by me, which is to found an Asylum, to be called *Hospice de la Reconnaissance*, a home for poor, aged workmen, whose numbers shall be determined by the amount of the fund which I shall leave for the purpose. To be admitted to it, a man must have worked at one of the trades which I have myself exercised. To enter it, he must be more than sixty years of age, never convicted of crime, and furnish proofs of a good, moral character, and show that he has no other means of living, and promise before entering to conduct himself like an honest man, and agree to be dismissed from the institution if his conduct therein is unbecoming."

On submitting this will to probate, it was found that he could not lawfully leave his nephews and nieces wholly unbenefited. The government assigned three hundred thousand francs to be divided among his nearest relations. The rest of his fortune, amounting to about five millions of francs, or one million of dollars, was devoted to the purpose designated in the will. The French government takes great care of endowments of this nature. Michel Brézin's property has been so well invested, and the institution so economically managed, that it now maintains in great comfort its three hundred inmates. Before his death he used to say that he should leave his money for the benefit of the workmen "who had helped him make it." His will accomplished this purpose. The French say that Brézin, a simple mechanic, was able, like Louis XIV., to found his *Invalides*.

We should suppose upon reading this will and visiting the Hospice, that Brézin must have been a very amiable and benevolent person, a dutiful son, a gentle citizen, a kind employer, a Peter Cooper kind of man. It seems he was of an extremely different type.

He was born in Paris as long ago as 1758, when Louis XV. was king of France. His father was a foreman in the mint of Paris, and brought up this child to follow his own calling. As his father could neither read nor write, and yet had risen to a high rank as a workman, he undervalued those accomplishments, and gave his son no school education at all. From the age of seven, the boy went to the shop every morning like a man. He picked up a little knowledge, however, in early life, although to the end of his days he wrote badly and spelled worse. He showed a particular aptitude for mechanical work, and became well versed, at an early age, in the operations of the mint.

In Louis the Fourteenth's time, each piece of money was hammered into shape on an anvil, very much as it was done in the time of Alexander the Great. But at this period the money-makers had got on so far as to strike out the coins roughly from a metal plate of the right thickness, and finished them by hand.

The young Brézin was not a model son. He was obstinate, passionate, and willful, and one day, when he was eighteen years of age, after a dispute with his father, he ran away from home, and made the tour of France as a journeyman mechanic traveling for improvement. He finally settled at Bordeaux, where lived one of his uncles, who procured him a place in the Bordeaux branch mint. Here he passed several years, until his father, having become old and infirm, gave up to him his position at the mint in Paris. Here again his stern and intractable character changed his career. Differing in opinion with his superiors in the mint, he resigned his place and set up in business for himself as a founder and worker in metals.

He was just in time to avail himself of the chances afforded by the French Revolution of 1789. Being a " democrat by anticipation," and one of the most pronounced character, he was employed by the revolutionary government in the manufacture of those enormous quantities of copper coin and debased coin which they vainly tried to substitute for good money. The most skillful coiner in France, he was also a hard man, a close calculator, strictly just to his workmen, but not gracious in his demeanor toward them. He made a great profit by this business, which was so pernicious to the people, and he had the good luck to escape the fate which overtook so many capitalists during the Reign of Terror. He not only saved himself, but his fortune also, which was the more difficult of the two in that impecunious time.

When the revolution became warlike, and had to defend itself against a continent in arms, Michel Brézin went into the business of founding cannon. Soon he had two foundries at Paris in full activity, which produced thousands of new pieces, and repaired thousands of old ones. An old-fashioned cannon was almost as dangerous to friends as to enemies. It was liable to crack and to burst. The touch-hole was continually enlarged by the burning of so much powder, until sometimes it was large enough to admit a hen's egg. Brézin was full of business; prompt, indefatigable, " harder to bend than any of the metals with which he worked."

All through his life he exhibited the same rigidity of character which he had shown in childhood.

Such a man was not likely to escape the notice of Napoleon Bonaparte when he seized the supreme power of the State. During the whole of Bonaparte's reign, Michel Brézin was the chief founder of those cannons to which Napoleon attached so much importance. There never was a time when a cannon-founder was likely to be kept so busy as during those twenty years. It was Brézin who set up the boring machines upon barges in the Seine, the machinery of which was turned by water power. Cannon, cannon, cannon, plenty of cannon, and then more cannon — that was the history of the reign of Napoleon Bonaparte, and Michel Brézin was the cannon-founder of the period.

In the midst of his activity came the Russian disaster, the invasion of France, the defeat, dethronement, and exile of the usurper. All the Brézin foundries were silent, and at the age of fifty-six he was condemned to repose. The return of Bonaparte from Elba called him once more to his old work, but the Hundred Days passed speedily, and France had no more need of cannon-foundries for many a year.

He retired from business with an ample fortune, which was much increased during the remainder of his life. He died in 1828, aged seventy years, but his Asylum was not fully established and organized until 1840. He was married, but died childless and a widower, as we have seen.

His character resembles in some respects that of the founder of Girard College, who was a hard, stern, close man, apparently destitute both of natural affection and human sympathy. My impression is that it is better for a man to be good and gracious as he goes along through life, rather than do all his generosity in a lump after he is dead. Still, there is room in the world for all the varieties of good people.

LOUIS JOLIET,

FUR-TRADER.

A BUSTLING, thriving town in Illinois perpetuates the name of the man who discovered the upper waters of the Mississippi. It was an honor well bestowed, and it were to be wished that all the towns in our wondrous western empire were as appropriately named as Joliet.

In 1645, when Boston was fifteen years old, and New York twenty-two, the whole of Canada belonged to a company of Frenchmen called the Hundred Associates, whose governor and manager was an enterprising, far-seeing man, named Jean Talon. Among the mechanics who came from France in the service of this company was a wagon-maker named Joliet. He settled in Quebec; where, in 1645, his son Louis, the explorer and pioneer, was born.

The Jesuit fathers, then all-powerful in Canada, received the boy into their school, and gave him what was then considered a superior education. Indeed, he was so enamored of the way of life in the college, and became so attached to his instructors, that, at seventeen, he resolved to join their order, and pass his life in its service. We hear of him, at the age of twenty-one, taking part in one of those philosophical debates which were once so much valued as a means and as a test of education. All the personages of the colony were present, and among those who are recorded as having distinguished themselves in the wordy encounter, we find the name of Louis Joliet.

But this man was formed for action. Soon after coming of age he renounced his intention of joining the Jesuits, and embarked in the great business of Canada, fur-trading with the Indians, in which he passed the next four years of his eventful life.

Jean Talon, for some time, had had his mind directed to the discovery of the place where the Indians obtained their supply of copper. All the Indians of Canada, from the lower lakes as far north as any one had ever gone, possessed implements and ornaments of copper, — even copper hatchets and knives, of as fine a temper, it is said, as our best steel. When the Indians were asked whence they procured their copper, they pointed toward that vast inland sea which we now call Lake Superior. In 1670, Governor Talon, looking about him for a man resolute and intelligent enough to search out the unknown source of this valuable metal, fixed his eyes upon the young fur-trader, Louis Joliet. Joliet accepted the commission.

With one companion he made a long canoe voyage upon the upper lakes, returning, after many weeks of adventurous navigation, without having discovered the copper mines of Lake Superior.

His failure will not surprise any one who has visited the copper region; for Portage, the centre of the quartz-copper mines, is hidden deep in the heart of an extensive peninsula, reached only by a narrow, winding stream; while the wonderful mines of mass copper are several miles from the shore, away near the western end of the great lake.

Jean Talon, when recalled to France, was succeeded by the vigorous Count Frontenac, who had ability enough to sympathize with Talon's plans, and to adopt some of them. Before sailing, Talon had recommended to the new governor Louis Joliet as a young man fit to be intrusted with enterprises demanding resolution, skill, and fortitude. A new scheme was then on foot. Talon's curiosity had been roused concerning a very great river in the far West, of which the Indians frequently spoke, and which, he thought, might prove to be the long-sought passage to the Pacific Ocean. Count Frontenac adopted from his predecessor the scheme of sending a party in search of this river, and accepted also his recommendation of Joliet as the fittest man in the colony to conduct it.

Joliet, twenty-eight years of age, in the prime of his life, familiar with Indians, their languages, customs, and arts, patient of toil, not easily turned from his purpose, and possessing whatever of knowledge had been gathered of the geography of the New World, willingly undertook the expedition. He was accompanied by the famous Jesuit missionary Jacques Marquette, who was aflame with desire to aid in wresting this western domain from the realms of the devil. The expedition consisted of Joliet, Marquette, and five men, who took with them two birch-bark canoes, in which they would navigate the lakes and rivers, and which they could carry over the intervening lands. In May, 1673, the little party, provided only with a little dried meat and corn, launched their light canoes in the Strait of Michilimackinac, and were soon on the broad and heaving bosom of Lake Michigan.

Across the lake they paddled to Green Bay, where they landed and told the Indians whither they were bound. The Indians strove to dissuade them from an enterprise so perilous. The Great River, they said, was full of monsters that would devour them, and at one place there was a devil whose roar could be heard at a great distance, and who lay in ambush to draw into the abyss wherein he dwelt all who presumed to descend the stream. Fierce tribes lived upon its banks, who tomahawked every stranger that approached their abode. Luckily the voyagers knew enough of the red men to disregard these wild tales.

Paddling to the head of Green Bay, they ascended the rapids of the Fox, dragging or carrying their canoes, until the tranquil Lake Winnebago opened before them. On they went, by lake and river, between forest and prairie, until they reached the great town of the Miamis and Kickapoos, where they halted to ask for guides to the river Wisconsin, the nearest tributary of the Father of Waters. The friendly savages furnished them with two, by whose assistance they reached the Wisconsin; floating down which they emerged, at length, upon the clear and rippling waters of the upper Mississippi — so different from the yellow, tumultuous flood of the lower country. It was the 17th of June, 1673, — just thirty-one days after they had stepped into their canoes upon the shore of the Strait of Michilimackinac. Since De Soto, they were the first white men who had looked upon the Mississippi.

It remained to explore the mighty stream. It remained to ascertain whether it did indeed empty into the Pacific.

Down the limpid, rapid tide they floated, by those bluffs so picturesque which travelers now daily admire; past those boundless prairies which are no longer, as then, dotted and streaked and blackened with buffaloes; stopping at night to cook their evening meal, but taking care to sleep in their canoes anchored in the stream. Fourteen days passed without their seeing a human being, or any sign of human life. But at last, in the mud of the shore, they discovered the print of Indian feet, and a well-beaten path leading across the prairie. Joliet and Marquette, unwilling to leave behind them an unknown danger, took the resolution, as wise as bold, to follow that path and see to what it led.

They left the canoes in charge of their five men, and walked briskly by the path for six miles. Then they descried, near the banks of a river, three Indian villages. With quaking knees and beating hearts, invoking the protection of Heaven, these two brave men kept on their way undiscovered, until they could hear the voices of the Indians in conversation. Standing boldly out upon the prairie, in full view of the village nearest to them, they shouted. Instantly the whole tribe swarmed out of the wigwams, and stood gazing at the new-comers. Soon four chiefs slowly advanced, holding up two pipes of peace; and when they drew near, stopped suddenly, and remained for some time gazing at the Frenchmen, motionless and silent. Great was the surprise of the white men, and greater their relief, to notice upon the persons of the chiefs some French cloth; for it seemed to denote that they were friends, who had traded with Frenchmen on the lakes. So indeed it proved. The chiefs conducted them to the village with every mark of respect; and there the principal chief, as the greatest proof of consideration that he could offer, received them at the door of his wigwam, naked, and pretended to be dazzled by the brilliancy of the light which their presence created.

"Frenchmen," said the naked potentate, affecting to shade his eyes from the blinding light, "how bright the sun shines when you come to visit us! All our village awaits you, and you shall enter our wigwams in peace."

All day and night the Frenchmen were feasted, and the next morning, when they returned to their canoes, the chief and six hundred of his people escorted them; and as they dropped down the stream grunted their farewells.

Down past the Missouri with its marvelous torrent of yellow mud; down past the beautiful Ohio; down the turbid monotony of the great river, until they had been just a month upon its waters; and still no end! They were then a few miles below the mouth of the Arkansas, with seven hundred miles between them and the Gulf. Feeling certain now that the river did not empty into the Pacific Ocean, but into the Gulf of Mexico, they deemed it best to turn their prows up the swift stream while yet there was time to reach Quebec before winter.

For eight weeks they toiled against that impetuous current, and only reached Green Bay after an absence of four months, Marquette utterly exhausted. The tireless Joliet, leaving his companion there to rest, pressed on to report the result of the expedition to Count Frontenac. Within sight of Montreal a sad mishap befell him.

"I had escaped," he writes to the count, "every peril from the Indians; I had passed forty-two rapids; and was on the point of disembarking, full of joy at the success of so long and difficult an enterprise, when my canoe capsized, after all the danger seemed over. I lost two men and my box of papers, within sight of the first French settlements."

After reporting to Count Frontenac, who gave him a generous welcome, he resumed his old way of life, and, two years after, married the daughter of a rich fur-trader. He subsequently settled upon the island of Anticosti, in the lower St. Lawrence, where he founded an extensive trading-post, and flourished for many years. In 1690, when Sir William Phipps sailed up the St. Lawrence to attack Quebec, he stopped on his way to sack and burn this establishment.

Louis Joliet, it appears, never recovered from the blow.

He became again an explorer, and afterward held the comparatively humble post of a pilot upon the St. Lawrence. He died, as it seems, in poverty, about the year 1700, aged fifty-five.

BARTHOLOMEW THIMONNIER,

TAILOR.

It is proposed in France to erect a statue in honor of Thimonnier, as "the inventor of the sewing-machine." Oh, no, Messieurs! No man was *the* inventor of the sewing-machine as we now have it in almost every house in the civilized world. It had a great many inventors, several of whom died before Thimonnier was born; and some of its devices were even patented in England as early as 1755. Thimonnier was a very meritorious person, and the story of his life is interesting and pathetic in a high degree. He did actually patent *a* sewing-machine in France in 1830, sixteen years before Elias Howe patented *a* sewing-machine in the United States. But there is a great difference between the definite and the indefinite article.

Bartholomew Thimonnier, the son of a Lyons dyer, was a journeyman tailor in a town near Lyons. He married an honest seamstress, and reared a numerous family upon the slender product of his industry. It had been better for him if he had stuck to his needle and his goose; but such was not his destiny. He was born to be an inventor, and he had the usual fate of his order.

In the beautiful part of France which he inhabited, the department of the Rhone, one of the principal industries in the villages and country places is the making of shawls and other articles by the use of the crochet needle. The women there carry on this elegant work during the summer in the open air, upon the piazzas of their houses, and at open windows. It was while observing the movements of the crochet needle that the idea occurred to him that such work could be done by a machine, and upon further reflection he concluded that his own work, the sewing of garments, was also capable of being done by a mechanical contrivance.

An unlettered man, living in a small town in a part of France three hundred miles distant from the capital, he had never heard of any previous attempts of this nature. He was as original and independent an inventor as Elias Howe himself, who was also an unlettered man, and wholly ignorant of all previous endeavors to invent a sewing-machine.

It was about the year 1825 when the inventor's mania took firm possession of our poor French tailor. He passed the whole of his leisure time, besides many hours both of night and day which were not fairly at his disposal, in a small, remote room working over his conception of a sewing-machine. He passed four years in this way, more and more absorbed in his secret labors. He neglected his business, spent all his little savings, lost his credit, and was regarded by his friends as little better than a lunatic. He did not have the advantage of our American inventor, who was a machinist by trade, and lived in an atmosphere of invention and science. Poor Thimonnier had to puzzle over a hundred difficulties which an apprentice boy in a machine shop could have explained to him. Quite unable to work in metals, he made his first machine of wood, and in the year 1829 he produced machines in this material which did actually, in some degree, answer the purpose intended.

His needle bore some resemblance to that of Elias Howe, in being pierced near the point, and in not passing completely through the material. He also sewed with a continuous thread. It was a step toward the production of an efficient sewing-machine, and bears sufficient resemblance to those now in use to justify the French people in supposing that Thimonnier's machine suggested them. At the French Exposition of 1855, the committee upon sewing-machines gave it as their opinion that the machine of Thimonnier, patented in 1830, "had evidently served as a type to all modern sewing-machines."

I had many conversations with Elias Howe, both

at his house in Bridgeport and at his office in New York, in the latter years of his life, when he had no interest to serve or to preserve by deception. He assured me that when he began to experiment upon a sewing-machine he had never heard of any former attempt of the kind. The idea came to him from a chance remark of his employer, who said, one day in the shop, that any man who " would invent a good sewing-machine would make an independent fortune." At that time Elias Howe was suffering from an inherited lameness, and his daily work in the machine shop fatigued and distressed him. He was supporting his family then upon nine dollars a week, at Cambridge, Mass. It was in these circumstances that he began to watch the movements of his wife while she was sewing, and to consider whether it was possible for those movements to be accomplished by a machine. Probably many hundreds of machinists had had the same idea, and we know that during the period covered by the labors of Thimonnier and Howe, several other persons put forth efforts to produce a machine that would sew.

To return to our French tailor. When he had finished his machine in 1829, his resources were quite exhausted, his credit was gone, and it was impossible for him to pay the expenses of a patent. An assistant teacher, almost as poor as himself, had faith in the invention, and entered into a partnership with the inventor, engaging to furnish the money for the patent and to defray the cost of making a second machine. Other partners joined them; the patent was procured; the inventor came to Paris; and a capital of eighty thousand francs was subscribed for the manufacture of machines and setting them at work. A large shop was hired in Paris, in which were placed eighty of the wooden sewing-machines, designed to work upon military garments, of which the French government has always required a prodigious number.

So far, all had gone to the satisfaction of the inventor; but when these eighty wooden machines began to work in a simultaneous movement, many unforeseen difficulties arose. The breakings and stoppages were distressingly frequent; for in truth, the machines were so crude, so imperfect, that it was not possible for them to work to advantage. Nevertheless, the tailors of Paris were in alarm. The machines worked well enough to give a promise of future and final success, and the cry arose that their craft was in danger. Tailors are a very numerous body, particularly in Paris, which makes clothing for distant parts of Europe. Moreover, the mobs and barricades of the revolution of 1830 were still fresh in the recollection of Paris workingmen. At length a mob of angry tailors assaulted the workshop, took possession of it, threw the little wooden sewing-machines out of the windows, and would have thrown the inventor after them, if he had not escaped just in time.

This disaster caused the company to dissolve, and Thimonnier returned to his home in the country with a few thousand francs in his pocket, the price of his shares which he had sold to the company. Some attempts were made to continue the business in Paris, but with no good results.

In his old home near the banks of the Rhone, the inventor still thought of little but his machine, and a year or two after he went to Paris again, carrying with him a machine which he considered the best he had yet made. He tried long to form a new company. Failing in this, and having expended all his money, he returned home on foot, a tramp of three hundred miles, carrying his machine on his back. When he was tired or hungry, he set it up in a village, and performed upon it as if it were a hand organ, glad to receive as a reward the sous and half-francs of the bystanders.

He resumed his trade of tailor, and used his machine for a while to sew up his seams. He obtained another friend and ally in a lawyer of a neighboring town, who advanced money for improvements and a renewal of the patent. He now made metal machines, which were better, and executed two hundred stitches a minute. The new firm sold a few machines in the neighborhood at ten dollars each, which worked well enough to excite alarm in the minds of the great multitude in that part of France who lived by the needle. He was attacked in one of the newspapers on the ground that he threatened the livelihood of millions of industrious French women. The inventor took pen in hand to defend his machine.

"My invention," said he, "enlarges the domain of woman and puts her upon an industrial equality with men. The workman who turns against machinery is like a child who rebels against and maltreats his nurse."

His defense was long and able, but the fates were against him. When he had some show of success in 1848, the revolution which drove Louis Philippe from the throne frustrated his hopes, and a few years after the admirable machines from America were introduced everywhere, and entirely supplanted the crude and imperfect devices of Thimonnier.

At the London Exposition of 1851, an English jury gave him the barren honor of priority of invention, and that was all. He died in his native village in 1857, poorer than he was when he began to invent, and leaving a widow advanced in life without provision, and four sons, journeymen mechanics. An industrial society of Lyons granted her a sum of six hundred francs, and some years after the government awarded her three hundred francs, which served but to defray the cost of her last sickness. She had, however, a kind of public funeral, and, as before stated, it is now proposed to erect a monument over their remains, surmounted with a bust of the inventor.

Such is the story of Bartholomew Thimonnier, which shows that the career of invention in France does not materially differ from the inventor's lot in America. It is necessary to succeed. When I knew Elias Howe he was deriving from his sewing-machine patents a revenue of two hundred thousand dollars a year. He succeeded. But for one Howe we have a hundred Thimonniers.

was, entered into partnership with this cautious old man of nineteen, furnishing the capital, and leaving to the youth the chief management of the business.

This seems strange. The explanation is, that George Peabody had a genius for making money, and Elisha Riggs possessed discernment enough to perceive it. The new firm had a rapid and striking success. On the return of peace, in 1815, the house of Riggs and Peabody removed to Baltimore, where it had such prosperity that in seven years, when Mr. Peabody was still but twenty-seven years of age, it had branch houses in New York and Philadelphia. In 1829, Mr. Riggs retired, and Mr. Peabody became the senior partner. As the house imported largely from Europe, Mr. Peabody was in the habit of going to London for the purchase of goods, and he saw such chances there that in 1837 he removed to London, where he established himself as a banker and merchant. He was forty-two years of age, and controlled a capital then considered large.

He was scarcely settled in London, when the most terrible and disastrous financial revulsion occurred which the United States has ever experienced. I can just remember it. About the middle of March, we heard the first clap of thunder in the news that a great cotton house of New Orleans had failed for eight millions of dollars. Within a month, the whole Southwest was bankrupt. In Mobile, nine tenths of all the mercantile firms failed.

In New Orleans, not one eminent house stood the test, and business was so completely paralyzed that three or four days would pass sometimes without a transaction in cotton or sugar. In New York, the merchants bravely resisted the pressure for six weeks, but at the beginning of May they failed by whole blocks in a day. There was a furious run on all the banks, until all except one were obliged to suspend. Of course, securities of all kinds, even of such solid States as Massachusetts, New York, Virginia, Tennessee, were borne down by the storm, and for several weeks some of them had scarcely any value in the market.

This was George Peabody's first great opportunity. He knew the causes of the crash. He knew its precise nature and extent. He knew that his country was sound in principle, and rich in all the elements of wealth. Knowing this, he acted upon it; and by investing freely in American securities when they were at the lowest point of depression, he did much toward restoring American credit, and at the same time laid the foundation, or rather expanded and strengthened the foundation, of his subsequent colossal fortune. He was then, as always, a cool, quiet man, not susceptible to clamor or panic. He bought boldly but wisely, and his profit was great. Continuing the career thus happily begun, he was able in 1857 to repeat the tactics which had been so successful in 1837. The revulsion of 1857 was little other than a panic — a sudden

GEORGE PEABODY,

BANKER.

How did he get so much money? That is the first question. For before we can properly praise a man for giving away millions of dollars, we must know whether in getting it he rendered the public an equivalent service, and whether he made a fair division of his gains with those who assisted him to make them.

One evening, in the spring of 1811, the cry of fire was raised in the streets of Newburyport, a noble old town on the coast of Massachusetts. Only an unoccupied stable was in flames; but the fire spread, and raged with astonishing fury for more than eight hours, until it had swept over a tract of sixteen acres and a half of the most closely built and densely populated quarter of the town. Two hundred and fifty buildings were consumed, among which were all the principal stores and public buildings. Among those who were burnt out on this occasion were three members of the numerous American family of Peabody. One of these was an uncle of the banker, who had been largely engaged in trade, and was totally ruined by this fire. Another was an elder brother, who had recently established himself in the dry-goods business; and he also lost his all. The third was George Peabody himself, then a lad of sixteen, a clerk in his brother's store. He was born, as we all know, at Danvers, in Massachusetts, in 1795, of parents in limited circumstances. As early as eleven years of age he was a boy in a grocery store, and at fifteen went to Newburyport to serve as clerk to his brother. It is not necessary to say that he acquired the rudiments of knowledge in a district school, because that is the case with all New England boys.

It is an ill wind that blows nobody good. It is probable that the three Peabodys, uncle and two nephews, thought themselves ruined on the morning after the great fire of Newburyport. To the youngest of the three, however, it proved a most fortunate event. The uncle, bankrupt by the fire, removed to Georgetown, in the District of Columbia, taking the youth with him, and there again established himself in business. But as he was still liable for his old debts, the business was carried on in the name of George Peabody, still a minor. But this lad, it seems, had an old head on his young shoulders; and it occurred to him that, by continuing in business with his bankrupt uncle, he would finally render himself liable for his debts. At the same time he had won the confidence of a Mr. Elisha Riggs, of Georgetown, who, capitalist as he fright, without adequate cause, and of short duration. But while it lasted it was severe, and it gave to a man like Peabody, established in London, far from the scene of disaster, golden opportunities which no man knew better how to improve than he. At the same time his ordinary business as a banker yielded him an ample revenue. With such chances, with such a head, it is not surprising that in a business career of forty-seven years' duration, he should have accumulated a fortune out of which he could give away seven or eight millions without impoverishing himself.

We must admit, therefore, that he gained his fortune in a way which the laws and usages of the modern world pronounce honorable. While he was making it, he was very far from being popular in the business circles of London and Paris. He had the name of being close and disobliging. He was not prone to grant those business favors and indulgences which less successful traders are sometimes compelled to ask of their more fortunate brethren. Still less was he disposed to give away small sums to persons in need; and I am informed, too, that he was far from lavish in gifts to his own relations. Indeed, he was not of what is commonly called a generous spirit. At least, he did not appear such to those associated with him.

Nevertheless, as he has since told the world, he had long before resolved, even while he was still a comparatively poor man, that if he should ever become rich, he would give away a portion of his wealth to promote the happiness of his kind. He had reached his fifty-sixth year before he began to execute his intention. His first striking gift was bestowed in 1851, for fitting up the American Department of the Crystal Palace. Contributions from America were strewn about a wing of the building, and the American commissioner had arrived without money to put up a platform or a counter, for Congress had made no appropriation for the purpose. At this moment of embarrassment and mortification, Mr. Peabody came to the relief of the commissioner, and by advancing him twenty thousand dollars enabled him to make a respectable show. Since that day his benefactions have been frequent and large. The following is an imperfect list of them: —

In 1852, when Mr. Grinnell lent a ship to Dr. Kane for an expedition to join in the search for Sir John Franklin, Mr. Peabody gave ten thousand dollars for the equipment and provisioning of the vessel. In the same year, when his native town, Danvers, celebrated its two hundredth anniversary, he sent twenty thousand dollars to found a library and lyceum, which he has since increased to two hundred thousand dollars.

In 1857, he made his first contribution toward the endowment of a similar institution in Baltimore, the funds of which he has since increased to a million dollars.

ABBOTT LAWRENCE,

MERCHANT.

Old merchants complain that the ocean cable and the swift freight-steamer have destroyed all chance for brilliant speculation in foreign commodities. If the price of indigo changes in Calcutta, it is known in London and New York on the same day, and dealers in the article can tell pretty nearly how much indigo there is in existence, and about where it all is. They are also promptly informed of every change in the prospect of the coming crop.

How different it was formerly! When the War of 1812 came to an end, there was a firm of young merchants in Boston called A. & A. Lawrence, composed of two brothers, Amos and Abbott. The business had been founded about the year 1800 by Amos, the elder brother, who had received Abbott first as an apprentice and then as a partner, the partnership dating from the year 1814, when Abbott Lawrence was little more than twenty-one years of age. This firm had so hard a time during the war, that Abbott Lawrence applied to the War

Department for a commission in the army; but before his application had been answered came the joyful news of peace, and the brothers prepared to improve the chance which the return of peace had offered them. The market was bare of almost all foreign merchandise, and at that time nearly all merchandise, except food, was foreign. Even pins and needles had become exceedingly scarce, and of many fabrics the supply had long since given out. The Lawrences were importers, and they had abundant capital for their business, as well as unquestionable credit, the elder brother having been highly successful before the war.

One of the first vessels to sail from Boston after the peace was the good ship Milo, and in this vessel Abbott Lawrence was a passenger. He was as handsome, as vigorous, and as enterprising a young man of business as Boston then could show. The passage of the Milo was short. He was the first to go on shore, and was probably the first Bostonian who landed in England after the return of peace. He hurried on to Manchester, made his purchases with prompt dispatch, and returned to Liverpool the evening before the Milo was to sail on her voyage home. There was no time to be lost, for the vessel was already in the stream and full of freight. He hired a barge to take him and all his purchases out to the vessel; but when he reached her the mate told him there was no room for his goods. Not only was all the cargo on board,

In 1862, he gave a hundred and fifty thousand pounds for the benefit of the poor in London, and the sum was expended in the construction of improved tenement houses. He afterward increased the fund to four hundred thousand pounds.

In 1866, during a visit to his native country, he gave away several millions of dollars: twenty-five thousand to the Phillips Academy at Andover; fifteen thousand to the Newburyport library; one hundred thousand to build a church in Georgetown in memory of his mother; sixteen thousand to the Georgetown library; one hundred and forty thousand to a scientific institute at Salem; twenty thousand to the Massachusetts Historical Society; one hundred and fifty thousand to Harvard College; the same sum to Yale College; twenty thousand to the Maryland Historical Society; twenty-five thousand to Kenyon College, in Ohio; and a million dollars to promote education in the Southern States, to which he afterwards added half a million more.

While thus endowing public institutions, he distributed, it is said, a million four hundred thousand dollars among his kindred, thus handsomely atoning for any neglect of which he may have been guilty in earlier years. He also made some superb and costly presents to his business friends and connections. To one gentleman in Boston, who had for many years been his principal correspondent in that city, he presented a magnificent service of silver; and wherever he went, he was prone to leave behind him some substantial memento of his visit. He never seems to have overcome his repugnance to ordinary charity. He was more apt to give a dinner service of plate to the master than a quiet fifty dollar bill to the assiduous, unknown housekeeper.

While the papers were filled with eulogies of this man and his gifts, I heard a good deal of detraction regarding him in conversation. I have heard his benefactions attributed to several motives. Some of our close-fisted business men assert that he gave away money for the gratification of his vanity, while others insinuate a motive still less creditable. Men seldom act from a single motive. If, in giving away his superfluous millions, he enjoyed the glory which it brought him, who should blame him? The praise of men is one of the proper and natural rewards of a virtuous act, and we ought not to censure any one for valuing and enjoying the good-will of others.

but the hatches were battened down. The young merchant persisted in the endeavor to get his goods on board. He told the mate that as this was his first voyage it was of the greatest importance to him to be successful in his mission, and he urged his case with so much ardor, that the officer, who had become very friendly to him on the voyage out, yielded to his desire.

The young man sprang to the tackle, and helped the sailors hoist the bales of merchandise on board. As soon as he had seen them safe on deck, without waiting to know how or where they were to be stowed, he returned to the shore, as it was not his intention to go back to Boston so soon. In eighty-four days from the time of her leaving Boston, the ship Milo discharged from her wharf the goods bought in England by Abbott Lawrence, and in less than a week they were all sold at a profit which one of his descendants describes as "enormous." His elder brother, who was of a calmer temperament, was greatly pleased with the good judgment displayed by the young man on this occasion, as well as by the rapidity of his movements.

Abbott Lawrence remained abroad for some time, and sent forward goods as his judgment dictated. He made a trip to the continent, where he saw the Prussian and English armies soon after the battle of Waterloo. During the few years following the general peace of 1815, the business of A. & A. Lawrence flourished exceedingly, and they laid the foundation of two of the largest fortunes ever gained by Boston merchants in legitimate business.

From this incident we can perceive what chances for inordinate gain foreign commerce occasionally afforded before there was electric communication between the continents. These chances, however, were rare, and became rarer. The occasional success of a timely venture made a great noise in business circles, and drew a great many men into attempting similar feats of enterprise. As time went on, it became evident that commerce was an uncertain basis of a business career, and the merchants of Boston turned their attention to manufacturing the fabrics which they had been accustomed to import from Europe. The firm of A. & A. Lawrence were among the leaders in this important movement. They became largely interested in the manufactures of Lowell, and were chiefly instrumental in founding the city of Lawrence, named after them. While Abbott Lawrence was still under forty years of age, his firm controlled a very large capital, and were among the chief business men of New England.

The late Lord Lytton wrote a novel with the singular title, "What Will He Do With It?" The question, I believe, relates to a young man who has acquired fortune, and with fortune the opportunity to accomplish something of benefit to the world. Abbott Lawrence, in the vigor of his age, had gained this opportunity, and he appears to have used it with a constant regard to his country's good. He lent the weight of his name and the aid of his capital to the early railroad enterprises of New England, which for some years had to contend with opposition, ridicule, and indifference. When, for example, it was proposed to construct a railroad between Boston and Albany, it was thought to be an enterprise for madmen only, and Abbott Lawrence was one of the able men who reconciled the capitalists of New England to undertaking it. The railroad between Boston and Lowell had just been completed, and was converting people to a belief in the system. Mr. Lawrence, in his speeches on this subject, pointed to the success of that road, and dwelt upon the effect of the Erie Canal upon the prosperity of the city of New York. He told the people in Faneuil Hall, in 1835, that the New York canals had doubled the value of real estate in the city of New York as soon as they were completed. Edward Everett spoke at this meeting, and in the course of his speech he said : —

"Don't talk of reaching Buffalo, sir. Talk of the Falls of St. Anthony and Council Bluffs!"

At the close of the meeting, Abbott Lawrence said to Mr. Everett, in his ardent and confident manner : —

"Mr. Everett, we shall live to see the banks of the upper Mississippi connected by iron bands with State Street."

At the time when these words were spoken, there were few indeed who believed them. The ability and public spirit which Mr. Lawrence had shown in advocating improvements caused him to be nominated to Congress in 1837. He was elected by the Whig party, and he supported its measures with ability and zeal. He served for a few years as minister to England, where he maintained a liberal establishment, and was highly popular. Like all able men of business, he was an advocate of giving just compensation to men of ability who are employed in the public service. In his speech urging the introduction of water into Boston, he scouted the idea of getting a cheap man to do dear work. He said: —

"I have done many things in my time. I have expended a great deal of money on buildings, machinery, canals, railroads, and such things. I cannot do these things myself. The first thing, then, that I have to do is to find a man in whom I can place confidence, a man of honesty, energy, and skill, and I found long ago that if I wanted such a man I must pay for him."

He was a zealous friend of education. He was strong in the conviction that no nation can play a leading part in modern times, and continue to play it, except on condition of educating the whole mass of its people. He used to enunciate this truth in his public addresses in England, when he was minister there, with much effect. Toward the close of his life he contributed largely to the foundation and endowment of the Lawrence Scientific School connected with Harvard College, the institution which enjoyed the services for many years of Professor Agassiz. Indeed, we may say with truth that he made a noble use both of his influence and of his wealth. There was scarcely any good cause or project of his time to which he did not lend a helping and often a munificent hand.

Like all other human beings, he had his limitations. Some of us think that his opinions upon the protective system will not be justified by events. But all men hold erroneous opinions. Abbott Lawrence was a virtuous man, and a great citizen — one of the best of the eminent men who have made Boston the beautiful and noble city it is to-day. He died in 1855, aged sixty-three years.

AMOS A. LAWRENCE,

SOLID MAN OF BOSTON.

"What would you do, if you were rich?"

Teachers have occasionally given out this question as a subject for compositions, expecting thereby to draw out the character of their pupils, as well as to call their attention to the proper objects of virtuous endeavor. Amos A. Lawrence was a rich man, one of those solid men of whom Daniel Webster used to speak. He was the son and nephew of rich men, the husband of a rich man's daughter, and he lived all his days the friend and companion of rich men. He did not, so far as is known, write any compositions upon what, as a rich man, he might, could, would, or should do; but he answered the above interesting question practically, and in a way that seems to me to be worth considering.

Let us take him up about the year 1850, at the age of thirty-six, while he was still in the prime of young manhood, while the love of pleasure and the capacity for enjoying it were still undiminished. He was then a member of the firm of Mason & Lawrence, commission merchants of Boston, the selling agents of some large cotton mills, with a business of several millions per annum, requiring what was then considered a large establishment of clerks and book-keepers.

Besides this business, he was a director in ten corporations of various kinds, some of them of great importance; as, for example, the Suffolk Bank, the Cocheco Manufacturing Company, the American Insurance Office, the Boston Water Power Corporation, the Amesbury Woolen Mills, the Middlesex Canal, and others. He was a director also in the Massachusetts General Hospital, Bible Society, and Board of Domestic Missions. He had charge of all his father's property, his father being Amos Lawrence, another very solid man of Boston. He had also a tract of land in the West of his own, and upon it he was building a seminary and the town of Appleton, which he found to be a complicated business. All his life long he was immersed in similar cares and trusts; at one time, treasurer of Harvard University; at another, founding a stocking industry at Ipswich; always busy, always absorbed; not with a mere view to add to his estate, for he was one of the most generous of men, but because these duties seemed fairly to fall to him as the son of his father and a merchant of Boston.

In addition to his business interests and philanthropic trusts, he was a man of public spirit, and did his share of public duty. On one occasion, when the old fire department of Boston, in a moment of pique, resigned, he became a volunteer fireman until the difficulty was arranged. He says in his diary : —

"It was hard work for a few nights, but we have slept quietly now for a week. Fires two mornings in succession at four and six o'clock, long before daylight, down in India Street. I turn out with my engine."

At another time, during the Know-Nothing riots, when a large number of inoffensive Irish people were injured and their houses pillaged, he joined the temporary force organized to maintain order. He shouldered his musket with the rest, and was kept on guard all night. Later in life, he took an active part in establishing a line of steamships between Boston and New Orleans, and was president of the company. Descended from Revolutionary ancestors on both sides, he was an officer of the Cincinnati. Few men were more efficient than he in the construction of the Bunker Hill Monument. It would be difficult, indeed, to name one benevolent or patriotic movement organized in Boston during his lifetime, of which he was not a promoter.

But this was not all. He made it a point of principle to preserve his health and cheerfulness by taking two hours of active, out-of-door exercise every day, riding to and from his country home on horseback, frequently stopping on the way in the winter season to enjoy half an hour's skating on Jamaica Pond. His son, who has written a beautiful little biography of him, which has only the extraordinary fault of being too brief, tells us how he passed his day so as to give due attention to his multitudinous duties.

He began the day with a few minutes' exercise before an open window with his twenty-five-pound dumb-bells. Then breakfast, punctually at seven, at which he could count upon meeting his whole family, — wife and seven children, — all well and cheerful, to greet the day. At a quarter before eight family prayers, at the end of which his horse was at the door, saddled and bridled. A seven-mile ride, taking Cambridge on his way, pausing a few minutes at his farm in Newton, brought him to his counting-room in Boston. Then he gave six hours to business, dispatching numberless affairs, and not refusing many a precious quarter of an hour to schemers, borrowers, and beggars.

This brought him to three o'clock in the afternoon, when his horse was again ready for him, and he galloped home to dinner. After dinner he slept for five minutes, for he had a delightful talent of taking short naps, and rising from them refreshed. After the nap came the recreation of the day, which might be a drive with his wife, a skate on the pond, a visit to his farm, or another ride on a fresh horse, returning after dark to tea, newspaper, and cheerful chat with his family and visitors.

This was something like his round of duty and pleasure for fifty years. His son tells us that his out-of-door life made him a familiar figure to all the people who lived in the neighborhood. He was a man so social and friendly that he was always ready to stop and have a chat with any one. He had a good word for every workman on the road. The men saw him coming and looked up, knowing that they would be recognized and saluted, and very often he entered into conversation with them about their work, and he rightly estimated the value of the knowledge which he derived from them.

There was one kind of town improvement which he always greatly favored — the laying out of playgrounds for boys and girls. He was himself a living proof of the value of innocent plays as a promoter of health and cheerfulness. He joined his neighbors in creating a skating-pond. He assisted in building the first floating bath-house in Boston, and he subscribed liberally to provide the Harvard students with a better and larger ball field. He was a constant promoter of parks and public gardens. He was a believer in the usefulness of beauty and peace. Once he joined his brother in offering a prize of ten thousand dollars to any one who should invent a system of signals which would silence forever the odious and terrific scream of the locomotive whistle.

Was this a perfect man? By no means. No doubt he had his share of weaknesses and faults.

But we can truly say of him that he lived up to the best ideal of a Solid Man of Boston which Boston had conceived in his day. He was the benevolent and enterprising Boston business man in his fairest aspect, sound in health, cheerful in disposition, a ceaseless giver of gifts, the soul of honor, and faithful in every relation of life to all the light he had. But as the world progresses, its ideals advance also. Probably the ideal rich man of the coming generation will be called upon to do fewer things, and those few much better. For example, he founded at Ipswich, with immense difficulty, the stocking industry, with a view to make a good pair of cotton stockings that could be sold by retail for twenty-five cents. He lost, as he says in his diary, a hundred dollars a day for eight hundred days — eighty thousand dollars in all. He lost so much money with his cotton stockings that, when he was troubled with a fit of indigestion, he would say that it was owing to " too much Ipswich."

After a struggle of twenty years, his efforts were crowned with striking success, so far as the stockings were concerned. As this article is written near the town of Ipswich, I may perhaps remark that the men, women, and children who make those stockings would be better and happier than they now are, if their employers lived near them and among them, and saw to it, in person, that they had a fair chance for a healthful and desirable existence.

The Ipswich stockings are good and cheap; but how is it with the weavers? The ideal rich man of the future will be chiefly concerned with *that* question. The commonplace rich man will not think much about it; but we are now speaking of the Boston ideals, men who mean to live in the highest way known in their time, and do their part in the special nobilities of their generation.

JOHN METCALF,

ROADMAKER.

IF the story of John Metcalf were not amply authenticated by documents still preserved in his native county and attested by solid work still existing, I should hesitate to relate it here. His life presents to us the most remarkable instance on record of four senses rallying to do the work of one that has been lost.

He was born at Knaresborough, in English Yorkshire, in the year 1717, of parents who held the rank of day-laborers. Near his native place is the famous Knaresborough forest, miles in extent, noted during many centuries for its herds of red deer and other royal game. I think the people who live near a tract of this kind — which furnishes a constant resource and playground to the inhabitants — are more vigorous, both in mind and body, than others. Sure am I that the addition to New York of the Central Park has improved the health and lengthened the life of the people who inhabit Manhattan Island.

This John Metcalf must have been indeed a vigorous creation. When he was six years of age, he took the small-pox, which totally destroyed his sight. As soon as he had recovered his health, his irrepressible activity began to assert itself. From groping about his father's cottage, he soon began to feel his way in the street, and in three years it was perfectly safe to send him on a message to any part of the town. At the same time he joined in the sports of the boys, climbing trees for birds'-nests, and becoming, in fact, one of the best climbers of the neighborhood. He roamed the fields and lanes alone, learned to ride on horseback, kept a dog, chased hares, snared rabbits, and learned to swim. On one occasion he saved the lives of three of his comrades who had fallen into the water, and on another, dived to the bottom of the river, and brought up the body of a drowned man. In the evening he learned to play on the fiddle, and at last became so well skilled that he was able to earn a portion of his livelihood by playing at country parties and balls.

Strangest of all, he was frequently employed to guide travelers in that part of Yorkshire. It was a rough country at that time; the roads were winding, intricate, and extremely bad; but in some mysterious way, this blind lad had acquired so familiar a knowledge of every crook and turn that he was one of the best guides in Yorkshire, whether by night or day. Sometimes the traveler was not aware of his blindness, after being many hours under his care.

"My friend," said a traveler to him one night, after arriving safely at a comfortable inn, "are you really *blind?*"

"Yes, sir," said the lad. "I lost my sight when six years old."

"Had I known that," said the traveler, "I would not have ventured with you on that road from York for a hundred pound."

"And I, sir," said the blind youth, "would not have lost my way for a thousand."

His fiddle and guiding bringing him in plenty of money, he bought a horse, of which he became extremely fond. It would come at his call, and answer him by neighing. Mounted upon this steed he followed the hounds, and showed himself to be one of the boldest of hunters. On one occasion he accepted a challenge to ride a race in Knaresborough forest, the ground being marked out by posts, which, it was thought, would be of little help to a blind man. But he was as ingenious as he was brave. He borrowed the dinner-bells from the neighboring inns, and, stationing a man at each post, gave him a bell to ring during the race. Guided by the sound, he came in winner.

He grew to be a man of splendid proportions and enormous strength, and there was no game of dexterity in which he did not excel. He even ventured upon long journeys, walking as much as two hundred miles over unknown roads, paying all expenses by his fiddle, and finding his way by an instinct that seldom led him wrong. Finally, he won the affections of a highly respectable innkeeper's daughter, married, and settled down to the enjoyment of domestic life.

He now engaged in business of a less vagabond and precarious character. He set up public vehicles for hire; he traded in fish; he speculated in hay; he went on peddling excursions, and still occasionally officiated at grand parties with his violin. When the Pretender landed in Scotland, in 1745, he joined the army as a volunteer, and did good service until the rebellion was put down. During his stay in Scotland, he discovered the extreme cheapness of the fabrics and articles of clothing manufactured there, and he used afterward to make journeys into Scotland, buy a quantity of cotton and woolen goods, and sell them in Yorkshire at a great profit. And thus he continued to push his way in the world, until he was nearly fifty years of age; changing his business as chances occurred — by turns guide, musician, soldier, peddler, horse-dealer, fish-dealer, wagoner, speculator, and stage-proprietor.

It was now 1765, the era when England awoke to the folly of not improving the extremely bad roads then universal in Europe. It is almost incredible how *very* bad the roads were, even in and near London, as late as the middle of the last century. Queen Caroline's huge coach used to be two hours in going from London to Kensington, a distance of three miles. Lord Hervey, who had a country-house at Kensington, wrote thus in 1736:—

"The road between this place and London is grown so infamously bad that we live here in the same solitude as we would do if cast on a rock in the middle of the ocean; and all the Londoners tell us that there is between them and us an impassable gulf of mud."

If that was the case near the metropolis, what must the roads have been in Yorkshire? They were rude tracks across heaths and fields, with deep ruts and awful quagmires, near which sometimes beacons were erected for the warning of travelers. These roads were perilous even for the packhorses which ordinarily traversed them; but for vehicles they were, during about half the year, all but impassable.

And now this state of things was about to come to an end, and John Metcalf, blind as he was, became one of the most skillful and successful contractors in Yorkshire for making the new turnpikes. For thirty years he was the chief road-builder of the county, and he invented many of the processes and expedients which have since been in general use. He proved to be one of the best judges of work that had ever been known. Walking over the line of country where the road was to be built, he was able to foresee its difficulties and to make a wonderfully correct estimate of the cost of overcoming them. He built bridges, culverts, viaducts; and, at the end of thirty years, he could point to his roads and boast with truth that all of his structures had stood the test of wear and flood.

In that part of England there is a good deal of boggy country, which appears to be almost unfathomable, as if the soil merely floated upon the surface of a deep quagmire. Having to construct a road across one of these swamps, he invented the only plan of doing it that has ever answered the purpose, and which was afterward borrowed by Stephenson in making railway bridges across similar swamps. He told his men to gather quantities of the coarse grass of the swamp, and bind it into long thin bundles, and to place them close together in rows, over the whole line of road. Then another layer was placed crosswise over them, and this process was repeated until there was a firm foundation for the stone and gravel of which the road was to be composed. The plan answered to admiration. It was, in fact, a floating road, and it was not merely one of the best, but also the dryest part of the road.

He continued to perform such labors as these with unfailing energy and skill until he was past seventy-five, when he gradually withdrew from active business, and retired to his farm for the remainder of his life. He had made a considerable fortune, and spent the evening of his days very happily with his descendants, amusing himself, occasionally, by speculating in hay and timber, and in the evening dictating a few pages of his autobiography. He died in 1810, aged ninety-three, leaving four children, twenty grand-children, and ninety great-grand-children.

THOMAS BRASSEY,
CONTRACTOR.

Mr. Carlyle invented, and I have borrowed, a happy phrase to describe the great employers of labor, who play so important a part in our modern world. He called them "Captains of Industry." But this Thomas Brassey, the famous English railway contractor, might more properly be styled a Generalissimo of Industry; for he and his partners had in their employment, at one time, eighty thousand men, whose wages amounted to sixty or seventy thousand dollars a day. He thought nothing of giving an order for three thousand wagons, or ten thousand wheelbarrows. In the course of an active life of nearly forty years, he constructed in whole or in part, a hundred and fifty railroads, — in England, France, Germany, Spain, Italy, South America, Australia, Canada, — which cost, in all, about four hundred millions of dollars. He had, at one time, as many as ten thousand men employed in Spain alone, besides thousands more in other remote countries.

As a specimen of his grand way of doing business, take this anecdote. In arranging the details of a contract with a Spanish banker, the Marquis of Salamanca, the nobleman proposed to issue bonds before the shares were taken; but to this Mr. Brassey, the nobleman by nature, objected, as not honorable. After much discussion, Mr. Brassey said to the marquis: —

"Look here, Mr. Salamanca; if you and your friends will put five hundred thousand pounds down on the table any day you like to name, I and my friends will do so too. Then the shares will be paid up, and there can be no possible objection to the bonds being issued."

The marquis did not see the matter in that light, and the project was given up. This incident shows something besides the mere magnitude of Thomas Brassey's operations. It is one more illustration of a truth which the whole history of business exhibits, that no business of the first class which has endured thirty years has had any other foundation than fair dealing. There never was a more striking case in point than the success of this man. On one occasion, when he was hurrying to completion an important railway in France, an enormous brick viaduct, one third of a mile long, a hundred feet high, and built at a cost of a quarter of a million dollars, suddenly fell in, and was utterly ruined. Within a few minutes after hearing of the disaster, he had set on foot measures for the reconstruction of the work; and although the downfall was not his fault, he refused to represent the facts to the company, in order to induce them to bear their fair share of the loss.

"No," said he. "I have contracted to make and maintain the road, and nothing shall prevent Thomas Brassey from being as good as his word."

That was the great secret of his lasting success. He was absolutely trustworthy. His word was as good as his bond. He put as good work in the bowels of the earth where no one would ever inspect it, as he did on the surface where thousands would see it every day. If he had engaged to open a line of railroad on a certain day, his part of the work was invariably done in time. In the whole of his career, he never missed once.

Next to this, the most important secret was his admirable treatment of those who assisted him. The greatest captains of industry, like the greatest captains of war, all excel in this particular. Brassey, besides taking great pains to surround himself with the right men, made their interest and honor his special and thoughtful care. He trusted them a great deal, liked to let them do their work in their own way, and judged them by results only. Nor would he ever hold one of his sub-contractors to a ruinous bargain. It frequently happens in constructing a railroad that a cutting turns out to be rock instead of earth, and the literal fulfillment of the contract would ruin a man. Brassey always took upon his own broad shoulders such losses as would cripple or crush a sub-contractor.

One example of this will suffice to show his way of doing it. Inspecting a road one day, he came to a cutting of this kind, the price of which had been fixed on the supposition that only clay had to be removed. Upon coming up to the work, and perceiving that the wagons were all loaded with rock, he said to the "sub:"—

"This is very hard."

"Yes," replied the man; "it is a pretty deal harder than I bargained for."

"What is your price for this cutting?" asked Mr. Brassey.

"So much a yard, sir."

"It is very evident," said the master, "that you are not getting it out for that price. Have you asked for any advance to be made to you for this rock?"

"Yes, sir," answered the man; "but I can make no sense of them."

"If," said Brassey, "you say that your price is so much, it is quite clear that you do not do it for that. I am glad that you have persevered with it, but I shall not alter your price. It must remain as it is, but the rock must be measured for you twice. Will that do for you?"

"Yes, very well indeed, and I am very much obliged to you, sir."

"Very well," rejoined Mr. Brassey; "go on;

you have done well in persevering, and I shall look to you again."

One of these walks along a line of railroad would sometimes cost the contractor a thousand pounds in rectifying similar mistakes. He greatly liked the principle of giving men a pecuniary interest in the work they were doing. He not only gave his chief agents a share in the profits of his contracts, but he liked very much the plan of letting out small contracts of mere digging to a dozen laborers, the proceeds to be equally divided among them, except a little extra allowance to the foreman. Several of his agents made considerable fortunes in his service.

Like many other men who have made colossal fortunes, he seemed to care very little about money. He was interested in his *work*, took pride and delight in doing it well, and was perfectly aware of the necessity of money as a means to that end; but when once the game had been won, he never seemed to value the stakes much for their own sake. And, in fact, to a man in his profession, millions are only what chisels and planes are to a carpenter — tools that he must have. One consequence of his being so free from the taint of avarice was that he could bear a large pecuniary loss, not with equanimity merely, but with cheerfulness and gayety.

"Mr. Brassey," said one of his agents, "never appeared so happy as when he had lost twenty thousand pounds."

One night, during a terrible financial crisis in London, which threatened to sweep away his whole fortune, he went home fully convinced that he must lose at least a million pounds sterling.

"Never mind," said he. "We must be content with a little less; that is all."

On another occasion, in Spain, he received a telegram, saying that a certain bridge had been washed down. Three hours after came another, stating that a large bank had been washed away. Other messages followed, of similar purport, and begging him to come at once to the scene. He turned to a friend and said, laughing: —

"I think I had better wait until I hear that the rain has ceased, so that when I do go, I may see what is *left* of the works, and estimate all the disasters at once, and so save a second journey."

On such occasions he often quoted the old proverb: "It is no use crying over spilt milk."

Thomas Brassey had none of those early struggles which mark the career of most able men of business. His father was a rich farmer of ancient family, and he served a regular apprenticeship to the business of land surveyor and agent. He gave such signal proofs of ability that his employer took him into partnership when he was but twenty-one; and he was already a thriving man, married, and twenty-nine years of age, before he ever thought of constructing a railroad. He was accidentally thrown into company, one day, with George Stephenson, who urged him to engage in the new enterprise. Being well established in business, he hesitated to change it, and especially for a business so new and untried. His wife's advice turned the scale, and he became the greatest contractor of his time.

He died in 1870, aged sixty-five, leaving three sons, one of whom is a member of the British Parliament. His life has been written by Sir Arthur Helps, who edited the works of Queen Victoria. It is not creditable to our publishers that a work so peculiar and interesting has not been made accessible to the people of the United States. It ought to be universally disseminated; especially in some factory towns that I could mention, where the mill-owners are apparently indifferent to the rights and feelings, the comfort and dignity, of those who work for them.

THOMAS TELFORD,
ENGINEER.

In Scotland, near the boundary line which divides it from England, there is a deep, narrow valley, seven miles long and two broad, which is inhabited by about six hundred farmers and shepherds. In the days of Rob Roy it was noted as a place whence parties of marauders issued, who went over the border and drove back herds of cattle and sheep stolen from the English. But in these later times its inhabitants have gained their livelihood by less adventurous and more honest ways. It is a sequestered vale, hemmed in by hills, and through it winds a stream, which gives life and picturesque beauty to the scene.

In the midst of this valley, Thomas Telford's father, in the middle of the last century, dwelt in a small mud cottage, consisting of two rooms and covered with a thatched roof. He was a herdsman on a sheep-farm near by, who lived and maintained his little family of wife and child upon six or seven shillings a week. A more humble abode could scarcely have been found even in Scotland, where, at that time, farmers of some substance lived in mud cottages of three rooms; and where laborers' families, in general, all herded together in one apartment. Thomas Telford was born in this hut in 1757, and when he was three months old his father died, leaving no provision whatever for his wife and son.

Certainly, this was a lowly beginning for a person destined, after a most useful and distinguished career, to be buried in Westminster Abbey, that venerable Pantheon of British worthies. The farmers, we are told, were kind and helpful to the widow and her boy, taking the child by turns to live with them at their houses, and giving her occasional employment in milking, hay-making, and sheep-shearing. She lived happily, healthily, and cheerfully; and the boy, who inherited her buoyant spirit, was noted in the valley for his frank and merry spirit, and went by the name of Laughing Tam. He, too, while he was still a small child, worked for the neighboring farmers, herding their cows and running errands, his wages being his food, a pair of stockings every winter, and five shillings per annum for a pair of thick shoes. A ruddy, healthy, merry Scotch boy was Thomas Telford, and a favorite with young and old.

Happily, there was in this poor parish that greatest blessing which a poor parish can have, a good common school, in which all the children were taught the rudiments of knowledge.

Here Laughing Tam learned how to read, write, and cipher, bringing every Monday morning, as the custom was, a fee to the teacher of one penny. At the same school he mingled with the children of farmers, professional men, and country gentlemen, which served to enlarge the sphere of his observation and assisted to cultivate his mind. With some of his companions in this parish school he remained on terms of intimacy as long as he lived.

At fifteen, when he was a stout, strong lad, he was apprenticed to a mason, who built farmhouses, barns, and small bridges. In this employment he passed his youth and early manhood; his wages as a journeyman averaging about thirty-six pence a day. It was always a passion with him to become perfect master of his business, and it was his constant habit to carry on at the same time his general mental improvement. If he worked in Edinburgh, he closely studied the fine architecture of the place, and the various engineering works in the vicinity, taking careful drawings of the critical portions, and studying them with the aid of the books in the public library. He thought no trouble too great if it either made him a better workman, or increased his knowledge of principles; and while thus striving after excellence in his vocation, he read with rapture the literature of his country, and frequently essayed to compose verses expressive of his enjoyment of nature.

So passed his life till he was twenty-five years of

age, when he was still a journeyman mason, who had rarely in his life earned more than two English shillings in a day, equal to about fifty cents of our present currency. Then he deliberately made up his mind to go to London.

"Having acquired," he once wrote, "the rudiments of my profession, I considered that my native country afforded few opportunities of exercising it to any extent, and therefore judged it advisable (like many of my countrymen) to proceed southward, where industry might find more employment, and be better remunerated."

His first object, as he afterwards said, was to make a better provision for the old age of his mother, and his second, to become *Somebody* by the exercise of his talents. Having arrived in London, he delivered a recommendation to a noted architect, who gave him work immediately as a stone-cutter, at which employment he obtained better wages than he had done at home. Here, too, as at Edinburgh, he took infinite pains to improve in his profession. Knowledge, knowledge, knowledge, was what he sought early and late. Not satisfied with the mortar commonly used, he went deeply into the study of mortar. He read, he observed, he drew, he meditated, he studied.

"I take care," he said, "to be so far master of the business committed to me, as that none shall be able to eclipse me in that respect."

He was extremely temperate and regular in his

mode of life, and thus obtained the strength necessary both to do his daily work and to carry on his schemes of improvement.

"I am chemistry-mad," he wrote to one friend. . . . "But, not to be confined to that alone, you must know, I have a book for the pocket which I always carry with me, into which I have extracted the essence of Watson's Essays, Black on Quicklime, but also facts relating to mechanics, hydrostatics, pneumatics, and all manner of stuff, to which I keep continually adding. It is my endeavor to unite those two frequently jarring pursuits — literature and business."

He said that he could not see why any man should be less efficient in business because he stored his mind with knowledge and cultivated it by literature. Let me not forget to add one most pleasing and creditable trait shown at this period of his life. He not only bore his mother constantly in mind, and sent her as much of his wages as he could spare, but, mindful of her defective eyesight, he took care to *print* the letters which he wrote her, so that she could read them with less difficulty.

"Let my mother know that I am well," he wrote to one of his old friends, " and that I will print her a letter soon."

Such a person, I need scarcely say, is not likely long to remain a journeyman stone-cutter. He was singularly engaging in his manner, having an admirable temper, and a most amiable, pleasing way with him; one of those happily constituted persons who make friends wherever they go. From being an ordinary workman, he was soon intrusted with small jobs as foreman, and ere long attracted the notice of a rich member of Parliament, who engaged him to superintend extensive works on his estate, and also obtained for him the appointment of engineer to the county.

From this time he rapidly made his way to be the first engineer of his time. He built an amazing number of costly and ingenious iron bridges in all parts of England and Scotland, some of which were the finest works of the kind in the world. He invented the improved Macadamized roads, such as we have in the Central Park, which led the poet Southey to call him the "Colossus of Rhodes." In short, he might be called the engineer of the coaching period of English history, as Robert Stephenson was of the railway period. It was Telford who created the roads, the bridges, and viaducts, which made England the most accessible of all countries before the invention of the railroad had superseded old methods of travel.

He remained the same genial, studious, painstaking Telford, at every portion of his splendid career. It is recorded of him that before he made his first suspension bridge, he performed more than two hundred experiments to test the strength of the various kinds of wrought iron; and it was his boast that his bridges, of wider span than any other which had ever been built, did not sag a quarter of an inch. To the last he kept his old tools in a closet as an honorable memento of his early days. "And besides," as he once said, " there is no telling what may happen." He was curiously free from avarice, and was even deficient in a love of acquisition, not sufficiently considering what he owed to others in the same profession. He darned his own stockings as long as he lived, and preserved, in all respects, the simplicity of his character and of his habits. He lived and labored to his seventy-seventh year. His remains lie near the middle of the nave of Westminster Abbey, next to those of Robert Stephenson, who expressed a wish to lie by the side of his great predecessor. The stone which marks his resting-place contains only the words — "THOMAS TELFORD, 1834."

JUNIUS SMITH, LL. D.,

PROJECTOR.

It seems right to affix the mystical letters LL. D. to the name printed above, for those letters were all the reward he ever received for doing the world an important service. It was Junius Smith, LL. D., who set on foot the system of navigating the broad ocean by steam vessels. It was a company formed by him which sent the Sirius across the ocean in the spring of 1838. It was he who built the British Queen. It was his faith, his courage, and, above all, his persistence, which overcame opposition, timidity, and indifference, and thus revolutionized the commercial system of the world.

And all he got for it was the privilege of writing himself down a Doctor of Laws.

In 1804, Junius Smith, descended from an old Connecticut family, was practicing law at New Haven, twenty-four years of age. He delivered the Fourth of July oration at New Haven in 1804, soon after which a mercantile firm of that city, to which a brother of his belonged, put into his hands a very important case, which proved to be the turning-point of his own career. Their ship Mohawk, trading to the West Indies, was captured by a British cruiser and sent into Tortola, one of the Virgin Islands belonging to Great Britain, where she was condemned as a lawful prize and sold for the benefit of the captors. The firm appealed to the English Court of Admiralty, and asked this young lawyer to go to London and argue the appeal.

He went, sailing from New York on Evacuation Day, November 25, 1805.

The law system of England had not then been reformed, and it was two years before he could get a hearing. However, his time came at length. He argued his cause before the Lords of Appeal, who reversed the decree of the court in Tortola, and ordered the proceeds of the sale of the ship and cargo to be given to the owners.

During this long delay the young lawyer, being a Yankee of the old energetic style, made some commercial speculations of his own, formed a connection with an important house in New York, and found himself, in fact, at the head of an important business. He made money, and occasionally lost some, but upon the whole was a prosperous merchant. He fell in love with an English girl, whom he met at the house of a friend in the country, whose family he had never seen. He describes her in a long letter of a later date as "an accomplished and elegant girl in every respect, as well as one of the best and most spiritually minded women that adorned Great Britain."

He plied his suit with the natural ardor of a Yankee lover, and, as he believed, with some success. Before he had made the acquaintance of any member of her family, he was obliged to return for a short time to America. No doubt he had come to a pretty clear understanding with the young lady, for he says: —

"I sailed in November, 1810, leaving my delicate domestic affairs in a loose, unsettled state; and yet I *thought* I should find my fair one single on my return."

He was gone seven months. Great was his joy, on reaching England, to learn that she was not only unmarried, but had rejected two good offers of marriage in his absence. He at once wrote to her father, and, in the true old-fashioned style, gave him plenty of " references " to American merchants in London and Liverpool. He found the father much more difficult to manage than the daughter. It was not until he had pressed him hard, and supplied him with " a large parcel " of commendatory letters, that the sturdy Briton took him by the hand, and pronounced the significant words: —

" I shall be very happy to see you at my house."

It was enough. The marriage took place soon after, and the victorious Yankee became a domesticated Englishman. Twenty years passed, during which he carried on business in London with varying success, and then occurred the experience which led him to enter upon the business of ocean steam navigation. In August, 1832, having business in New York, he set sail with his family in the English bark St. Leonard, which he had himself chartered for the voyage. The passage was rough and extremely tedious, being protracted to more than eight weeks. As he paced the deck, impatient, and possibly irritated by the complaints of his one hundred and fifty passengers, the thought occurred to him :—

"Why not do this by steam?"

The more he reflected upon it, the more satisfied he became that crossing the ocean by steam was not only practicable, but was better, safer, and more economical than the transit by sails. It is evident that Junius Smith now caught the mania of the improver. As soon as he reached New York, he began to discuss the project with merchants and others, but without meeting the least encouragement. He grew more confident by meeting the arguments of his opponents. He says :—

"I answered all objectors to my own satisfaction, and gathered strength in the combat, although I knew that they remained unconvinced, for incredulity was visible upon every feature."

He at length resolved, before leaving New York, to propose to leading merchants and capitalists the formation of a company for carrying out the project. He called upon Philip Hone, Goodhue &

Co., and several others. The answer he received in substance was: —

"Try the experiment when you get back to London; and if it succeeds, we will come in and join you."

On reaching London, he tried first to bring over to his views the directors of steamship lines plying between London and Scotland. His letter to one of those boards, and their very positive and uncompromising refusal, have been preserved to this day, together with a mass of similar proofs of his zeal and the indifference of capitalists. Then he tried to charter a small steamship himself. After some days of negotiation, he found that the ship had sixteen owners, and he renounced forthwith the project of inducing sixteen men to accept so audacious a scheme.

He next tried to form a company for the purpose, and, on June 1, 1835, issued his prospectus, proposing to raise one hundred thousand pounds, in shares of five hundred pounds each. This he sent to every merchant and capitalist in Great Britain who could be thought of as likely to favor such a project. Not one share was applied for. Not one encouraging response was received. On the contrary, the plan was treated with something more than the ridicule which ordinarily assails schemes that are considered to belong to the bubble species. Merchants engaged in American commerce were hostile and abusive, so that he made up his mind to seek for aid outside of the circle of American shippers.

I take pleasure in stating that the first individual to indorse the scheme was George Grote, historian, banker, liberal politician, and member of Parliament. Junius Smith says of him: —

"He saw the scope of the plan clearly, remarked that he thought it a fair, legitimate, and noble enterprise, and no bubble; but he declined accepting either the chair or a seat in the direction, as being incompatible with their business as bankers."

The zealous projector ran all over London seeking a chairman, and finding none. He discovered, however, that the idea was making its way in the British intellect, which is sometimes slow, but generally sound. Men began to talk like Sir John Reed, another banker and M. P., who said: —

"I approve of the plan, sir, and have no doubt it will succeed; and as to raising the money, sir, it is nothing at all, sir; you will have no difficulty whatever."

"But," asked the protector, "will you allow me to insert your name as chairman?"

"Why, sir, you know I am a member of Parliament for Dover. I have six hundred letters to answer every session, am director of the Bank of England, and have a large concern here to look after. I am afraid it will not be in my power to give my time to it."

At length, however, he found his long-sought

chairman in Isaac Selby, an important business man of London, and himself a bold projector. At the second interview Mr. Selby said, in the frankest and heartiest manner : —

"I will be your chairman."

"I thank you, sir," said Junius Smith.

That was the whole of this momentous interview. The rest of the way was comparatively smooth sailing. Applications for shares poured in by every mail. The proposed capital was now half a million sterling, and a whole million was promptly subscribed. In October, 1836, the contract for the first vessel was signed — a steamship of two thousand and sixteen tons, named the British Queen, in recognition of the recent accession of Queen Victoria. The failure of the engine builders causing a vexatious delay of many months, the company chartered the Sirius, of seven hundred tons burden, and dispatched her to New York from Cork, April 4, 1838.

The Great Western sailed from Bristol four days after, and both arrived in New York on the same day, April 23, the Sirius in the morning and the Great Western in the afternoon.

I remember the arrival well. It was one of those beautiful days of the New York spring when thousands of people now go to the Central Park, but then they went to Hoboken. I was one of many thousands who, from Hoboken and the Battery, saw these vessels steam up the bay and cast anchor in the stream, and thus crown the long labors of our Connecticut Yankee with an immortal success. He came out himself in the British Queen soon after, and was back at his own house near London in just thirty-two days.

This ever-memorable success not proving advantageous to himself, he spent many of his remaining years in endeavoring to domesticate the tea-plant in South Carolina. He had a large plantation near Greenville, S. C., and while engaged in the enterprise he was the victim of an assault by which his skull was fractured. He died at Astoria, N. Y., in January, 1853, aged seventy-three years.

FREDERIC SAUVAGE,

SHIP-BUILDER.

There was a grand launch at Glasgow some time ago of the Etruria, a new "ocean greyhound," which was expected to do nineteen miles an hour, and cross the Atlantic within six days. One of the builders made a speech on the occasion, in which he drew a comparison between the present Cunarders and the first of the line that ever crossed the Atlantic — the once famous Britannia, which sailed from Liverpool on the 4th of July, 1840. This was the vessel in which Charles Dickens first sailed to America in 1842. He describes the voyage in his most amusing manner in "American Notes."

The Britannia, as the speaker remarked, was considered, at the time, one of the greatest triumphs of the ship-builder's art. She was 207 feet long; her tonnage 1,155; her horse-power 850; her speed eight and a half miles an hour; and she had accommodations for 120 passengers. The Etruria is 500 feet long, and her tonnage nearly 8,000. Her engine is of 14,000 horse-power, and she carries 2,500 tons of coal, 5,000 tons of cargo, 1,500 passengers, and a crew of more than 200 men.

Many interesting speeches were delivered at the launching banquet, and many striking things were said; but there was one serious omission. The first vessels that crossed the ocean, the Sirius, the Great Western, the Britannia, and others, were side-wheelers. The screw was not applied to large vessels until 1847. But the wonderful speed of recent steamers could never have been reached by vessels propelled on the side-wheel system.

Besides the constant waste of power by the paddle-wheel from its form, one of the wheels in a sea-going steamer is frequently out of water; sometimes wholly, often partly. The wheels, moreover, are exposed to all the violence of the waves, and liable to create formidable accumulations of ice. In truth, the application of the screw was the most important single improvement that has been made in steam navigation since the Clermont sailed up the Hudson in 1807. It is the fundamental secret of the superiority of the new Etruria over the old Britannia. A side-wheel steamer probably could not be forced across the Atlantic, in the most favorable circumstances, in less than ten days. Builders in Glasgow hope to launch screw vessels which will do the voyage in five days.

It becomes, therefore, an interesting question, To whom are we indebted for this masterly device? Most of us have supposed that it was the work of

Captain Ericsson, although he did not claim it himself. I read in Lippincott's " Biographical Dictionary " the following paragraph: —

" Smith (Francis Pettit). An English inventor, born at Hythe, Kent, in 1808. He invented the mode of propelling steamboats by the screw, which was employed in the royal navy about 1838."

In the French city of Boulogne, however, there is a marble monument, surmounted by a bust in bronze, erected by the city authorities in memory of Frederic Sauvage, a native of that city, as the inventor of the screw propeller! A public funeral was decreed to him for the same reason, and there are still living at Boulogne several aged persons who remember witnessing his early experiments with screw propulsion. Above all, there is at Paris the official record of his patent, dated in March, 1832, which patent was also recorded in England in the sense of a patent " Applied For," according to the American expression. It is not claimed that no one had previously conceived the idea of propelling a steamer from behind by means of a screw. The friends and descendants of Frederic Sauvage have established beyond reasonable dispute that he was the inventor of *the* screw which first proved successful, and which is now employed on all sea-going steamboats. Baron Ernouf, a French author of reputation, has recently stated the facts bearing on the claim of Frederic Sauvage in a narrative of great interest.

Pierre Louis Frederic Sauvage, born at Boulogne in 1786, was one of a long and honorable line of ship-builders. He was one of the great crowd of ship-builders who were employed by Bonaparte in 1801 to assist in constructing his famous flotilla for the invasion of England. Sauvage was then but a forward boy of fifteen. During the preparation of the invading fleet he pursued mathematical studies, became a musician of much skill, and gave many proofs of his being a born inventor. One of his youthful inventions was an alarum to wake him early in the morning from the deep sleep of youth. It was a see-saw, which had a tin vessel at one end of it with a small hole at the bottom, from which water escaped one drop at a time. It was so contrived that when the tin vessel was empty the canting of the see-saw upward set six bells ringing. They rang with such force, as the inventor once wrote, "that it would have waked the devil, *if the devil ever slept*." If he wished an early call, he had only to lessen the quantity of water. He could sleep a pint or a quart, according to his need or discretion.

Like many other inventors, he was too ingenious for his own profit. Having inherited the ship-yard of his father, he built his ships with a care and thoroughness which was more advantageous to the owner than the builder, and he was continually drawn away from his legitimate labor to unprofitable enterprises requiring ingenuity and time, such as raising sunken vessels. As he was a married man with three children, he found himself obliged to change his business. He bought a marble quarry near Boulogne, and invented the machine, now so familiar to us all, for sawing marble by power. This was in 1821, as we learn from an " Honorable Mention " and a gold medal awarded to him by the Society of Arts at Boulogne. He perfected his marble-sawing machine to such a point as to saw fourteen slabs of marble at once with the oversight of one man. Every one advised him to take a patent for this wonder; but he was not yet satisfied with it, and while he was laboring to perfect his machine the idea of it was spread abroad and copied everywhere.

His marble works, however, were profitable to him, and he enjoyed for a time a period of tranquillity which he had never known before, and unhappily was never to know again. He still amused himself with inventing. He invented a machine for cutting likenesses in profile, and another, not less ingenious, for reducing statues to statuettes with the precision of mathematics. At length, in the year 1831, when he was a man forty-five years of age, he began to experiment upon the mode of propelling steamboats. From early life he had watched the development of steam navigation with an interest almost amounting to passion. He early perceived, as Fulton himself did, the unavoidable waste of the paddle, and he continually reflected upon the possibility of a substitute which should act on the vessel more directly and simply.

It is a tradition among his descendants that the first idea of his invention of the screw was suggested to him by watching the movements of a gold-fish in a glass globe. He saw the fish moving about in its prison of glass, darting upwards and downwards, circumnavigating his globe, all by easy movements of his tail! As he watched the fish, he observed the similarity of its movements to that of a scull at the stern of a boat. He was himself an expect sculler, having practiced that mode of propulsion very frequently in his youth. It became clear to him that the propelling power of a steamboat could be more advantageously applied at the stern than at the sides.

Having reached this conclusion, he constructed a little vessel about a foot in length upon which to try experiments. His power was derived at first by the descent of a small weight down the mast, but he afterwards found it better to use a watchspring fixed in the hold. He directed his attention to making a stern wheel or wheels which should act upon the water with the force and directness of a scull.

"Knowing," says Sauvage, "the power of a scull, I endeavored to produce the same effect by continuous motions capable of being produced by the steam-engine. I imagined then an oar used as a scull placed in the most favorable position (an angle of forty-five degrees). I then traced a screw of which the outer line inclosed all the space traversed by the oar working in the best way, and the result was *a screw of which the diameter was equal to its length.*"

His first screw was made of a little piece of elder wood with common needles stuck into it, upon which were fastened pieces of oiled silk in such a way as to form an approximation to the screw desired. Upon careful experiment he found that his silken screw propelled his little boat about three times as fast as paddle-wheels, and the screw had the immense additional advantage of being buried in the water beyond the reach of most accidents.

In January, 1832, he invited his fellow-citizens to a public exhibition of his experiments. In March of the same year he patented his invention in Paris, where also he had a small canoe made, which he propelled up and down the Seine with remarkable rapidity by means of a screw. He explained his invention to all comers who manifested an interest in it. He even sailed in his screw canoe from Paris to Havre, stopping often by the way, relying always upon the protection of his patent in France, and his application for a patent in England.

Unfortunately, he was unable to make the annual payments in England which were then necessary to continue the application in legal force, and hence Francis Pettit Smith, a noted English engineer of the day, formerly a resident of Boulogne, built a screw tow-boat on the Thames, patented the invention in England as his own, and came himself to Paris to secure a French patent. There he was confronted with the patent already issued to Frederic Sauvage. Nevertheless, he obtained the glory and the profit of the invention in England, while Sauvage came very near starving in France, and died in a mad-house.

It is agreeable to read of victorious men, but we do not often have that pleasure in surveying the lives of inventors. One reason is that the qualities of mind which give the inventive faculty are rarely found in conjunction with worldly wisdom. This appears to be the explanation of the tragic failure of Frederic Sauvage, the inventor of the screw propeller.

He had no sooner satisfied himself and his friends at Boulogne of the value of his invention, than he sold his marble works for a price much below their value, and gave himself wholly up to the work of introducing the device which he justly felt to be of first-rate importance. Away he sped to Paris with his plans and models in March, 1832, and as soon as he had taken out his patent he explained his invention to the French Secretary of the Navy. He dwelt upon the advantage of having the propelling power of an armed vessel wholly under water, invisible to the foe; and he also demonstrated the greater propelling power of the screw over the paddle-wheel. After a very long delay, he received a reply from the ministry, to the effect that his invention could not be given a trial by the navy department because experiments recently made in the United States had proved that the screw was a failure when applied to large vessels.

This reply was the more stunning as the inventor had never before heard of experiments with the screw in America nor anywhere else. Such experiments, however, had been made both in America and in England, but not with screws of the Sauvage form. The Sauvage screw was as long as it was broad, and was based upon the idea of *a revolving scull*.

The screws attempted on the Thames and at New York were of great length, five times the length of their diameter. They turned almost horizontally, and were not completely immersed in the water. It was in vain that the inventor explained the difference between his screw and those of Fitch, Ericsson, and Stevens. He had had his hearing, and his application had been passed upon. Moreover, secretaries of the navy have rarely been appointed in any country for other than political reasons, and hence the arguments of poor Sauvage were addressed to men incapable of appreciating them. One of the government commissioners appointed to witness his experiments asked him, after seeing the performance of his little screw boat: —

" Why don't you place the screw in front of the vessel, instead of behind ? "

If Sauvage had been the kind of man to succeed in the world, he would have answered this question so as not to wound the self-love of the commissioner who, for the time, had the fate of the invention in his hands. Instead of doing so, he bluntly answered: —

"For the same reason that a fish does not have his tail at his head."

The young official who was thus repulsed happened to be a favorite aid-de-camp of the minister, and was continually about his person. It is supposed that the inventor's satirical reply closed the door to the further consideration of the screw. Eight months were consumed by these experiments and delays, at the end of which period an important part of the price of his marble works had been expended, and he was no nearer success than when he began.

At that time, as now, the city of Havre, a hundred and fifty miles down the Seine from Paris, was the seat of the ship-building industry, and accordingly our inventor launched his screw canoe upon the languid tide of the Seine, and made the voyage to Havre in it, turning the screw himself by a crank. As no paddle-wheel was visible to people on shore, the little vessel excited great wonder, as she seemed to move rapidly along without any means of propulsion.

At Havre he exhibited his boat, and explained his principle to the ship-builders and machinists.

His explanations were well received, but he had against him the known rejection of his device by the ministry. The commissioners at Paris had not denied the success of his canoe. They merely asserted that American experiments had demonstrated that the same principle had failed when applied to large vessels. He replied to this objection in a very expensive way for a man of his small means. He bought or hired a twenty-ton barge of clumsy form, only used for carrying sand, and having applied a screw to the stern of the old tub and a kind of capstan for the propelling power, he made an experiment in the harbor in presence of a great number of intelligent ship-builders and captains. The success was as great as could have been expected by the most sanguine inventor with such a vessel.

Nevertheless, it did not induce any capitalist to join him in his enterprise, while it aroused a violent opposition from the towing interest, then very powerful at Havre. All towing of vessels was then done by large, heavy boats propelled only by oars, and hence he had not merely prejudice to contend against, but the interests of a powerful and numerous body of men. He did not himself yet perceive that his principle was the best possible for Havre tugboats, of which hundreds may now be seen there propelled by the Sauvage screw. He said to the ship-masters : —

"The tow-men will indeed lose by my invention, but commerce will gain by it."

This last consideration, however, did not console the men who gained their subsistence by rowing towboats. The inventor had now spent the whole of his capital, and exhausted his credit besides. His baker gave him notice that he could no longer furnish him with bread on credit, and in France, to a poor man, bread is truly the staff of life. He was in danger of starving to death in his room at this time, for he was incapable of asking alms in any extremity whatever. One of his friends, however, informed the inventor's brother of the condition in which he was. The brother sent him assistance in time, and he at once began again to exhibit the power of his screw in the waters of Havre.

Nevertheless, he could not make headway against the obstacles which opposed the introduction of his invention, and he was compelled to turn his attention to some other mode of gaining money. He introduced, and with success, his Reducer, an apparatus for reducing large statues to any smaller size desired. He had now an interval of ease, during which he attempted to revive the force of his screw patent in England, which had lapsed through his failure to pay the annual fee. This attempt appears to have called attention to his claims, and the British Navy Department offered a price for the exclusive right to his invention. Sauvage, *being an inventor*, made such a reply as we should expect.

"The screw propeller," said he, "is a French invention, and French it will remain."

This was very fine, no doubt, but a few months after, a polite and well-informed Englishman called upon him, and asked him to explain his system of propulsion. Sauvage was as willing to talk upon his favorite device as the Englishman was to hear. He showed the stranger all his working models, and likewise his screw-propelled boat upon the Seine. He gave him a sail in this boat, after which the stranger took his leave, with many compliments. His brother reproached him for his imprudence, but the inventor replied : —

"My experiments have been public, and everybody could see them. Besides, is it not too evident that all French inventions must be put out to nurse in England ? "

In three months there was a screw tugboat of the Sauvage pattern upon the Thames, and the owner of it, in the following year, came to Paris to get a French patent for the invention. This, of course, was refused ; but in the mean time, an enterprising Englishman, F. P. Smith, launched a screw steamer, the Archimedes, of 237 tons burden, which, in spite of many defects of construction, proved the utility of the screw principle beyond question. The Archimedes made a trial trip to Boulogne, the very birth-place of the French inventor, beating several paddle-wheel vessels on the way. This success calling attention to the screw, a vessel on the same principle was built in France. It was called the Napoleon, and it confirmed the success of the principle. But the inventor was so indignant at the many departures from his principle in the construction of the ship that he refused to come on board of her, although he was, in effect, requested to do so by the king, Louis Philippe.

In the midst of these events, Sauvage was thrown into prison for debt. A national subscription for his benefit was proposed, which he haughtily declined, and remained in prison until he was legally released. The only advantage he ever received from an invention upon which he had expended two hundred thousand francs, the earnings of his lifetime, was "an indemnity" of twenty-five hundred francs from the French Navy Department.

I cannot relate the long series of misfortunes which befell this ill-starred genius. In 1850, when it became manifest to every intelligent engineer in the world that the propelling screw on the Sauvage pattern was about to supersede the paddle-wheel on all sea-going vessels, the inventor's mind gave way, and he was confined in an asylum. Strange to relate, his last three years, spent among lunatics, were the happiest in his life, for he was cheered by the most delightful illusions. He believed himself the king of the ocean. In his disordered imagination, he saw great vessels approach as if to salute the master whose genius had given them their means of swift propulsion. He saw them sail away in tempest and in calm, propelled by screws of his own fashioning. Occasionally, when his reason partly returned, he was plunged into gloom, but these intervals grew shorter as his days grew near their end.

He had always been fond of birds. He now had cages of singing birds in his room, and he would amuse himself for hours by playing to them upon his violin. He would sometimes point out to visitors that the wings of his birds acted upon the principle of his beloved screw. He died peacefully in 1857, aged seventy-one years, and a monument to his memory adorns his native city.

WILLIAM ELLIS,

INSURANCE AGENT.

"OTHERS may keep a carriage, but I prefer to keep a conscience."

So said William Ellis, manager of a London insurance company. But he did not make this odd remark with any reference to his business. He was thinking of his hobby, which was the reform of education in England. He was one of those happy men who lead two lives in one, and have two distinct careers, one private, the other public: one by which they acquire leisure and independence; the other by which they utilize these for some public object to which they attach *infinite* importance.

First, as to his business life, which was as extraordinary as his public career. In 1824, when he was twenty-four years old, he was appointed clerk in the office of the Indemnity Mutual Marine Insurance Company, at a salary of two hundred pounds sterling per annum. The business of insurance being hereditary in his family, he took to it as a duck takes to water. He had, indeed, a genius for judging of a marine risk, and rarely made a mistake. Long before his head was gray, he was regarded in London as the first man in the world in the marine branch of insurance. He was often called the king of the underwriters.

Three years after entering the office, he being then twenty-seven, he was invited to take the post of manager, which gave him the practical direction of the whole business. The stock rapidly rose in value, and in a very few years it was held at three times its par value. The foundation of his success was, no doubt, the soundness of his judgment, which indeed is, and must ever be, the cause of permanent success in all large operations. When, for example, the gold began to come in from Australia in great quantities, the marine men were afraid of the risks; but he, on the contrary, took them freely at the high premiums offered, sometimes insuring as much as half a million dollars in one ship. He said to himself: "Gold is a safer risk than most things; it is easier to save from a shipwreck, and if it goes to the bottom, it can often be recovered."

Now it so happened that the very first ship upon which he had taken a large gold risk was lost. But he was so sure of the correctness of his reasoning that he continued to insure the gold as freely as before, and this he did for many years. The profits of the company were immense, for they seldom had an important loss.

The directors of the company showed themselves to be intelligent business men, for they gave him a fair portion of the profits of his skillful management. This they did, not by raising his salary, which would have been, perhaps, an inconvenient precedent, but by making him a present every year of fifty thousand dollars. He, in his turn, showed high business sense by declining to accept this unless every one under him, down to the porters and messengers, received an annual bonus proportioned to his salary.

He had been a frugal man from the first, because, as he explained one day to his daughter, he meant to put himself as a reformer "beyond the reach of oppression for opinion's sake." He thought that "the luxury of thinking for one's self, like other luxuries, must be paid for." To this he added the remark quoted above: "Others may keep a carriage, but I prefer to keep a conscience."

His conscience, I may add, guided him aright in some difficult problems of management. It was he who introduced into the business of insurance the system of paying losses with alacrity when the insurer, by some accident or forgetfulness, had omitted one of the legal conditions, such as, for example, neglecting to renew an old policy, which the insurer had fully intended to do. Nor would he avail himself of any other legal technicality to avoid paying a loss. There was a great fire in a distant seaport, which extended to some of the vessels lying alongside the wharves, or anchored near them. The question at once arose: Are we liable for a disaster which did not occur "at sea" according to the letter of the policy? Without one moment's hesitation, he paid the total loss on every ship which he had insured, and this compelled the other companies to do the same, besides establishing a precedent which has benefited insurance companies quite as much as it has merchants. All insurance business is now conducted, more or less, in this spirit.

At the same time, he was strict and firm in exacting the rights of the company. He would have his due, and he obtained it all the easier, because he had an absolute command of his temper. One day, after a tremendous scene in his office between himself and an infuriated broker, a person who had witnessed it asked him how he had managed to keep his temper with such a man.

"The easiest thing in the world," was his reply. "I said to myself: 'Hush! There is a fool in the room.' Then I said to myself: 'Shall I double the number? No; that would be a pity.'"

With such qualities and such a chance to exercise them, he was not long in acquiring the independence upon which he had set his heart as a means to a noble end. From early life, when he was a member of the circle of young men, Mill, Grote, and others, who surrounded Jeremy Bentham in his old age, he had reflected deeply and constantly upon the causes of human misery, and especially upon the poverty and distress he saw around him in London. He asked himself: "Why does the huge wealth of Great Britain bless so few of its people? Why does it injure so many, both among those who have too much of it, and those who have little or none of it?"

He came to the conclusion that it was the almost universal want of right education. He saw that children and youth were taught many things, but not taught the causes of human welfare.

"Education," he once wrote, "is not to be confounded with the mere teaching of reading, writing, and arithmetic, nor with what goes by the name of history and geography. It means the teaching of *the conditions of well-being, and the training of youth to an observance of those conditions.*"

He spent the leisure of fifty years in the endeavor to convince the people of England of this truth. He wrote eighteen volumes, delivered hundreds of lectures, taught thousands of pupils, held numberless conversations, all having the same general purpose, all inculcating the same lesson, namely, that the general cause of human misery is the defects of human character, and that, therefore, the great object of all education should be to create, strengthen, and exalt character. He wanted every child and every student to know the true causes both of national prosperity and personal welfare.

He had considerable success in awakening public attention to these truths. Still they made their way but slowly. One reason for this may be gathered from an anecdote. At the time of the

Irish famine, some one asked him if he had seen the beautiful prayer just issued by the Archbishop of Canterbury for the relief of the sufferers, which, he thought, could not fail to be heard and answered.

"Do you expect," asked William Ellis, in his quiet, good-tempered way, "that the Almighty will send another potato crop before next year, or that He will diminish the capacity of the human stomach?"

Indolent and thoughtless mortals have in all ages preferred the easy method of calling upon God for supplies to the hard way of William Ellis, which was to avoid waste, practice forethought, comply with the natural conditions of welfare, perform the common duties of every day, and train the young to industry, obedience, and self-control.

Among those who watched his career with interest and approval were Prince Albert and Queen Victoria, whose children he instructed in political economy and the natural causes of prosperity, public and private. These lessons were given weekly for two seasons, at Buckingham Palace, in a series of familiar conversations, something in the manner of Socrates and his friends. One of his most appreciative pupils was the Princess Royal of England, now called the Empress Frederick of Germany. It is not improbable that the worthy efforts of the young Emperor William to improve the condition of workingmen and to reform schools may be traced to the instruction which his mother received from William Ellis.

The Memoir of this excellent man by his daughter Ethel is dedicated to the Empress Frederick, as " the Royal Lady who has done far more than can here be told, at once, to improve and to diffuse education, who has borne with her through life a vivid and a loving memory of her teacher, William Ellis."

SIR JOSEPH WHITWORTH,

TOOL-MAKER.

THIS famous maker of great guns, which throw two hundred and fifty pounds of iron six miles and a half, was a mechanic of the old school; one of those who mastered their art by slow degrees and heroic painstaking. There are still many old men in English Manchester who remember him when over the door of a small shop could be read the sign : —

JOSEPH WHITWORTH,
Tool-maker, from London.

This modest sign was put up in 1833, when he was already a man thirty years of age, and a mechanic of twelve years' standing.

He was a country boy, born in Cheshire, the county of cheese, and came out of school for good at the age of thirteen and a half years. Then he was placed in his uncle's cotton mill as boy of all work, and began to pick up a little knowledge of machinery, and to understand the mysteries of the steam-engine.

Machinery attracted and fascinated him to such a

degree that, at the age of eighteen, he left the cotton mill and entered a machine shop, where he worked for four years, learning and practicing the business of making machinery.

To perfect himself in his business, which is the most difficult and varied of all the mechanical trades, he went to London, at the age of twenty-one, and obtained employment with a firm renowned throughout Europe as machinists and toolmakers. Here he worked eight years as a journeyman, and became the most skillful mechanic in the establishment. He was noted as an extremely *exact* workman, and the first great success of his life was an effort to produce greater exactness in machinery. He was the first man to make a perfect plane in metal. Before his day, plane surfaces were produced by a laborious and expensive process of filing and grinding with emery powder and water; and this process was never quite successful. A very slight departure from a true plane spoils a steel plate for engraving, a stereotype plate, or a printer's table. Whitworth invented a machine for planing and scraping a metallic surface, by which he succeeded in producing the first perfect plane ever made in metal. By his machine iron plates can be made of a surface so perfectly even that if one be placed upon the other the weight of the upper plate will expel the air between the surfaces very slowly, and it will seem to float over the lower one without touching it. When at length the film of air is expelled, the plates will adhere, so that when the upper one is lifted it will carry the lower one up with it.

The beauty of this invention is as apparent as its importance, but the economy of the process is also very remarkable. To make a true plane in the old way of filing and grinding costs a dollar and a half for a square foot. The Whitworth machine does it better for two cents.

Having reached this point in his career, he returned to Manchester, and set up in business on his own account as a maker of tools. His business could not fail to prosper, and he continued his progress as an inventor, always selecting, as if by instinct, problems the most difficult and the least likely to attract attention. One of his inventions was a measuring machine, which is capable of measuring a millionth part of an inch. By the aid of this machine, it can be shown that a bar of steel a yard long is lengthened a millionth of an inch by the heat imparted to it from the touch of a finger. By the aid of his two inventions, the planing machine and the measuring machine, some machinery is now produced of absolute accuracy.

Once an inventor, always an inventor: that is the usual rule. Forty years ago, in an interval of leisure, he invented a street-sweeping machine similar to those which we have seen operating in the streets of New York. His machine did the work of thirty men, and it was said at the time to have changed Manchester from being one of the dirtiest towns in England into one of the cleanest. The revolving brooms of his engine swept the dirt from the street up an inclined plane into the cart. This, however, was a mere episode. He rendered a great service to all the machinists of the world by introducing the system of uniformity in the threads of screws and the uniformity of parts of machinery,— an American idea. He also anticipated, at least in thought, some other American inventions. In 1857, he wrote : —

"I don't hesitate to say that all the harvest operations will very shortly be performed in one quarter of the time required by the hand-labor now expended, by the further application of machines worked by horse-power. This is my conviction, based upon the experience I have had in the successful working of the machine I constructed for sweeping the streets, and at the same time filling the cart, by horse-power."

Readers who have visited a great prairie farm in harvest-time do not need to be told that this prediction has been already more than fulfilled.

The rude blast of the Crimean war diverted his attention from this line of experiment. It became a question which was the best rifle in existence. Joseph Whitworth entered upon a series of most ingenious experiments, to ascertain the best form of barrel and bullet, and the best system of rifling. He is not a man to take anything for granted. He discovered at length what he was in search of, and produced a rifle which sent a bullet through thirty-four elm boards half an inch thick, while the old Enfield rifle penetrated but twelve. He not only produced the rifle, but discovered the law and reason of its power, and invented machinery which could produce his rifles with unvarying perfection.

The secret of making a projectile penetrate is to make it revolve with great rapidity. Some of Whitworth's projectiles revolve at a rate almost inconceivable, making a thousand rotations in a second, or sixty thousand in a minute. The fastest wheel in a machine shop rarely makes more than two thousand revolutions in a minute. It is this extreme rapidity of rotation which enables the Whitworth bolts to penetrate steel plate many inches thick.

Having completed his rifle, he applied its principles to large ordnance with extraordinary success. He sums up the results of his experiments in these words: —

"In 1860, I penetrated a four and a half inch armor plate with an eighty-pound, flat-headed, solid steel projectile. In 1870, I penetrated with a nine-inch gun three five-inch armor plates, interlaminated with two five-inch layers of concrete."

When he had brought his projectile to this point of perfection, he directed his attention to the production of a steel plate capable of resisting it, experimenting with the various ores, and aiming at a process which should free steel from every kind of defect. He made twenty-five hundred experiments in the purification of steel, and succeeded in very greatly increasing its tenacity. He appears to have come nearer than any other man to realizing the professor's old joke of hurling an irresistible against an impenetrable mass.

Personally, Sir Joseph Whitworth was the least warlike of men. He consoled himself for having invented these terrific engines of war by the conviction that the more destructive war is made, the more governments will be afraid of beginning it. He said once: —

"Believing in the pacific influence of the most powerful means of defense, these long projectiles of mine I call *the anti-war shell.*"

He might have gone on forever making peaceful inventions without deriving from them any public honor; but when he began to invent instruments for destroying his species, the Queen of England made him a baronet, and did him the honor to fire off his first rifle by pulling a silken cord attached to the trigger.

Though himself a man of little schooling, he had the highest opinion of the value of scientific knowledge acquired in early life, and he founded thirty scholarships, which give to thirty young men five hundred dollars a year each for three years, while they are studying the theory and practice of mechanics. He was also much interested in the welfare of the numerous mechanics in his employment. He adopted the system of making the best of his foremen, draughtsmen, workmen, and clerks, shareholders in the concern, but on such conditions as to retain the control in the competent hands which created the business.

CHARLES KNIGHT,

PUBLISHER.

One day in the year 1823, two gentlemen, living in the outskirts of London, fell into conversation, while walking to the city, upon the cheap publications of the day, a great number of which were written by scoffing and unprincipled men, and had a widespread demoralizing effect. These two gentlemen were Mr. M. D. Hill, Member of Parliament for Hull, and Charles Knight, a publisher, and a member of the Society for the Diffusion of Useful Knowledge. It seemed to both of them unnecessary that a periodical should be coarse because it was cheap; and at length Mr. Hill said:—

"Let us see what something cheap and good can accomplish. Let us have a Penny Magazine!"

"And what shall be its title?" asked Mr. Knight.

"The Penny Magazine," was the reply.

They went at once to Lord Chancellor Brougham, the president and great promoter of the Society for the Diffusion of Useful Knowledge. He cordially entered into the scheme. A committee of the society was called, and although some members argued that a penny weekly sheet would be something below their dignity, the work was decided upon. Mr. Knight undertook the pecuniary risk, and was appointed editor. The first number was issued March 31, 1832, and before that year closed it had reached a circulation of two hundred thousand. Many remember "The Penny Magazine," in which the useful and the entertaining were so happily blended, and to the columns of which some of the first men of the period contributed. It was the great forerunner of cheap publications of an elevated character, and it was an important event in the mighty movement which will finally place all the treasures of literature, art, and science within the reach of every person on the globe capable of appreciating them.

The whole life of Charles Knight was employed in similar labors. It was he who projected and carried on the Library of Entertaining Knowledge, the Penny Cyclopædia, Half-Hours with the Best Authors, the popular History of England, the Cyclopædia of the Industry of all Nations, and a large number of other works having the same general object — to diffuse and popularize knowledge.

The father of this excellent man was a printer and bookseller, who kept a shop close to the principal gate of Windsor Castle, the most imposing and magnificent royal residence in Europe. There the boy grew up, at a time when England was engaged in her long struggle with Napoleon Bonaparte, which made life so heavy and so bitter to the industrious people of Europe. He saw a great deal in his boyhood and youth of King George III. and his family, the king frequently coming into his father's shop to look over the new publications. One summer morning, before the shop was fully opened, the voice of the king was heard under the windows, calling: —

"Knight! Knight! Knight!"

His father came down as soon as possible, and found the king deeply absorbed in reading a work which had come down in a parcel from London the evening before. What was his horror and consternation to discover that the king had taken up Thomas Paine's "Rights of Man," in which the author defended the French Revolution, and attacked the institution of monarchy. The king continued to read for half an hour, at the expiration of which he laid down the book and left the shop without a word, but also without offense, for he continued to be as friendly and frequent a visitor as before. Mr. Knight also reports that the king was as much amused as any one at the caricatures of the day in which he was broadly burlesqued, and that he was quite capable of being amused at Peter Pindar's poems of the Apple Dumplings and Farmer George.

He was indeed, in private life, as good-natured

and amiable a gentleman as ever misgoverned a kingdom or spoiled a family. Mr. Knight tells an amusing story in point. One evening, after having joined the family in the drawing-room, the king went back to the library where he had been writing, and found the wax candles still burning. It was a curious rule of the palace, as of great houses generally in that day, that a wax candle should never be lighted a second time, and the unconsumed portions were usually the perquisites of some servant or officer of the household. These particular wax candles blazing away in the king's library were the perquisites of the king's page, named Clarke, whom the king met on his return to the drawing-room.

"Clarke, Clarke," said the king, in his rapid manner, "you should mind your perquisites. *I* blew out the candles."

It cost the English people at that time ten thousand pounds a year to provide Windsor Castle with wax candles. The government of the royal household was as wasteful and corrupt as the government of the city of New York used to be.

The boy once saw William Pitt and George III. walking up and down the terrace of Windsor Castle, side by side, talking earnestly together; and what he then saw gave clearness and precision to his conceptions of their characters when he came to write his "History of England." Speaking of Mr. Pitt, he says: —

"The immobility of those features, the erectness of that form, told of one born to command. The loftiness and breadth of the forehead spoke of sagacity and firmness."

The lad also had a lively recollection of seeing the king and queen at the little Windsor theatre, which was so small a place that one half of the lower tier of boxes was occupied by the royal family and their attendants. The king and queen sat in large armchairs, with satin playbills spread before them. The orchestra was large enough to hold half a dozen fiddlers, and the pit was so near the boxes that the king could have shaken hands with half the people in it. At any amusing point in the play, the king would applaud the actor by name.

"Bravo, Quick! Bravo, Suett!"

At which the pit and gallery would clap and roar in sympathy. At the end of the third act, the royal family were regaled with coffee, while pots of ale circulated in the gallery. When the curtain fell at the close of the performance, and the court had retired, the pit would surge over into the boxes, and scramble for the satin playbills, which would be framed and hung up in the parlor of the fortunate possessors.

These glimpses of the great world had much to do with forming the mind of this observant and studious youth, who passed his days browsing among the multitudinous books of his father's shop, and following with most attentive mind the vicissitudes of the great contest proceeding on the continent, in which figured Wellington, Nelson, and Napoleon, and which seemed to the people of England a contest between the powers of darkness and the powers of light. From an early age he was struck with the ignorance of the people of Windsor.

"An atmosphere of *proud ignorance*," he records, "was surrounding the whole region."

A mushroom gentility had grown up, as he explains, about the royal palace, each class and each profession cherishing the foolish delusion of caste superiority. The canons of Windsor and the dignitaries of Eton College looked down upon the brewers and the dealers in grain, who in turn despised shopkeepers, who held their heads high above mechanics; and they too found somebody to despise, no doubt. He well names this ridiculous feeling *proud ignorance*. Believing that he could do something to dispel this "fog," as he also terms it, he formed a dozen young men of his own class into a Reading Society, which hired a room, procured lectures, and gathered books. At that time, he tells us, the general feeling of the educated class was against such proceedings as this, and it was an accepted belief in Windsor, as in Europe generally, that for workingmen to read books and listen to scientific lectures was to make them dangerous members of society.

Thus it was that Charles Knight began his long

and most honorable career as a public instructor. His first venture in business was in the same direction. It was a periodical called the "Plain Englishman," in which he endeavored to show that a paper could be instructive without being dull, and cheap without being wicked. He was powerfully aided in his endeavors by Henry Brougham, the greater part of whose life was spent in the destruction of hoary abuses and the diffusion of civilizing knowledge. That Lord Brougham had the misfortune to outlive his better self should not blind our eyes to his very great merits and services.

Mr. Knight had every kind of success in life except one. He was happy in his home; he was honored by his countrymen; he greatly served his generation; his life in all respects was honorable to human nature. There was one thing, however, he did not accomplish, and that was the accumulation of money. He was not a good business man, and he expended a large portion of his force in writing the books which it was his business to sell. Few men can carry on successfully two careers so different as the writing and the publication of books, both of which are invested with peculiar and great difficulties. Mr. Knight passed the last few years of his life in comparative poverty, though, I believe, he possessed enough for the gratification of his simple wants.

He died at an advanced age, and a monument has been erected over his remains.

PHILIP HONE,

AUCTIONEER.

It is sometimes said, and even by pretty good Americans, that an hereditary nobility is a handy thing to have in a country, to perform public duty, entertain distinguished visitors, and serve generally as an ornamental class. But what better nobleman could a country ordinarily have than Philip Hone, that courtly, good-humored, hospitable, and public-spirited citizen, who, from 1825 to 1840, was the most conspicuous inhabitant of the city of New York?

Like all the rest of human kind, he had his defects and his limits, but I should not know where to look for a nobleman of twenty descents who better served or more satisfactorily adorned the place of his abode. Yet this highly ornamental New Yorker made his fortune in the unromantic business of an auctioneer. Even that noisy business served his turn, for it developed his naturally fine voice, afterwards so often heard and admired at public meetings.

Sixty years ago, he lived at No. 235 Broadway,

near Park Place, and opposite to what was then called "The Park." We had but one park at that time, and it was still surrounded by its primitive picket fence. Mr. Hone thought it a grand improvement when the shabby and rotten old pickets were taken away, and neatly painted posts connected by chains were put in their place. He looked out of his library windows and rejoiced at the improved prospect.

His house was among the most spacious and handsome in the city. Passers-by pointed it out to their country cousins with pride as a specimen of New York magnificence. But the cost of it did not run up into the millions, as conspicuous houses now do. In 1821 he bought it for twenty-five thousand dollars, and in 1837 sold it for sixty thousand, about the present price of an average house in Madison Avenue. He was himself much surprised at the magnitude of the sum for which he sold it, and spoke of it with respect as "a great deal of money." At present, a New Yorker draws his check for about the same sum when he pays for a promising colt.

In this stately abode, as it was then esteemed, he entertained home and foreign notabilities, particularly if they were distinguished for something besides rank and wealth. He gave a dinner to Fanny Kemble and her father, of which the lady wrote a very saucy report in her published Diary. Fanny Elssler had also the pleasure of dining with him.

Dickens, Wallack, Irving, Clay, Webster, were his frequent guests; particularly Webster, who would sit five hours at a time in his house, telling stories and sipping Madeira.

But this was only the ornamental and agreeable part of the duty appertaining to his position. He was president or director of almost every public institution, literary, scientific, or charitable, which the city then could boast, and he attended to this branch of his public duty with a vigilant and conscientious regularity seldom equaled.

Of some of the most useful of those institutions he was the founder, or one of the founders, notably of the first savings bank and the Mercantile Library. It was no part of his scheme of life to serve any of these establishments as a mere figurehead or ornamental appendage. Mr. Bayard Tuckerman, who has recently edited two most agreeable volumes of the " Diary of Philip Hone," after giving a list of about twenty associations and corporations with which Mr. Hone was officially connected, from Columbia College to the Union Club, uses the following language: —

"In these positions he worked with the same assiduity that a man could apply to his own business. An ordinary day's occupation for him was to ride out on horseback to the Bloomingdale Asylum, to return and pass the afternoon at the Bank for Savings, thence to attend a meeting of the Trinity Vestry, or to preside over the Mercantile Library

Association. He was never voluntarily absent from a meeting where the interests of others demanded his presence, and many were the good dinners which he lost in consequence."

He lost those dinners because the fashionable dinner hour at that time was four o'clock, which was much too early for a gentleman so full of business as he was.

Most New Yorkers are aware that the marble bust of this genial and generous man still adorns one of the halls of the Mercantile Library, but very few of them know just why the bust was placed there. It was a testimonial from a number of his fellow-citizens, to commemorate his honorable conduct in sacrificing two thirds of his large estate in his old age to discharge obligations which he had assumed for his sons. He spent several of his last years in embarrassment and anxiety, in the effort to make good his indorsement of their notes. He felt obliged also to return to active business, and became president of a fire insurance company, the interests of which were greatly promoted by the weight and attraction of his name. By the second great fire of New York the company lost its whole capital, and he was a well-nigh ruined man. He stood by the ship, however, until every claim was liquidated and the business honorably closed.

Even the third time he went into business by accepting the office of Naval Officer at the port of New York, an office which he held till the day of his death. Through all these vicissitudes he preserved his cheerfulness, his good temper, and his public spirit.

It was in 1846 that twenty of his friends united to procure the bust for the Mercantile Library. They sent out the commission to Italy, where it was executed by Hiram Powers, and the secret was so well kept that he knew nothing of it till the bust was placed upon its pedestal. Among the twenty subscribers were many names still well known. In their letter to him, they expressly said that their object in placing the bust in the library was to convey to "the future merchants of New York" the high example which he had set them in sacrificing a large portion of his estate to meet obligations incurred on behalf of others.

One of the most pleasing traits in the character of Philip Hone was the warmth of his affection for his friends, and, generally speaking, he loved them in proportion to their worth. Of all the men who lived in New York in his day, the one whom he held in the profoundest esteem and affection was Chancellor Kent, the author of the well-known "Commentaries." He never mentions the Chancellor in his Diary without becoming eloquent in his commendation. In one place he says: —

"I venerate him as a father, while I love him as a brother; and the reverence I feel for him as an instructor is sanctified by my affection for him as a friend. The hour I pass in the twilight of every

Sunday evening with Chancellor Kent and his amiable family affords me the highest gratification, and I come away as delighted with my visit as a young lover from the society and the smiles of his mistress."

At the same time he was a vigorous hater, though never except for public reasons. Many of the leading Democrats of his day he regarded with intense disapproval, particularly Andrew Jackson and William Cullen Bryant, then editor of the "Evening Post." He happened to be looking out of his window one morning in 1831, when he saw the famous fight between Mr. Bryant and Colonel W. L. Stone, of the "Commercial Advertiser." The poet began the attack by striking Stone over the head with a cowhide, after which the two men clinched, and Stone wrested the cowhide from his antagonist and carried it off.

Many years after, Mr. Hone wrote of the poet in severer language than he ever employed toward any other individual.

"How such a black-hearted misanthrope as Bryant," he writes, "should possess an imagination teeming with beautiful poetical images astonishes me; one would as soon expect to extract drops of honey from the fangs of a rattlesnake."

This means that Mr. Bryant, as editor of a Democratic newspaper, had opposed and denounced the United States Bank, and in his obituary notice of its president, Nicholas Biddle, had expressed the opinion that if justice had been done him, he would not have spent his last days at an elegant country seat on the banks of the Delaware, but in the penitentiary. Mr. Bryant, perhaps, was not far from right, though it was a rough thing to say in an obituary notice, even of a man whose mismanagement of the bank had reduced to beggary many hundreds of aged widows and helpless orphans.

Philip Hone died in 1851, enjoying life and the society of his friends almost to his last day. He belonged to a New York which has passed away as completely as the city of Athens has, in which Socrates conversed and Plato wrote. But it lives again for the New Yorker who reads Philip Hone's Diary, and who discovers therein that the New York of 1835 was not half so good a place as the New York of 1891.

JAMES LENOX,

BOOK COLLECTOR.

NEW YORKERS are familiar with the large, costly, but not attractive edifice near the Central Park which contains the results of the lifetime's toil of James Lenox. Many New Yorkers also know the extensive brown stone house in the Fifth Avenue, in which Mr. Lenox lived for forty years, and stored away by the roomful the books which he accumulated.

He was a strange man, difficult to describe, more difficult to explain. Very rich, very handsome, high-minded, generous, polite, he was also shy, unsocial, difficult of access, and utterly averse to every sort of publicity. He was an old bachelor, his family consisting of his sisters, of whom there were originally seven. If he knew beforehand that any action of his was to be praised in a newspaper, he avoided looking at it, and he charged his family on his deathbed not to furnish for the press any particulars of his life.

He did this not merely from instinctive aversion to publicity. He was himself scrupulous to state the exact truth on all occasions and to every person. He hated a lie. He hated also fractional parts of a lie and approximations towards a lie. He detested exaggeration and all undue emphasis. Those who had dealings with him, men as honest as himself, thought sometimes that he carried this virtue to excess; and, in truth, few men know how to make their favorite virtue attractive to others.

The way he came to be so rich was extraordinary. His father, a Scotch Philadelphian, removed to New York at the close of the Revolutionary War. He prospered greatly in business there as a merchant, at No. 59 Broadway, where his son James was born in the year 1800. The elder Lenox, about the time of his son's birth, bought a small farm near the site of the present Lenox Library for a few hundred dollars, and afterwards, to oblige a friend, he took another tract of land in the same region for a debt of a few thousand. In his will he apologized to his numerous family for the supposed worthlessness of this investment, but expressed the hope that they would make allowance for his feelings towards an old friend. He thought, however, that this land, if they kept it long enough, might prove to be of some value. He had, he said, "a firm persuasion that it might, at no distant day, be the site of a village."

Long before his son had reached his prime, the land was worth several millions of dollars. The site of a small Presbyterian church which Mr.

Lenox gave, some years before his death, on the upper portion of this farm, was valued in the assessor's books at a hundred thousand dollars. It was this tract of land, in addition to his father's other investments, which made James Lenox so rich that he was able to gratify his taste for the curiosities of literature, and get together one of the costliest, one of the most interesting, and one of the least useful libraries in the world.

A rich man, unless he is very dull and very ignorant, must and will have some employment. James Lenox spent the leisure of a long life, and a considerable portion of his immense revenue, in gathering together books which had the charm of rarity. Although he was a graduate of Princeton, he could scarcely be called a learned man nor even a student. What he wished was to make a collection of *book curiosities*. These he stacked away in a vacant room of his great house, until there was just space enough left to shut the door. Then he locked that room and proceeded to fill others, until, toward the close of his life, he began the erection of a building in which to place them for the use and entertainment of the public.

Rarity was what he was after. He once ordered from Germany a tract which was, by a misprint, priced in the catalogue at one hundred and fifteen francs. His honest bookseller, the late Henry Stevens, sent him the tract with the price corrected to fifteen francs. Lenox sent it back to his agent as "not wanted," because he had ordered it under the impression that it was a "rare book." On another occasion, he returned to London a very rare, ancient New England tract, expensively bound, because it had been marked "uncut" in the invoice, but the leaves "had manifestly been cut open and read." His agent had to explain to him that the bookseller's word *uncut* means only that the edges have not been trimmed or reduced to a uniform size. He then accepted the rarity, saying very modestly: "I learn something every day."

Nor was he at first acquainted with the market value of the famous rarities. His first idea in collecting was to get together curious Bibles, and in gratifying this taste he sent an order to his London agent to buy for him a copy of the "Mazarin Bible," a Latin version, in two volumes, of the year 1455, accounted a great prize. As he had fixed no limit, his agent kept on bidding for it till it was knocked down at twenty-five hundred dollars, which the London papers ignorantly pronounced "a mad price." When the book arrived at the New York Custom House, the whole cost, including fees and duty, amounted to three thousand dollars, and the millionaire refused to take it.

After a long correspondence, he discovered that the Bible was in reality worth more than its cost. He paid for it, took it home, and soon learned to regard it as the chief ornament of his collection.

His pride in it was greatly enhanced when he learned, some time after, that a copy not so good as his own had brought nearly nine thousand dollars at a London sale.

After collecting a vast number of rare Bibles, he began to gather works relating to America and the voyages which led to its discovery, including all the editions of books concerning Marco Polo, Mandeville, Columbus, and the others. Then he undertook to collect every edition and translation of The Pilgrim's Progress, by John Bunyan, who was his favorite author. In this he had remarkable success. He also made a wonderful collection of Miltons. Mr. Stevens, his agent, remarks that the Lenox collection of Miltons excels that of the British Museum and the Bodleian Library put together. He bought in one lump, for six hundred pounds, four folio and forty quarto editions of the works of Shakespeare. There were single years of the forty during which he was a collector when his rarities cost him more than fifty thousand dollars.

It sometimes required many years of hunting to find a rarity upon which he had set his heart. Long he desired to possess a perfect copy of the "Bay Psalm-Book," the first book printed in the American Colonies; date, 1640. He told Mr. Stevens that he was willing to go as high as a hundred guineas for it. After a seven years' search, Stevens found an excellent copy at an auction sale. It required great self-command to conceal his exultation; but when bids were called for, he had the nerve to say in a natural, quiet tone, "Sixpence." The book rose by six-penny bids until it was knocked down to this astute Yankee for nineteen shillings. He immediately put it in his pocket and called out "Delivered," which fixed the bargain beyond retreat.

"What rarity have you got now?" inquired the auctioneer.

"Oh, nothing." said Stevens, "but the first English book printed in America."

He found four leaves missing, which, however, he was able to supply from another imperfect copy of the psalm-book. Having thus completed his copy, he had it bound in the best manner, and sold it to Mr. Lenox for four hundred dollars, which proved to be much under its value.

Mr. Lenox, who was a Presbyterian like his father before him, was a most strict observer of the day of rest. Only once in his life was he known to attend to a matter of business on that day.

On a certain Saturday afternoon in Paris, his agent sent him word that he had an opportunity to buy for fifty guineas a copy of what is called the "Wicked Bible," from the circumstance that the word *not* was accidentally omitted from one of the commandments. The temptation was great. Mr. Lenox had either to write a business note on Sunday, or run the risk of missing this ridiculous treasure. He wrote the note, and secured the prize.

The incident shows at once the strength of his passion for collecting and the essential childishness of the pursuit.

James Lenox wore himself out in forming his library. His agent describes his labor as "prodigious," for he allowed no one to assist him. He toiled ten hours a day for years. He could not bear to have any stranger in the house, and hence his labor, to use the language of Mr. Stevens, was "absorbing and immense." At length his memory began to fail, and he was quite unable to use or find the curious treasures that he possessed.

He died in the year 1880, when he was eighty years of age, leaving the whole of his collections, with the edifice that contains them, to the city of New York. He created also an endowment for the care and increase of the library.

The institution might better be called a book museum. The books are almost as little used or seen as when they were locked up in Mr. Lenox's own house. Nevertheless, they *can* be examined upon proper conditions, and to the few who are able to appreciate them they afford extreme pleasure and some solid advantage. The rivalry of wealthy collectors has long ago placed early editions and rare tracts far out of the reach of working authors; but here they are, in the Lenox Library, free to all who live within easy reach of the city of New York.

The agent of Mr. Lenox was a man as remarkable as himself, and seemed made to serve him. He wrote his name thus: "Henry Stevens, G. M. B.," which used to puzzle his English customers very much. He meant by those mysterious letters Green Mountain Boy. Although he passed forty years of his life in London, he remained always an ardent patriot, and kept up a lively correspondence with friends in his native land.

He was truly a Green Mountain *boy*. Beside being a native of Vermont, he retained to old age a certain boyish vivacity and jocularity which are characteristic of the true Yankee. I heard an Englishman say, some time ago, that cricket was a game for men, and base-ball for boys.

"That may be true," said an American present, who knew nothing of cricket; "but every good American, you know, has something of the boy left in him."

It was certainly true of Henry Stevens, who managed to get a great deal of boyish fun out of his business. He loved his work. He had the singular happiness of pursuing all his life a calling which he had chosen in his youth for his recreation in holiday time. He was one of those Horace Greeley boys of Vermont who begin to read by the light of pine knots, and pick up a great deal of miscellaneous education by the time they have done driving cows and doing chores. He learned some Latin in his youth and a little Greek, and so worked his way to Middlebury College at the age of twenty.

That is the way boys in Vermont used to manage half a century ago; and, in truth, many are doing very much the same at the present time, some of whom will doubtless be heard of in the future. After studying at Middlebury a year, and coming near the end of his resources, he was lucky enough to get a well-paid clerkship in the Treasury Department at Washington. He obtained in a single year at Washington money enough to complete his studies at Yale College, and he graduated with credit. He then entered the Harvard Law School, during the presidency of Judge Story, and made some progress toward the bar, which, however, he never reached.

During these years, he was gratifying his taste and paying a part of his expenses by picking up rare and curious books, which he sold to collectors and libraries. He spent all his vacations in this way for five years, sometimes on his own account, but usually as an agent of Colonel Peter Force, who was then compiling his "American Archives." From Maine to Virginia he traveled and trudged, finding his treasures, as he himself related, in disused churns, old cradles, dilapidated hencoops, empty flour barrels, and dusty garrets. In Virginia and the Carolinas I have myself seen heaps of pamphlets and musty books, which had been tossed aside forty, fifty, sixty years before, unvalued and quite forgotten. I remember in the little law-office in North Carolina, where Andrew Jackson studied law soon after the Revolutionary War, seeing a wagon-load of such old-fashioned literature rotting in the damp, from which I was invited by the lady of the house to "help myself," for there was not a soul in the family then living who cared for such things. Henry Stevens swooped down on many such collections, just as Bishop Meade, of Virginia, afterwards did, picking up things for nothing which to-day are worth their weight in gold.

In this way he not only acquired an extensive knowledge of literary rarities, but he became acquainted with a small number of rich collectors. He knew what each of them was looking after, what gaps in his collection he was longing to fill, or what special subjects he was preparing to treat. He also knew what many of them already possessed, and how able or disposed they were to pay a proper price for rarities. Provided with this valuable kind of knowledge, and finding himself possessed of three hundred dollars, being also of the mature age of twenty-six, he flitted across the sea, and began to explore the old book-shops of London for such odd and curious books as he knew how to sell to advantage in America. He was a very good-looking young gentleman, well-formed, somewhat tall, and of a full-orbed countenance, set off by abundant hair.

He reached London with about forty pounds in his pocket, his sole capital for beginning life in the Old World. He found that he had struck a bonanza.

On a single morning in that July of his arrival, he sometimes found in shops and bookstores two hundred rare old books on America at as many shillings a volume as they are now worth pounds sterling. Before he had been in London two weeks, he had bought or discovered more than five thousand dollars' worth of odd old books, which he at once reported to his American customers.

"They were scrambled for," he afterwards wrote, "in Boston and New York, like hot buckwheat cakes at a college breakfast. It was hardly possible to sweep them together fast enough. The books were sorted, invoiced, packed, and shipped at Mr. G. P. Putnam's, and paid for by drafts attached to the bills of lading."

This was an auspicious beginning for a young man upon a capital of two hundred dollars, and thus was founded a business which has flourished for nearly half a century, and which still flourishes under the direction of Mr. Stevens's son. More good fortune followed. Soon after his arrival in London, his friend Putnam mentioned one day that he was executing some orders for a certain Mr. James Lenox, of New York, who had recently begun collecting old Bibles and early voyages. Putnam suggested his offering Mr. Lenox some of the American treasures he was daily discovering.

He did so by sending an invoice of about a thousand dollars' worth of old books to Mr. Lenox "on approval." The return ship brought an order from Mr. Lenox for every book on the list except one. From this time until the end of Mr. Lenox's long life, the Green Mountain Boy acted as his European agent in the formation of his library, greatly to the advantage of both. Lenox had the money, and Stevens had the knowledge; so between them they got together a wonderful collection of odd, ancient, rare, and curious books.

One mishap befell this ardent and fortunate book-hunter. When the war broke out in 1861, he had just concluded some very heavy purchases of valuable books, including one large library of German oddities and rarities, relying upon his American "clients," as he called them, for reimbursement; but the war, for a time, paralyzed the chief collectors. Like other great capitalists, Mr. Lenox was a timid man, and although the war, after the first few months, did not diminish his revenue, he bought very few books. The Green Mountain Boy was unable to meet his engagements, and had to suspend payment for a time. He recovered himself, however, and was afterwards engaged by Mr. Lenox to make a catalogue of his library. This project was abandoned, and he soon resumed his usual employment in London.

Near the close of his life, he wrote for an association of librarians a paper on his recollections of Mr. Lenox, which he afterwards expanded to the proportions of a small volume. This work he did not live to complete. He retained his interest in the employments of his life to his very last day. His son records that the night before his death he talked of work he proposed to complete in the spring, when he hoped to be in better health. He also discussed, and finally approved, a proof-sheet of his little volume upon Mr. Lenox. The next morning he passed away. His small book on James Lenox is a quaint and singularly interesting work, affording us a chance insight into character and transactions not usually opened to the public. Some future Stevens may discover a stray copy of it two centuries hence, and sell it for an enormous sum to some future Lenox.

ALVAN CLARK,

TELESCOPE MAKER.

It is a mystery to the nonscientific mind how a magnifying glass three feet in diameter should cost fifty or sixty thousand dollars. We are all familiar with magnifying glasses, and we see boys playing with them as we pass in the street. A pretty large one, such as old ladies use in reading the Bible, costs but a trifling sum, and it is therefore by no means clear why the object-glass of a telescope, which weighs but a few hundred pounds, should represent and include so many thousand dollars' worth of human labor.

But glass, like many other commodities, varies greatly in quality. We see in the same window a wineglass worth three cents, and another one, not half as large, worth two dollars. There is a similar difference between the steel of a watch-spring and the steel of a rail. If a large rail were made of watchspring steel of the finest kind, it would cost several thousand dollars.

In the whole world, there are but half a dozen firms who will undertake to make the glass for a large telescope. The constructors of the Lick Observatory had to wait several years after ordering the two rough disks of glass required, before they actually arrived in the United States. They were made in Paris, and cost seven thousand dollars each, — the mere glass, cast roughly into the form required. Optical glass, whether made of sand or flint, is a very peculiar product, and it is a matter of the greatest difficulty to make it pure and of uniform quality in every part. We may almost say that the sand or the flint of which it is composed has to be inspected and selected grain by grain, and when at length it is fused in the melting pot, a skillful hand must stir it continuously until the decreasing heat makes it impossible. The least impurity, the slightest error in combining the ingredients, the smallest flaw, is fatal to the composition.

When the glass is moulded into the required shape, a new series of difficulties begin, and they are so great that there are very few persons living at the same time who have the patience and skill to overcome them. The late Alvan Clark, of Massachusetts, was famous throughout the civilized world for his skill in perfecting telescopic glasses. In this work he was unequaled. Several of the largest telescopes now in existence owe their power and excellence chiefly to the skill of this modest son of New England, who had no education in the schools of science, and never saw the object-glass of a telescope till he was past forty years of age. Since his death, which occurred a few years ago, many highly interesting particulars of his life and character have become known.

A Yankee farmer's son, he went to school in the winter, and worked on the farm in the summer, all in the good old-fashioned way which formed so many of the men who created the United States. He worked in the country until he was of age, which was about the time when the factories of Lowell were getting under way, and beginning to attract from country places young men of enterprise. During his boyhood, he had developed a talent for drawing and carving, and had even painted a little. In 1826, being then twenty-two, he obtained employment in one of the Lowell mills as a calico printer, and remained there nine years. During this period of his life, he became a married man, and the father of those worthy sons who afterwards lent him such intelligent and important assistance.

The artist feeling remained strong within him, and in the course of time he attained such skill in the only branch of art then profitable in the United States, the painting of portraits, that he had the courage to abandon the mill and become a miniature painter. His portraits, executed with extreme care and patience, are still to be seen in many old Boston houses, exhibiting the quaint fashions of fifty years ago. They preserve their color and clearness perfectly. In those days, if a lover was going to sea, to St. Louis, or any other distant part of the world, he asked his sweetheart to be so good as to sit for her miniature, which he bore away with him, and was supposed to look at tenderly several times a day. The picture cost him fifty dollars. Alvan Clark had considerable success in this branch in Boston, and was giving his boys a somewhat expensive education. He sent one of them to Andover to study engineering, and there the boy, as boys often do, became intensely interested in the telescope, and in the heavenly bodies which the telescope reveals to us.

It happened one day that Alvan Clark came upon this boy while he was engaged in polishing a metal plate. He asked him what he was doing. The lad replied that he was making a plate for a reflecting telescope. The youth was, in fact, endeavoring to make a telescope of his own, very much as the great Herschel did in the last century, when he found he could not afford to buy one. The young man succeeded in polishing his plate, and the father himself became interested in the subject. He began to study mechanics and astronomy, in order, as he once said, " to instruct my boy;" and from that time father and son experimented and worked together. They produced a reflecting telescope of considerable power, with which they viewed the heavenly bodies with much satisfaction.

Professor Newcomb is mistaken in supposing

that the efforts of the portrait painter and his son met with no encouragement until they had been recognized in a foreign country. Mr. Clark himself said to a reporter, in 1881: —

"One of the Cambridge professors was much pleased with some instruments we made, and when we suggested to him that we would like to manufacture improved instruments, he gave us great encouragement, and we went ahead."

Indeed, the father and his two sons, as early as 1846, gave up all other employments, and entered upon the manufacture of telescopes, obtaining such celebrity that an order reached them from a noted astronomer in England for an object-glass. This was only seven years after the establishment of the business. The instrument sent to England proved brilliantly successful, and from that time Alvan Clark was recognized as the first artist in his line. Orders came from several countries, and when the war interrupted the pursuit of science, they manufactured those admirable field-glasses which were of such use to officers in the open country.

The process of grinding and polishing the large telescopic glasses continues during many months, and frequently changes as the work approaches perfection. The rough grinding and smoothing are done by machinery, two levers working in opposite directions, so arranged that the artist can reach any part of the surface that he desires. This stage of the work, though it requires the hand of a master, is the least difficult, and it is done with considerable rapidity. But when the preliminary grinding is done, the delicate part of the task begins. The human hand is the only instrument fine enough to give the last polish, and one revolution of the hand too much would, in a perceptible degree, impair the correctness of the glass. When he was testing the great object-glass which he and his sons made for Russia, the men working the instrument turned it a little with their hands. The master said, as his sons were about to make another trial: —

"Wait, boys; let her cool."

The reporter who was present asked him what he meant by this. He explained that the poise of the glass, so to speak, was so delicate that the heat from the hands of five men who had held the metal case would lessen its correctness.

Besides his great skill in his vocation, Alvan Clark was a man of peculiar and admirable traits. One of his neighbors mentions his extraordinary aversion to every sort of push and advertising. He never did one thing or said one word by way of getting an order or extending his business. He could not be persuaded to send specimens of his work to the Centennial Exhibition at Philadelphia, and, although his largest transactions were in furnishing object-glasses of immense size, he did not conceal his opinion that the huge telescope is a delusion. When he was interviewed by reporters, and knew that his words would be published, he told them that telescopes of moderate size, not exceeding fifteen inches in diameter, were better for the highest purposes of astronomical observation than the renowned instruments of Herschel, Rosse, and the Lick Observatory. As a matter of fact, the great telescopes are not yet associated with one discovery of the first order.

JEAN BAPTISTE COLBERT,

CABINET MINISTER.

The French habitually call this able minister "The Great Colbert," because there are seventeen other men of the same name and family who are distinguished in the annals of France. The last Exposition at Paris recalled to mind no man more forcibly than this minister, who protected and encouraged the arts which Paris exhibited to the world. He is another illustration of a remark I have often made, that despotic and aristocratic governments are saved from self-destruction by men of lowly birth and great talents who make their way to positions of controlling power. Jean Baptiste Colbert assisted to save France from the ruin with which she was threatened by the folly and ignorance of Louis XIV.

The Colberts were of Scotch origin. In a church at Reims there is an ancient tombstone of Richard Colbert, who died in the year 1300, on which we can still read two doggerel lines, to the effect that "Scotland gave Richard his cradle and Reims his tomb." The great Colbert entered upon life as an apprentice in his uncle's grocery store, in the old French city of Troyes. This uncle married a grocer's daughter, throve in his business, was churchwarden of his parish, became a wholesale dealer in grain, wine, and fabrics, and at length a great merchant, with agents and storehouses at Frankfort, Venice, Florence, Paris, from which the rich products of the Champagne country were distributed over the earth.

Having thus become a person of influence, he placed his nephew as a clerk in a bank at Paris, which was owned by two Italians, who transacted the financial business of the Cardinal Mazarin, prime minister. The young man was thus thrown into frequent communication with the cardinal, who perceived that he was a person of great capacity and instinctive fidelity. The cardinal at length took him into his own household, gave into his hands the management of his private affairs, and accustomed him to public business. A few days before he died, he spoke of Colbert to the king, assuring him that he was a man of an industry which nothing could fatigue, of an honesty proof against all temptation, and of a capacity equal to the transaction of public business.

"Sire," said the dying minister, "I owe everything to you; but I believe that in some sort I discharge my debt to your majesty in giving you Colbert."

The king accepted the gift, but he was determined to have no more prime ministers. As soon as the cardinal was dead, he summoned his council, and told them that henceforth he was going to govern the kingdom himself. Addressing the secretaries of state, he said : —

"I warn you, gentlemen, not to sign anything without my command, to report to me every day personally, and to favor nobody in your monthly pay-rolls."

Then addressing Fouquet, his finance minister, he added : —

"I beg that you will employ the services of M. Colbert, whom the late cardinal recommended to me."

Thus Colbert was introduced to the public service. The first use he made of his influence was to assist in destroying that very Fouquet, who was rolling in wealth wrung from the people of France by the most corrupt and shameful means. The young king meant to have the spending of all the public money himself, and he was easily brought to perceive that he could not do this while he had a minister who spent a king's revenue. Fouquet invited the king to a festival which cost forty thousand crowns. A play by Molière, the greatest comic genius France has produced, was performed for the first time in the theatre of the château. The tables were covered with vessels of gold and silver. As the king moved about with his mother among the splendors of this festival, he whispered in her ear : —

"Ah! madame, shall we not make all these fellows disgorge?"

The king was so incensed that he was strongly inclined to have the minister arrested that very hour. His mother restrained him.

"The poor man," said she, "is ruining himself in entertaining you, and would you have him arrested in his own house?"

It is the king himself who relates this story in his memoirs. He adds: —

"I put off the execution of my design, which caused me incredible pain, for I saw that during that time he was practicing new devices to rob me."

Four months later, however, when all was ripe for so decisive a measure, Fouquet was arrested, deprived of all his offices, and detained in prison the rest of his life. This was chiefly the king's own act, but he did it in such close and obvious concert with Colbert that the minister had the odium of the king's severity, and all the more, as he immediately succeeded to the vacant place. The new minister, incorrupt and efficient, restored some order to the finances: he reduced many grievous public burdens, and at the same time increased the public revenue. He put an end to much jobbery and waste; and above all he introduced and encouraged new manufactures by inviting from foreign countries men well skilled in various trades, and assisting them to set up in business by royal bounties.

He may be said to have created in France the manufacture of several articles, in which France for a century and a half surpassed the rest of the world; namely, fine broadcloth, lace, silk fabrics, glassware, linen, and fine cutlery. The skillful artisans whom he brought from Holland, Italy, and Spain were required by him, in return for the royal bounties, to take a certain number of apprentices, and thus the knowledge of their arts was retained in the country and spread abroad in it. Some recent writers object to the severe rules and regulations which he imposed upon those branches of business. He instituted, for example, a system of inspection which confiscated all goods not of the required quality. A man who offered in the market a piece of cloth, lace, or silk, which was not up to the standard, was liable to have his looms broken, his cloth burnt, and fines imposed. He was obliged, also, to enter into a solemn agreement never to cheat again. If this minister proceeded in the old-fashioned, despotic manner, it was simply because he lived in the seventeenth century, and not in the nineteenth, and lived in a country where nothing was known either of the nature or the power of liberty.

He was not content with merely making his country rich. He desired to render it great also, and illustrious in the eyes of other nations. To this end, continuing the policy of Richelieu, he established a national observatory, enlarged the botanic gardens of Paris, reorganized the Academy of Painting, the School of Architecture, and the French art-school at Rome. He greatly increased the royal library, and caused several men of learning from Italy and Holland to settle in France. I have before me a list of thirty-two men of learning and literature to whom he induced the king to give small pensions for their lives, enough in those simple times to enable them to devote their whole time to their several subjects and arts, and to free their minds from anxiety concerning the future. Corneille, for example, had two thousand francs ($400) a year; Molière, one thousand; Racine, eight hundred. Some of these pensions, it is true, fell to the wrong men, who were long ago forgotten. Upon the whole, however, they were given with pretty good judgment.

If this man had only had a king worthy of him, France would have been saved from unnumbered woes, both then and since. But the money poured into the treasury by Colbert's prudent and patriotic administration was wasted by the king in needless wars, and in an extravagant self-indulgence almost unparalleled. He wasted two hundred millions upon Versailles alone; and, more than once, he came within an ace of losing his kingdom. Colbert opposed these wretched doings to the utmost of his power. Especially, he warned the king against a public debt; and when Louis had found a more complaisant adviser, Colbert said to that adviser, when they were alone: —

"You triumph! But do you believe that you have done an action worthy of a virtuous citizen? Do you suppose I did not know as well as you that we could get plenty of money by borrowing? But do you know, as I know, the man with whom we have to deal, his passion for display, for great enterprises, for all kinds of expense? The system of borrowing has begun, and you will see in consequence expenditures and taxes unlimited. You will answer for it to the nation and to posterity."

The last years of Colbert were a sad and ineffectual struggle to keep France solvent. The king was extremely displeased with his pertinacious opposition. We have a very ill-spelled but cutting letter which the king wrote to him after a cabinet counsel, in which Colbert had remonstrated more boldly than usual. Only the beginning and the ending of this royal epistle can be given here:—

"I was sufficiently master of myself, the day before yesterday, to conceal the pain I felt at hearing a man whom I have loaded with benefits speak to me in the manner in which you did. . . . Profit by my self-control; do not again risk offending me; for when I have heard your remarks and those of your colleagues, and when I have pronounced upon the matter in hand, I do not wish ever to hear another word said upon it. . . . Speak freely; but when I have decided, I wish not a single reply."

The minister never worked cheerfully at his vocation again. A violent fever, caught while accompanying the king to Holland, weakened his constitution, and terminated his life before the disasters came upon France which marked the latter half of Louis XIV.'s reign. During his last sickness, the king sent him a letter of sympathy by one of his gentlemen, but it gave no consolation to the dying patriot.

"If," said Colbert, "I had done for God what I have done for *that man*, I should be saved twice over; as it is, I know not what will become of me."

When the king's gentleman came to his bedside, he pretended to be asleep, and after he was gone, he still refused to read the letter, saying: —

"I do not wish to hear the king spoken of any more. Let him now, at least, leave me in peace."

Colbert lived sixty-four years, dying in 1683, having spent about twenty years of his life in mitigating the horrors of personal government. An uneducated man, he did more for learning, art, and literature than any minister of his time, and himself learned Latin, after he was fifty, while taking his daily rides in a carriage. His tutor rode with him, and made him keep his distance, too. "M. Colbert tried to be familiar with me," this tutor used to say; "but I kept him off by my respect."

ERCKMANN AND CHATRIAN,

LAWYER AND RAILWAY CASHIER.

A LITTLE volume lies before me, a French novel, called "Madame Thérèse." I open it at a place where a battle is described between the French and their allied enemies of 1794. A village of Alsace has been sacked, and the dead are lying in rows, white and rigid, with their eyes staring into the sky. An old man of the village stands in the midst of the desolation, transfixed with sorrow and amazement. A boy is with him, his nephew, Fritzel, to whom he speaks with sudden vehemence: —

"Behold what war is, Fritzel; look, and remember! Yes, this is war: death and destruction, fury and hatred, disregard of all human feelings. Yesterday we were at peace; we asked nothing of anybody; we had done no harm; and, suddenly, strange men came to strike, to ruin and destroy us. Fritzel, remember this: war is all that is most abominable on earth. Men who do not know, who have never seen each other, rush suddenly together to tear each other to pieces."

These words we may take as the moral of this book, as well as of a long series of other books by the same authors. They exhibit to us the wars of Napoleon, not as they appear in his false bulletins; not as they glitter in the pages of Thiers; but as they were seen by the conscript torn from his relations and his sweetheart; by the prisoner; by the wounded soldier left to die in a ditch; by aged parents robbed of the staff of their declining years. The scenes of war are presented in them with simple fidelity and truth. It is enough. To hold war in the deepest abhorrence, it is only necessary to see it as it is.

The authors of these books are two Frenchmen, natives of Alsace, named Emile Erckmann and Pierre Chatrian, or, as they are printed in their title-pages, Erckmann-Chatrian. Since Beaumont and Fletcher, the alliance of these two men is the most famous of literary partnerships, and it is a far worthier one than that of the English dramatists, whose plays the world could well spare. The novels of these men promote the great end of all worthy exertion, which is that of making the human lot less hard.

Erckmann, born in 1822, the son of a country bookseller, was a law student who did not relish his law books. Chatrian, the son of a glass-maker, educated at a local college, learned his father's business, and practiced it for some time in Belgium. He too preferred intellectual pursuits, and took the place of assistant teacher in a school of his native town. It was there that Erckmann and Chatrian met and formed a friendship which issued in their collaboration.

They began, when Erckmann was twenty-six and Chatrian twenty-two, to write patriotic plays, one of which was actually performed. It was entitled "Alsace in 1814," and the local journal informed the public that it was "written by two young people of the province."

This play the French describe as being "full of gunpowder and action." Probably we should use the words "blood and thunder." It was of such an inflammatory nature that, after the second performance, the mayor ordered it to be withdrawn. They wrote another military play, which was never produced, and then one in the style of Schiller's "Robbers," which also never saw the footlights. Erckmann at this time wrote a pamphlet against the military conscription, and Chatrian sent articles to a newspaper which was sufficiently described by its name, "The Democrat of the Rhine." Already they had begun to sign their productions with their joint names, though as yet the conjunction brought little fame and no profit.

It seems, however, that their local writings had success enough to encourage them, in 1848, to seek their fortune in Paris. Upon reaching the metropolis, they took a very sensible course: Erckmann continued his study of the law, and Chatrian obtained a small clerkship in the office of a railroad company, in which he has remained ever since. He has labored for thirty-five years in the same office, promoted from time to time, until now he is the cashier of the company. Erckmann, I believe, turned his legal knowledge to account in some way, although he does not appear to have regularly practiced the profession.

Ten years passed, during which they gained their subsistence by honest labor, and spent their leisure hours in cultivating their talents. They wrote short pieces occasionally, in which the Alsatian legends were expanded into strange, fantastic tales, and now and then one of these was published in a periodical, without attracting any particular notice. At length, in 1858, they published a volume called "The Illustrious Doctor Mathéus," a story in which the homely life of an Alsatian village was relieved by a mixture of the marvelous and the fantastic, as in the "Rip Van Winkle" of Washington Irving. This work gave them a standing in the world of letters. They followed up their success with half a dozen similar tales, which increased their reputation.

Then they struck their true vein. "Yégof the Fool," a story of the invasion of France after the retreat of Bonaparte from Moscow, when the peasants of Lorraine fled to the mountains and fiercely defended the passes against the invader, attained a sudden and intense celebrity, and this led to the production of "Madame Thérèse," which gave them permanent classic rank in the literature of France. Of the female characters in fiction produced in our day in France, Madame Thérèse is the one most to American taste. The child of a peasant, unlettered, but admirably educated, endowed with the qualities which give charm, dignity, and worth to the home, she is the woman that is indispensable to human happiness.

Since this incomparable work, the two authors have made many successes as novelists and as dramatists, always faithful to their chief message. They have waged war against war, given no quarter, and granted no truce.

Some years ago, Sainte-Beuve, the chief critic of Paris, met the collaborators in the office of the paper to which he contributed his celebrated Monday articles, and said to them:—

"I have read your books. I wished to devote to you one of my Mondays. I shall not do it; I find that your romances are the Iliad of fear."

Chatrian smiled. He replied to the critic thus:

"Monsieur, my colleague and myself spring from families who have been under fire in foreign wars, and given their blood for France. Our fathers fought for their country; and if we celebrate peace, it is not from cowardice, it is from horror of those butcheries. It is because our fathers saw in our own Alsace invasion and war. I do not wish that our predictions may come true, and the foreigner once more stand upon our soil; but if that day comes, look for Erckmann and Chatrian; you will not find them among the tremblers."

I must try and find room for one more anecdote tending to show how faithful they have been to their art and to the multitude of readers whom their genius has attracted. It is a story we may all consider with advantage, whether we labor with the pen or the pickaxe.

Some years ago, the two partners had finished a romance for an important paper, after having worked upon it for six months. It would have brought them many thousand francs. Before delivering it to the "Journal des Débats," they met to give it the last deliberate reading. As the chapters passed in review before them, neither of them felt satisfied, and when at length the last leaf had been read, there was a melancholy silence, which was broken by the impetuous Chatrian.

"Shall I tell you what I think? Very well, then, it is a failure. We have labored much upon it, I grant you; but we have deceived ourselves. Come, now, this story represents a pretty large sum of money; but suppose we had it in our hands: we should not be so very much richer than we are, and we should have to carry ever after the dead weight of an inferior book. I know well what these pages have cost us to cover them with ink; but after all, men do not always execute what they conceive. And as at this time we are both in a bad vein, you take the train to-morrow and go to your mountains and rest; take the air and put yourself in vigor again. As for me, I will remain here; and before you go we will burn this manuscript to the last leaf, so that we may not be tempted to make use of a tale which does not satisfy us."

"You are right," said Erckmann, "we will burn it."

Next day, silently in the chimney corner, the two friends threw into the fire, leaf after leaf, the book which for half a year had been the object of their labor, their thoughts, and their hopes. When the last spark was extinguished, the friends embraced and parted.

SIR FRANCIS CROSSLEY,

CARPET MANUFACTURER.

ONE of the greatest pleasures mortals know is a well-planned and well-executed journey. What a delight in the anticipation, in the start, in the progress, in the hardships, in the arrival near the presence of some magnificent natural object! and what an endless pleasure in recalling and relating the manifold incidents! And all this may be much more than pleasure: it is often a lasting increase of mental and moral power.

Wonderful good has come to our race through journeys. If we trace the movements that have benefited humankind most, we often find that they began in a journey, or a series of journeys. The most impressive instance of this is the journey of Marco Polo into Asia, in the thirteenth century, which led directly to Vasco da Gama, to Columbus, to the discovery and exploration of a new continent and all the islands of the sea. To an intelligent mind, long immersed in the routine of business, traveling is a stimulus and a restoration, like nothing else.

Even one of our dainty little trips through the prettiest parts of Great Britain is not to be despised, if the traveler has no stomach for the continental vastness and variety of his own country.

A very curious and interesting story was related some time ago by a well-known business man, which shows the inspiration that a journey may be to a man long accustomed to the monotonous cares of an extensive business.

He was a wealthy English carpet manufacturer and Member of Parliament, named Francis Crossley. Being at Quebec, in 1855, on a holiday tour with his family, he paid a visit to our White Mountain region, about a day's journey from the quaint old Canadian city. Although he was then but thirty-eight years of age, he had been so early inured to industry that his business life was almost as long as his natural one. As a boy, he had earned his pocket-money at a loom expressly set up for him in his father's shop, and he had kept close to his work ever since. It was his firm of John Crossley & Sons that took the lead in making carpets by steam power, which, during the last thirty years, has covered with carpet half the floors of Europe and America. Their business had grown so rapidly that the vital energies of the father and three sons had been exerted to the uttermost, merely to keep up with their ever-widening opportunity.

But there was Francis Crossley, one of the "Sons," enjoying, at last, one of those inspiring journeys spoken of above. During the afternoon of September 10, 1855, he found himself winding through the White Mountains, viewing a series of the most entrancing scenes which our new railroad system had then rendered accessible to the traveler. The atmospheric conditions, which are all-important in a mountain region, were highly favorable, bringing out the tumultuous sea of mountains in the most bewitching light.

On reaching Gorham, the party repaired to the hotel. The ladies obeyed the summons to the tea-table, but Francis Crossley, still under the spell of what he had seen from the train, preferred to take a walk, and view, more at ease and in greater quiet, the range of mountains spread out before him. It was one of the September sunsets so well known to the frequenters of the region. The sun was just hiding behind Mount Washington, and there was presented to the young Briton, accustomed to the more sombre hues of his native landscape, all that pomp of illuminated clouds and those indescribable splendors of color with which early autumn floods the deep valleys and acclivities of our mountain ranges. Here and there, too, the foliage was touched with the gorgeous hues of September. No one who has not seen the mountains just at that season, when the glories of summer and of autumn are both at their best, can form any adequate idea of their impressive and captivating beauty.

The young man was deeply moved. His mind was wrought up into a religious exaltation. He was lifted out of himself, and above himself. As he stood looking out upon the scene before him, his thoughts wandered back across the sea to the English town of Halifax, where his manufactory was situated, and he thought of the many thousands of laborious men, women, and children going through their long day of toil. At that period, all branches of carpet making were more trying to human muscle and patience than they now are. The cruel old day's work, from half past 5 A. M. till 8 P. M., had been shortened; but it was still much too long, and the men had not yet become reconciled to the new power-loom, which had displaced many who were too old to learn new ways. Visitors to Halifax had remarked a tone of defiance in the voices of the men, and an expression of discontent, and even fierceness, in their countenances. There was as yet little sympathy between employers and employed, but, on the contrary, much latent and much avowed hostility.

And so, on this beautiful September evening, in far-off New Hampshire, the young employer of labor thought of the people who were toiling for him at home. He said to himself: "What can I do for *them?* I cannot bring those thousands of laborious people to see this beautiful range of mountains; but perhaps I can create something beautiful for them to see and enjoy near their home. It may be possible to take a piece of rough ground in Halifax and convert it into a public garden, so near the workingman's home that he can stroll into it when his labor for the day is done, and get home again without a fatiguing walk." To use his own language: —

"That seemed to be a glorious thought. My prayer that night was that, in the morning, I might be satisfied when I awoke that, if it was only a mere thought fluttering across my brain, it might be gone; but that if there was a reality about it, there might be no doubt, and I might carry it into execution. I slept soundly that night, and when I awoke, my impression was confirmed. On the 10th of September, when I went to the White Mountains, I had no more idea of making a park than any one here had of building a city; and never from that day to this have I hesitated for a moment."

On reaching his Yorkshire home again, he did not allow this project to grow cold, but proceeded at once to buy the ground and prepare to lay it out. Besides creating a garden, he endowed it with a fund large enough for its maintenance and improvement, spending in all about a quarter of a million dollars. When presenting the garden to the city, he mentioned this incident of his conceiving the plan while gazing in rapture on the White Mountains, but in the same speech he attributed his original latent inclination toward such schemes to the character of his mother, who, in the early years of her married life, had labored in a carpet mill, working from four o'clock in the morning until eight in the evening. One morning, he said, as she was going to her work in a new place, in conjunction with her husband, she made a vow, and put it in these words : —

"If the Lord does bless us at this place, the poor shall taste of it."

The vow was faithfully kept. She was always looking out to ameliorate the lot of the people. One winter, when times were very hard and mills were closing all around them, she gave this advice to the firm : —

"Do not sell your goods for less than they cost, for it will ruin you without permanently benefiting any one; but if you can go on giving employment during the winter, do so, for it is a bad thing for a workingman to go home and hear his children cry for bread when he has none to give them."

This was a homely way of stating the case, but it answered the purpose, and was all the better for its simplicity. The old lady lived to see her sons employing five thousand persons in making carpets, and all working a reasonable number of hours. One of her great pleasures in her old age was to fix a looking-glass in her room in such a way that, while lying in bed, she could see the cheerful faces of the people going and coming to their work. It was a pleasure to her, perhaps, even to see the late-comers pay a fine of one penny, because all the fines were given to the fund for the benefit of the sick and aged.

So we see that Sir Francis Crossley, as he was afterward called, inherited the propensity to benevolent action from his mother, but this propensity might have remained latent but for the ecstasy and inspiration derived from the view of the White Mountains on that September evening.

ELIZABETH FRY,

WIFE AND MOTHER.

In the ancient part of the city of London, no building more strongly attracted the attention of the stranger than Newgate Prison. I never saw an edifice so black, gloomy, and repulsive. No one needed to inquire what was its purpose, for every stone and grated window bore the unmistakable stamp of JAIL. It was from the front of this prison that prisoners, until recently, were executed at eight o'clock on the Monday morning after their trial; when thousands upon thousands of the reprobates of London gathered in the wide, open space below, to witness the horrible scene.

In former times, this famous jail was, if possible, more hideous within than without. There was one part of it, comprising four small rooms and a yard of no great size, which was called the "Untried Female Ward," in which three or four hundred women were usually confined while they were awaiting trial, — old women and young women, hardened criminals and the unjustly accused, — many having broods of children with them. The government provided them with nothing except food. Half clad in filthy rags, without bed or bedding, they slept upon the floor of the rooms — in which they lived, cooked, and washed. Some of the children were almost naked, and most of them were pining and miserable from want of such food and exercise as children require.

Many of these women seemed complete savages. If they got a little money, they could buy gin and beer from the prison tap-room; and whenever it happened that a new prisoner came in with a few shillings, the inmates gave her no peace until she had "stood treat;" and there would be a scene of riotous debauch for some hours. There was no one to keep them in order except a man and a boy, though sentries walked along the roof far above their reach. The governor himself never entered this part of the prison unless his duty compelled him. When visitors came near the grating, the women gathered near in a tumultuous, infuriate crowd, begging for money, which, if they obtained it, was immediately squandered in gambling or drink. One visitor says that when double gratings were afterward so arranged that the women could not get near visitors, they fastened their wooden spoons to long sticks, and thrusting them forward, redoubled their outcries for money.

"Thus they remained," this visitor remarks, " in an unchecked condition of idleness, riot, and vice of every description. The women were of the lowest sort, — the very scum both of the town and country, — filthy in their persons, disgusting in their habits, and ignorant, not only of religious truth, but of the most familiar duties of common life."

Another lady, who visited this ward about the year 1813, afterward described the scene thus : —

"The railing was crowded with half-naked women, struggling together for the front situations with the most boisterous violence, and begging with the utmost vociferation. I felt as if I were going into a den of wild beasts."

Another lady describes the women as "squalid in attire and ferocious in countenance, seated about the yard. One of them," she adds, "rushed round the area yelling like a wild beast," and "tearing everything of the nature of a cap from the heads of the other women."

It is difficult for us, with the humaner feelings of these days, to believe that such scenes could have been exhibited in a Christian city so recently as the year 1813, thirty years after Howard had published the results of his tours among the prisons of Europe. But so it was. Some prisons had indeed been purified and reformed, and several penitentiaries had been built, containing many of the improvements which Howard had recommended. As late, however, as the year just named, and for some years later, the female inmates of Newgate Prison were in the condition which I have described.

In January, 1813, four benevolent Quakers visited the prison, for the purpose of solacing the last hours of some convicts who had been ordered for execution. It was not uncommon in those days for as many as five, six, and even twelve persons to be executed on the same Monday morning; nor was the execution of women unfrequent. These four gentlemen, having accomplished their benevolent errand, passed within sight of this deplorable women's ward. It was a cold, bitter day in January. The three hundred female prisoners and their forty or fifty little children were crouched and huddled together, presenting a scene of suffering and horror which excited in these excellent men the profoundest emotion.

A day or two after, one of them, in the course of a conversation with a lady of their congregation, Mrs. Elizabeth Fry, described what they had seen. Mrs. Fry was the daughter of one of those wealthy Quaker families whose great estates are transmitted from father to son as regularly as those of the nobility. She had married into another great Quaker house, and was well known throughout the denomination for her systematic and conscientious philanthropy. She was a great entertainer of Quaker preachers and emissaries, a liberal subscriber to charities, and had been admitted in the Quaker meeting to the office of preacher. She was not one of those philanthropists who content themselves with subscribing money for benevolent purposes. She had been accustomed, all her life, to visit the abodes of wretchedness, and she had personally assisted in the educational movement begun by Lancaster.

Amazed and appalled at what she heard, she determined to go herself to the scene of so much depravity and woe. Accompanied by one lady, she visited the prison, and applied to the governor for permission to enter this ward. He did not refuse them, but he advised them, before entering, to leave their watches at his house, for fear some of the women should snatch them from their sides. The two ladies preferred, however, to retain their watches. They went in, and the gates were closed behind them.

Mrs. Fry was then thirty-three years of age, a tall, elegant, and stately woman, in the full lustre and freshness of matronhood. Her presence was dignity itself. Nor did she appear among those poor creatures as a fine lady, covered with the fashionable decorations of the time. The sober garb of the Quakeress, in such a scene as that, had something of the effect which the dress of a Sister of Charity has when she moves among the abandoned and the suffering, protected only by her garb and the sanctity of her mission. These two Quaker ladies were regarded by the inmates with curiosity and respect. They gathered about them. Mrs. Fry addressed a few words to them, which, unfortunately, have not been preserved, and her companion also followed her with some kindly remarks. The tradition is, that Mrs. Fry invited them to join with her in prayer, and that such was the majesty and power of her presence, and so irresistible the music of her voice, that the greater portion of them knelt down upon the pavement, and remained in the attitude of prayer, while Mrs. Fry poured forth one of those tender and eloquent supplications for which she was so famous. The ladies then withdrew.

Mrs. Fry was not one who would think it sufficient to meet such a case as this with exhortations and prayers alone. A few hours after, all her household that could ply a needle were busy making warm woolen garments for these poor women, and they were kept busy at this work until, with the assistance of other Quaker households, the most pressing wants of the women and children were supplied. Other visits followed similar to the first, and various plans were set on foot for the mitigation of the physical sufferings of the female prisoners.

But this did not satisfy her. At a later period, she requested one day to be left alone in the female ward, for she was determined to lay before the prisoners themselves a plan she had formed for the benefit of their children. When the women, as usual, had gathered about her, she read, in her silvery tones, the parable of the Lord of the Vineyard, in which those who had begun to work late in the day received the same reward as those who had toiled from the morning. This parable she applied to their case, and she proceeded to discourse at length upon the blessed truth, that no matter how guilty a person may have been in his life, IT IS NEVER TOO LATE TO MEND. When she had secured the attention and good will of the women by her address, she pointed to their suffering children, and enlarged upon the grievous consequences resulting to them from passing so many idle days, hearing the words they heard, and witnessing the scenes exhibited in the prison, and she proposed, if the mothers were willing, to establish a school for the children. Tears of grateful joy glistened in many a mother's eyes at this proposal, to which they all assented by acclamation. She cautioned them, however, to think over the plan; for, as she had no authority over any of them, the school could not flourish without their coöperation. She told them that if, upon reflection, they still approved the plan, she wished them to select a governess from their own number. On her next visit, they had elected a schoolmistress, — a competent and well-disposed young woman recently committed for stealing a watch.

The sheriffs, the chaplain, and the governor, though they regarded the scheme as hopeless, gave their approval, and assigned a cell for the school. It was at once filled to overflowing with little children, girls, and young women. The success of the school surprised every one. It not only kept the children out of mischief and instructed them, but it humanized the mothers, and exerted a powerful civilizing influence upon the whole ward. "Already," as Mrs. Fry wrote in her diary, at the end of three months, "from being like wild beasts, they appear harmless and kind." The inmates of the other female ward of the prison begged that they too might have a school, and their request was granted, with results equally striking.

In order to continue and systematize these labors, a society was formed for the express purpose. The city authorities coöperated. The worst evils of the jail system were suppressed. The reform spread to other jails, and Mrs. Fry's efforts led finally to a total revolution in the prison and criminal systems of Great Britain. The change in Newgate was such that it became a topic of conversation throughout the kingdom, and the benefit of her labors was spread all over Europe. A matron was at length appointed, and what we may call Mrs. Fry's system was accepted by the government and legalized. She afterward traveled extensively on the continent of Europe, calling the attention of kings and magistrates to the condition of female prisoners and their children. It was directly through her labors that the criminal code was revised, and that the wholesale executions of malefactors ceased.

It was a practice then, when convicts were going

to Botany Bay, for the women to have a riotous debauch before leaving Newgate, during which they would break the windows and the furniture; and when they were going through the city to the ship, in open wagons, they would shout and sing and bandy indecent jokes with the hooting crowd. The convict ship, of course, was a scene of misery and depravity. All this was changed through the labors and influence of Mrs. Fry. She prevailed upon the governor of the prison to have them conveyed to the ship in hackney coaches, and induced them to behave in an orderly manner. She provided needlework for the women during the long voyage; she established a school in each ship; and set all her children, and many of her friends' children, to dressing dolls for the amusement of the little girls on the voyage. Thus the six months' passage to the other side of the globe was made a blessing to young and old.

This admirable woman wore herself out in such labors as these. She died in 1845, aged sixty-five years, and went to the grave followed by the benedictions of Christendom.

THE EARL OF SHAFTESBURY,

PUBLIC SERVANT.

I USED to see this famous man occasionally when he was in the prime of his prime, a member of the House of Commons, and known as Lord Ashley. If any friend of aristocratic institutions had desired to present a favorable specimen of the kind of man an aristocracy can produce, he could scarcely have found a more striking example of manly grace and beauty than this heir of the ancient earldom of Shaftesbury. He was a superb young man, a perfect type of the beauty which we call " manly: " tall, nobly formed, of winning countenance, bland and dignified in demeanor, and without the least appearance of haughtiness. Almost all clothes look well on a well-formed person; but he was well dressed, and with perfect simplicity.

I have seen him stroll into the House of Commons within a few feet of broad and burly Daniel O'Connell, with his ruddy countenance glowing with Irish health and Irish good humor; one the ideal nobleman, the other the ideal Irishman and man of business. It was not alone upon me, a youth and a stranger, that young Lord Ashley made this impression. One of his fellow-students at Oxford, afterwards Bishop Short, of Adelaide, said of him, sixty years after, at a great meeting in London: —

"I well remember watching Lord Ashley day after day, walking up the great hall of Christ Church College on his way to lecture, assiduous in his duties, diligent in his studies, and thinking, 'If that is a specimen of the English aristocracy, we have in the House of Lords an institution which has no rival throughout the world.'"

If is an important word here. How many fine and comforting things would be true, if we could only get out of the way a few of those troublesome little *ifs!* The late Earl of Shaftesbury was very far indeed from being a representative of his order. He was an exceptional man in most particulars. His great distinction was that, being himself rich and distinguished, he devoted his life, his powers, and his prestige to ameliorating the condition, not of the poor merely, but of the *most* poor, the *most* forlorn, and the *most* repulsive, of all his countrymen. This exceptional trait of character he did not derive from his aristocratic ancestors, nor from the University of Oxford, nor from his association with the most favored class of his fellow-citizens. He has himself told us who and what it was that caused him to take so deep an interest in the poor, the miserable, and the degraded.

It was the influence of a noble-minded maidservant that first lifted him above his order. Her name was Maria Millas. She was a lady's maid at Blenheim, before his mother's marriage; his mother being a daughter of the Duke of Marlborough. After the marriage, Maria Millas became housekeeper to his father and mother. Very soon after the birth of the late earl, the care of him devolved almost entirely upon the housekeeper, which is not unfrequently the case in great houses, where the mother has multitudinous occupations of business and pleasure.

Now this Maria Millas was one of those women who are not only good themselves, but have an extraordinary power of infusing goodness into others. Many of my readers, doubtless, have had the good fortune of knowing such a woman, and to them it is not necessary to explain how this housekeeper could inform, exalt, and ennoble the mind of a susceptible boy. To those who have never been so happy as to be acquainted with such a person, no explanation could really explain the mystery. Maria Millas died when the little lord was seven years old.

"But," he once wrote, "the recollection of what she said and did and taught, even to a prayer that I now constantly use, is as vivid as in the days that I heard her. The impression was, and is still, very deep that she made upon me, and I must trace much, perhaps all, of the duties of my later life to her precepts. I know not where she was buried. She died, I know, in London, and I may safely say that I have ever cherished her memory with the deepest gratitude and affection."

Such a fact as this is of peculiar interest. It explains to us how a man could be so nobly developed on the moral side, and yet remain to the end of a long life somewhat narrow and intolerant on the intellectual side. He could not endure the smallest departure from the theological beliefs in which he had been trained, and he used to regard some famous books, generally deemed sufficiently orthodox, with a disapprobation approaching horror. But every human being has his foible, and we may well forgive this one to a man who was chiefly instrumental in reducing the hours of factory labor from fourteen hours a day to ten, and rescuing millions of little children from the most cruel and merciless treatment to which children have ever been subjected in any age or land.

When Lord Ashley was urging his bills for the relief of factory children, he was not content to sit in his library and read about them in the newspapers. He went down to factory towns, such as Leeds, Manchester, and Bradford, got up at four o'clock in the morning, took his stand at the factory gates, and saw the miserable line of hurrying operatives, men, women, and children, go in to their long day's work. He would stand at the same gates to see them come out, noting especially the crowd of little children.

"A set of sad, dejected, cadaverous creatures they were," he once said in Parliament.

It seemed doubtful to him sometimes whether any of the little wretches had strength enough left to get home.

"In Bradford," he said in the same speech, "proofs of long and cruel toil are most remarkable. The crippled and distorted forms might be numbered by hundreds, perhaps by thousands. A friend of mine collected a vast number together for me; the sight was most piteous, the deformities incredible. They seemed to me, such were their crooked shapes, like a mass of crooked alphabets."

It is almost beyond belief what men, calling themselves Christians, and called by their neighbors respectable persons, could inflict upon little children. Lord Ashley told the House of Commons in 1842 that, in several of the English counties, it was common for children to be sent to the factory, for a full day's work of fourteen hours, when they were but seven years of age. In other counties, he said, "some begin as early as six years of age; many begin at five." In Yorkshire, it was not uncommon for infants even of five years old to be sent into the coal pits.

"Near Oldham," continued Lord Ashley, "children are worked as low as four years old; and in the small collieries, some are so young that they are brought to work in their bed-gowns."

Many of these children, besides working fourteen

and sixteen hours a day, had to labor in an atmosphere heated above a hundred degrees, and frequently poisoned with the fumes of drugs. The tobacco manufacturers employed numbers of little children seven years of age, and the bleachers kept their boys at work in rooms charged with the fumes of sulphur. Strangest of all, the parents, the *mothers*, of these little children were eager to send them to the factories and the mines; such was the ignorance that prevailed, such the pressure of poverty, such the force of appetite.

Whenever man does his worst to his fellow, we can generally say of him, with much truth, *He knows not what he does.* The factory system, driven by steam, had come upon the world so suddenly that the evils of it grew faster than men's consciousness of them; and men of business, at all times, are too deeply absorbed in their difficult affairs to attend properly to the needs and rights of their workmen. Hence, workmen must learn to protect themselves, chiefly through the instrumentality of just and enlightened laws.

It cost Lord Ashley and his friends many years of close attention and well-directed labor to get the worst of these evils remedied. They did finally secure the ten-hour law, and kept little children out of the mills and the mines.

It was he who also founded the Ragged School system, which was of great use in its day, though now superseded by better methods. It was he, too, who reformed the numerous class of street peddlers of vegetables, called in England costermongers. They presented the earl with the finest donkey they could buy in London, named Coster, an animal which was for some years to be seen in Lord Shaftesbury's park. In his house also may be found a marble bust of himself, bearing the following inscription: —

"Presented to Emily, wife of the seventh Earl of Shaftesbury, by the operatives of the manufacturing districts of the north of England, as a token of their esteem and regard for the persevering and successful efforts of her noble husband in promoting by legislative enactment a limitation of the hours of labor, of children, females, and young persons employed in mills and factories."

When this bust was presented on a festive day in 1859, seven thousand persons insisted on kissing the hands of the person whom the bust represented. He died a few years ago, aged eighty-four years. His family was of the good old number of ten, — six sons and four daughters, — most of whom are still living, and parents of numerous broods. If I were one of them, I would find out where Maria Millas was buried, and mark the spot in some suitable and permanent way.

MRS. COSTON,

SHIPS' SIGNAL MANUFACTURER.

———•———

About forty years ago, in the city of Philadelphia, a young widow of great beauty and force of character found herself face to face with a terrible problem. Though but twenty-one years of age, she was the mother of three children. Her husband, an officer of the United States Navy, had died recently, and other misfortunes befell, which had reduced her to poverty; and there she was in a home no longer her own, penniless, with three children dependent upon her.

How many women wake from the stupor of sudden bereavement to find themselves in a similar condition! Her husband, a young man of genius and knowledge, had been a successful inventor, much to the advantage of our navy in many ways; but he died too soon to reap much reward from his labors outside of the department, and dying in the very dawn of a most promising career, left his children without provision. His name, a very proper one for a Philadelphian, was Benjamin Franklin Coston.

A thought came to the widow. She remembered that her husband, during his last days, had mentioned a certain box of papers as being of considerable value, and it occurred to her, with a force she could not account for, that in that box she should find hope and help. The lady has since written of these events in a volume published recently called " A Signal Success." She says that it was on a dreary afternoon in November, when her spirits were at the lowest ebb, and the rain was falling heavily against the window panes, that the idea came to her of opening this box. She found it, unlocked it, raised the lid. It proved to contain many packets, sealed and labeled, containing the record or plans of inventions unfinished, and experiments in chemistry designed to be further elaborated.

At last she came upon an envelope full of papers relating to a system of signals, to be used in the night at sea, for the purpose of communicating messages from ship to ship, and from ship to shore. She remembered that her husband had been strongly impressed with the great need there was of better night signals, and that he had made some experiments toward their invention at Hampton Roads in the year 1840. She remembered, too, that he had been greatly encouraged by Commodore Stewart and other naval officers, who had experienced, both in war and peace, the need of such signals. In the envelope there was a chart of all the signals proposed to be used, neatly colored, with ample explanations of the manner of use.

Readers of Fenimore Cooper's novels cannot have forgotten the stirring scene in the "Two Admirals," in which the day signals play such an interesting part. Two flags appear upon a distant ship, — a red one above, and a green one under it. The admiral looks into his "signal-book," and discovers that this means, Look at message No. 14, which the same book interprets into the intelligence that there are vessels in sight from a distant masthead. Another arrangement of flags, which appears soon after, directs him to No. 382, meaning, "Strange sails, — enemies."

We learn from the animated chapter in Cooper that every vessel in the navy had a signal-book, which contained all the messages which would ordinarily be necessary between vessels, and that these were numbered from one to thirteen hundred. By a certain arrangement of flags, the number of a message was signaled, and the other captain, on receiving it, had only to refer to his signal-book to see what the message was. No. 10 might mean, "We are short of water;" No. 91, "Can you spare us a foresail?" No. 13, "What longitude do you make?" There was also a system by which the letters of the alphabet were designated, and thus any message could be slowly spelled out.

The invention of Coston, which his widow held in her hands, made it possible to use this system of signals by night. Instead of colored flags shown in a certain order, his idea was to show colored lights of great brilliancy, such as he had used in compounding rockets and other naval fireworks. As a chemist, he had experimented frequently in the production of brilliant illuminated colors, and he indicated in his plan what means he proposed to use to produce colors of the requisite force.

As she sat examining the contents of the package, she remembered more about this invention. A naval officer had visited her husband as he lay upon his death-bed, to whom the dying man had given some of the completed signals for the purpose of having them tried. This officer had promised that if they proved successful he would interest himself in making the invention a benefit to the wife and children Coston should leave behind him. She made up her mind at once to attempt to develop and complete this invention, — she, who had hitherto done little but accept the good things of life without effort as they were showered abundantly upon her.

She closed the box and sat down at her writing-desk. She wrote to the naval officer, asking what had become of the signals. After some time, the box of specimens arrived, but without the recipes for the manufacture of the colors. Anxious, but resolute, she applied to the stanch friend of her family, Admiral Charles Stewart, then commanding at the Philadelphia Navy Yard, for advice how to proceed. She went to Washington, where the Secretary of the Navy, Mr. Isaac Toucey, at once consented to give the invention a trial.

A few signals, imperfectly made, were placed on board a vessel of war and subjected to a trial at sea. A letter soon came from Admiral Paulding, telling her, in kind but uncompromising language, that they had proved good for nothing; but he added that the *idea* was an excellent one, and that she ought to be encouraged by the department to develop it.

Mrs. Coston now entered upon a series of labors and journeyings which kept her in the fullest activity for more than thirty years. It required months of work and worry to get colors made of the indispensable brilliancy. She happened to be in New York at the time when the successful laying of the cable across the Atlantic was celebrated by a display of fireworks at the City Hall, and the idea flashed upon her mind that the men who made those splendid colors could produce some which would answer her purpose also. She wanted but three colors, a pure white, a brilliant red, a vivid and unmistakable green.

"In ten days," she records, "I received a package containing the desired colors, and I persuaded a friend to drive to a mountain five miles distant, and burn them to show me the color. The trial was a success; the green fire brilliant and intense."

She soon had a supply of signals which she was confident would realize her husband's idea; and so it proved. She was present herself, in deep mourning, when a board of naval officers gave them their second and decisive trial. Their success was such as to extort exclamations of delight from all who witnessed it, and the officers gave to the department a most favorable report. The Secretary of the Navy received her with great cordiality, saying:—

"Now, what is the next step, and what can I do for you? But, first, what are those signals worth?"

"I cannot tell you," she stammered out.

"There you show the woman," Mr. Toucey replied; "but after this long period of labor you should begin to reap some reward. Consult with your friends, fix on a price, not forgetting you deserve a fair one, and call here to-morrow."

Next day, as Congress alone could authorize the purchase of the patent, the secretary gave her an order for signals enough to supply every ship in the navy, at a price which would amount to six thousand dollars for the whole. She entered into partnership with a manufacturer, and the work began.

This, however, was only the late beginning of a very slow and imperfect success. All persons who have to do with governments find themselves obliged to take the advice of the poet Longfellow,

"Learn to labor and to *wait*." Mrs. Coston had to wait a long time to get much beyond the barest subsistence by the manufacture of her husband's signals. The premium upon gold during the war made the price inadequate, and it was only after a long delay that Congress voted a small appropriation for the purchase of the right to make them for the navy. The sum was twenty thousand dollars, which scarcely covered the expense attending the development of the idea.

The signals came to the navy just in time; for nearly all the blockade runners that were caught during the war were caught by the use of the Coston signals. Admiral Farragut and Admiral Porter, and indeed all the admirals who held important commands, testified to their great and constant utility.

In the course of time, this resolute lady made her way to almost every court and cabinet in Europe, in order to bring to their notice the excellence of the signals. She procured their adoption in the French, the Italian, the Danish, and the Swedish navies, with a fair prospect of their being finally adopted by every ship that sails the sea, and every life-saving station on its tempestuous shores. Some of her journeys tested her powers of endurance to the uttermost. and she displayed in many strange scenes a high degree of ability and tact.

The most striking benefit of these night signals is seen at the life-saving stations, which are enabled by their use to hold a continuous conversation with the officers of a stranded ship, and to convey, as well as to receive, that precise information upon which success in relieving them often depends. Certainly, Mrs. Coston is justified in claiming for her husband's brilliant invention a " signal success."

JOHN DELAFIELD,

MERCHANT.

OF the writings of Washington Irving, probably the favorite piece with the majority of readers in his own day was "The Wife," the fourth article in the "Sketch-Book," the one that comes just before the immortal and universal "Rip Van Winkle."

It is the story of a young and rich merchant, who, a few months after his marriage to a lovely girl, was suddenly reduced to poverty. The terrible news had not yet gone abroad, and the husband lived in mortal dread of the hour when his wife, born and bred in luxury, would be obliged to face the toils and mortifications of the common lot. He revealed his sad perplexity to Irving, who advised him to take his wife into his confidence, and make her acquainted with the whole extent of their misfortune. She bore it "like an angel." They removed to a cottage in the country, covered with vines and honeysuckles, to which they transferred only one object that spoke of their former grandeur, — her harp.

The story is told in the best manner of the author, and exhales an air of the olden time, when both wealth and poverty meant more than they now do.

It was not, indeed, a very uncomfortable poverty to which this adorable wife was reduced, and the author was kind enough, at the close of the tale, to inform his readers that the pair subsequently regained their fortune, and lived happy ever after. But the husband assured his friend that he never experienced a moment of more exquisite felicity than when he was welcomed to his modest cottage in the country by his wife with a cheerfulness and cordiality never quite equaled in the days of their splendor.

Two generations of readers have enjoyed this story without knowing that it was almost a literal transcript of the experience of John Delafield, one of Irving's oldest friends, and, I believe, a friend of his father also. The New York Delafields are among the most interesting and honorable families that have ever lived upon Manhattan Island. Its founder here was John, the father of Irving's friend. He was celebrated, in his day, for an act of commercial integrity of an extraordinary character. After retiring from business, in 1798, one of the richest men in the city, he risked an immense sum in insuring vessels. During the troubles of 1799, when both French and English preyed upon American commerce, almost every underwriter in this city was obliged to suspend payment. John

Delafield paid all his losses on demand, although it required the whole of his available capital, besides obliging him to mortgage his real estate.

Irving's friend and the hero of his story was also named John, and he had a life almost as strange and full of vicissitudes as his father. After graduating at Columbia College in 1802, he at once entered a counting-room as confidential clerk. In a few years we find him a merchant in full activity, shipping cargoes of American produce to Spain during the tremendous conflict between Bonaparte and the allied powers.

Very early in his career, his adventures began. While acting as supercargo on one of his own ships, he was driven by bad weather into the harbor of Corunna, in Spain. From the deck of his ship, he witnessed the storming of the town by the French army; and soon after, the French having opened fire on the vessels lying at anchor, he was obliged to cut his cables and put to sea, carrying with him a noble Spanish family who had sought refuge on board his ship. Short of provisions and in a leaky vessel, he directed his course to England, which he reached with the greatest difficulty.

This was in 1808, which was a bad time for almost every class except soldiers and financiers. John Delafield, then twenty-two, remained in London, where he established a banking business, in which he greatly prospered, until he was caught once more in a crisis of war. When President Madison declared war against Great Britain in 1812, John Delafield, then conspicuous as an American banker, was claimed as a prisoner by the British government, and was held in restraint throughout the contest. Powerful friends used their influence in his favor, and he was permitted to remain at large and continue his banking business, upon giving his parole not to go beyond fifteen miles from home. He was still a very young man when the events occurred which are related by Washington Irving. He had made money with great ease and rapidity, lived handsomely in London, with an elegant country seat a few miles distant, and had every reason to suppose himself solidly established. But the sudden cessation of a war of long continuance is always followed, sooner or later, by disturbances in the world's business, which make and mar many fortunes. John Delafield lost his whole estate, and by doing so, enjoyed the thrilling experience so movingly related by his friend Irving. The pretty little cottage to which he removed after his failure was probably near Uxbridge, a short distance from his former country residence.

The Delafields have had a remarkable way of falling upon their feet. A few years after his London failure, we find John Delafield in New York, his native city, cashier of the Phœnix Bank, of which he afterwards became president. He was a generous and public-spirited citizen, founder and first president of the Philharmonic Society, founder of the Musical Fund Society, one of the founders of the New York University, and a most liberal benefactor of the Historical Society. He was also an enthusiastic gardener and horticulturist, as was shown by the extraordinary beauty of his country place near Hell Gate.

Later in life, he again lost his fortune, and entered upon a new career near Geneva, N. Y., where he bought land, and gradually converted it into a farm that was famous all over the State for its productiveness. He was one of the first farmers in that part of the State to apply science to the cultivation of the soil. He was careful to find out with precision, by chemical analysis, what elements a soil lacked, and with what fertilizing substance he could best supply the lack. He died in 1853, at the age of sixty-seven, after a life full of usefulness and honor.

There are many living descendants among us of the first John Delafield, who left seven sons and four daughters, affording another proof that one of the best and greatest services a man can render his country is to rear a numerous family of virtuous and intelligent children.

HENRY FAWCETT,

PUBLIC MAN.

We were all very much astonished some years ago to hear that Mr. Gladstone had appointed a blind man to the office of Postmaster-General. Still more surprising is it to find, now that Henry Fawcett is dead, that he is regarded in England as the ablest Postmaster-General Great Britain has ever had. He added many new and valuable features to the post-office system, making it a greater blessing than ever to the people, and particularly to the frugal and industrious poor. All parties in England united to do honor to his memory.

The story of his life is of singular and deep interest. He did not lose his eyesight until he was twenty-five years of age, when he had graduated from Cambridge University, and was making his way toward public life. His father, a wealthy farmer who lived near Salisbury, was a public-spirited politician, a member of the famous League which gave to England the inestimable blessing of free trade. He was a friend and ally of Cobden and Bright, an excellent popular orator, who still spoke effectively after he was eighty years of age. He was a man of admirable constitution of body, an advantage which he imparted to his son.

From his boyhood, Henry Fawcett excelled in all athletic exercises, was fond of field sports, a good cricketer, skater, and swimmer, blessed also with a remarkably keen eyesight. He was fortunate in his schools, having been for some time under the tuition of Professor Tyndale, who had a genius for inspiring the young with a love of knowledge and a generous ambition to use it. After spending four years at Cambridge, he graduated in 1856, the seventh in mathematical honors out of a class of four or five hundred.

Two years later, in the midst of his studies in law and political economy, occurred the terrible accident which deprived him of his sight. He was spending some time at home during the shooting season, and was out on the fatal morning with his father, shooting partridges. His father fired. A portion of the charge from his gun struck the young man in such a way that the exact centre of each eye was penetrated by a shot. In an instant he was stone blind. His face was turned at the moment towards the city of Salisbury, the cathedral of which sends a slender, graceful spire more than four hundred feet into the air; and this was the last object on which his eyes ever rested.

For some days he was prostrated, and it was difficult to decide whether the father or the son was the more to be pitied. He soon rallied, however, recovered his usual buoyant spirits, and determined that he would not allow the accident to frustrate the career he had marked out for himself. He returned to Cambridge, took into his service a competent reader, and continued his studies.

Some years after, he contracted a most fortunate marriage with Miss Millicent Garrett, a lady who was already fond of the very studies to which he was most strongly attached. She became not merely a helpmate to him, but an author and speaker on her own account. They wrote essays together and separately. In the volume into which these were afterwards gathered, the husband begins his preface with this remark: —

"In the following pages my wife and I have collected some of the essays and lectures written or spoken by us within the last three or four years."

Her subjects are Woman Suffrage, the Education of Women, Free Schools, and similar topics, while he writes upon Pauperism and its Remedies, Modern Socialism, and Agricultural Laborers. Nor do they always agree in opinion. She opposes and he favors free education.

All such work was comparatively easy for a blind man who had a wife's intelligent eyes to see for him, and money to employ readers and an amanuensis. His public life demanded rarer qualities. In one year from the time when he lost his eyes, he recited, before the British Association at Aberdeen, a discourse, full of facts and figures, upon the effects of the gold discoveries in California and Australia. If the discourse itself was a great surprise, the members were still more astonished at the readiness with which he answered objections in the discussion which followed.

From this time, he was a public man. We find him taking part in public meetings, delivering speeches upon such topics as Coöperation, Capital and Labor, Strikes, and similar subjects. He published also a "Manual of Political Economy for Beginners," and contributed frequently to reviews. In 1863, he was elected Professor of Political Economy in Cambridge University, in which capacity he delivered lectures which, I am sure, will have an effect upon the future policy of England. He showed himself the friend of everything liberal and humane, provided it was also practically wise. His writings are free from the taint of brilliancy. His style is the plainest and clearest, well suited to the subjects upon which he loved to discourse.

During our war, he supported the cause of the Union most warmly, and ever since the war both himself and Mrs. Fawcett have shown a particular interest in the welfare and happiness of the United States. Mrs. Fawcett perhaps understands the politics of the city of New York better than some of our aldermen do.

Three times Henry Fawcett ran for Parliament before his election for Brighton in 1865. He proved himself an efficient member on the extreme liberal side, going as far in radicalism on every question as was reasonable and safe. The most distant portions of the empire did not escape his serious attention. His labors for the native people of India made him exceedingly popular in that country. He received a few years ago an elaborate silver tea service from Calcutta, inscribed : —

"Presented to the Right Hon. Henry Fawcett, M. P., by his native friends and admirers in Bombay, India, June, 1880."

On home measures he was perfectly independent. When it was voted, for example, to grant to the Princess Louise a marriage portion from the public treasury of a hundred and fifty thousand dollars, there were three hundred and fifty *ayes* to one *no*, and the *no* was that of Henry Fawcett.

In 1880, when Mr. Gladstone was forming his ministry, he gave the postmaster-generalship to Mr. Fawcett, who began at once to introduce improvements, which, no doubt, he had long contemplated. He lowered the charge for money orders, improved the postal notes, made it easier for poor men to deposit small sums in the postal savings banks, established a new parcel post, and reformed the telegraphic service. His most important addition to the system was a scheme of post-office annuities and life insurance, by which it has been rendered easy for a poor man, by small payments, to provide an annuity for his old age, or to insure his life for the benefit of his family.

In introducing this system, Mr. Fawcett was careful to state that the idea had been suggested to him by post-office officials whom he named. At the time of his death, he was meditating further improvements, some of which were of great promise.

Not less remarkable, considering his blindness, was the manner in which he joined in out-of-door sports. He walked, skated, rode, swam, hunted, fished, and all of these with boldness, grace, and skill. One of his friends reports that he would skate for hours over the frozen marshes about Cambridge, fearless of the thin ice and air-holes which abound in such places. Mounted upon a fleet horse, he would follow the hounds over hedge and ditch, guided only by the occasional word of a companion, and ride, too, with an audacity rarely surpassed. As a fisherman, his skill and success were extraordinary. He showed, also, a strange coolness in facing election mobs, the noise of which must have been more alarming to a man who could not see. While he was speaking, his audience perceived that he was blind, both from his impervious spectacles, and from a certain pose of the head which showed that he was not looking at his hearers, nor at anything else.

With all his strength of constitution, he died at the early age of fifty-one years, from a sharp attack of pneumonia. He rode fourteen miles, caught a violent cold, and died in a few days. The English people, according to their custom, raised a fund to rear a monument to his memory, — not a tasteless and stupid heap of stones, but some kind of institution to promote the higher education of the blind.

His wife lives to mourn his departure, and to continue his work His daughter lives also, the winner in 1890 of the highest rank in mathematics at the University of Cambridge.

JOSEPH HUGO,

MASTER CARPENTER.

Philip, King of Macedon, is said to have kept a herald about his court whose duty it was at regular intervals to say to the king, " Philip, thou art a man."

Kings may need to pay for such a monitor, but private individuals are spared the expense. A man may be at the pinnacle of popularity, and many nations beside his own may render homage to his name, but there is always some one who makes it a point to remind him that he is a fallible mortal like the rest of us.

There used to be, as I remember, an individual who wandered about among the newspaper offices of New York and London, whose great object in life seemed to be to write and say ill-natured things of Charles Dickens. Some readers may recall this singular person. He had probably received a slight from the great novelist, or fancied that he had, and it rankled in the shallows of his mind.

For some years, no Frenchman enjoyed or endured so intense a popularity as Victor Hugo. He was for sixty years a famous poet, but during the last ten years, after his return from an exile of nineteen years in the Channel Islands, he stood before France as the brilliant representative and powerful exponent of her liberal ideas and republican aspirations.

It is not in the power of one of our unimaginative and too critical race to realize how this man was adored by the people of Paris.

A banquet was given to him, to celebrate the fiftieth anniversary of the production of one of his plays, — "Hernani." It was a splendid occasion, at which almost every person in France who is high in the public regard was present, — authors, artists, legislators, actors. At the head of the table sat the aged poet, robust in person, his cheeks ruddy with health, his hair standing up from his great forehead as white as the snow. In spite of his eighty years, his physical force seemed quite unabated. He had a strong, guttural voice, and he looked the very picture of a plain, solid, honest, thoughtful man.

After the banquet, at a signal, the joyous roar of conversation ceased, and there was deep silence in the room. M. Emile Augier, the dramatist, rose with his glass in his hand. He made no speech, as we should have done on a similar occasion. What could have been expressed in oratory which every one did not already know and strongly feel? He simply said, in a clear, deep voice, holding his glass aloft : —

"The Father!"

The poet attempted no reply. None was necessary; none was expected. The object of the banquet was completely accomplished without speaking, and no eloquence could have enhanced the lustre of the festival. On that evening, Victor Hugo, the head of French literature, received the homage of the French intellect.

A still more remarkable tribute was paid to him by the people of Paris — nay, by the people of France — on his eightieth birthday, when, as it is computed, six hundred thousand persons passed by his house during the day and evening, saluting him and his grandchildren as they moved by. Some one said at the time: —

"To-day, while still alive, Victor Hugo enters upon his immortality."

Well, this man, old, illustrious, the idol of his countrymen, found some one to give him *gratis* the information which Philip, King of Macedon, received from his paid herald. The name of this individual is Edmond Biré, a member of the monarchist party, and he accomplished his mission by writing a book at the old man, of five hundred and thirty-three pages, entitled "Victor Hugo Before 1830."

This author has made a collection of the most agreeable and flattering things that have ever been written of Victor Hugo by his admirers, relations, and friends, and subjected them to a close and critical examination, testing them by documents and official records. The book was an attempt on the part of a devoted Royalist to neutralize the influence of the most eloquent Republican of his time. In the execution of his task, he brought to light some interesting and curious facts, of which I will give one specimen.

Among the nobility of Lorraine there flourished for centuries a family of the name of Hugo, which produced from time to time eminent soldiers and ecclesiastics. Victor Hugo and his wife appear to have been under the impression that he was descended from these Hugos, and such has been the opinion of Europe generally. General Hugo, the father of the poet, left his native Nancy while he was still a boy, obtained soon after a commission in the revolutionary army, lost his brothers in the war, and remained during the rest of his life quite severed from his early connections. Perhaps he shared in the most universal foible of human nature, and did not mention, when he was a general, a count, and an officer of the king's household, that his ancestors were very far from being either generals or counts. Thus, it may well have been that Victor Hugo remained in ignorance to a late period of the remote origin of his family.

M. Biré pounces upon this claim of the poet's admirers and proves that it has no foundation in truth. He went to Nancy, the birthplace of the poet's father, and found in the registers of a parish church the original record of General Hugo's birth: —

"November 15, 1773, Joseph-Léopold-Sigisbert, son of Joseph Hugo, master carpenter, and of Jeanne-Marguerite-Michaud."

This was an interesting discovery. Further researches were not without their reward. He found the record of the two marriages of this Joseph Hugo, grandfather of Victor Hugo, from which he learned that July 1, 1755, Joseph Hugo, master carpenter, had married the daughter of Dominique Béchet, master shoemaker, and that January 22, 1770, the same Joseph Hugo, widower, had married Marguerite Michaud, governess to the Count of Rosières.

It was of this last marriage that our illustrious poet was born, and the fact has interest as suggesting the possible origin of his talent. The governess of a nobleman's children in that age would almost inevitably have been an educated woman, and it may be that from this governess he derived his aptitude for literature.

Looking further into parish records, M. Biré discovers that Jean Philippe Hugo, father of Joseph, was a farmer in the neighborhood, and that *his* father was a farm-laborer.

Thus we find that the poet, Victor Hugo, son of General Hugo, is descended from an honorable line of mechanics and farmers, who compose nineteen twentieths of the honest portion of the human race.

I need not say how M. Biré exults in this discovery, nor why he does so. He accuses the poet of having claimed lineal connection with the Counts Hugo of former centuries. Madame Hugo does indeed make this claim, and several other biographers of the poet also make it. There are passages in the poems of Victor Hugo from which we may infer that he, too, once supposed himself descended from the noble Hugos of Lorraine.

This seems to us a wonderfully trifling matter to make a to-do about. Nevertheless, some good results from it. We now know that this poet, like the other greatest poets, including Shakespeare and Goethe, sprang directly from the people, — the common people who build houses, work farms, make shoes, fell trees, and carry on the daily business of the world. I offer M. Biré my thanks for this agreeable information.

In truth, Victor Hugo looked much more like a master carpenter than a romantic poet. One of his friends, looking at him one day, and being struck with the solidity and strength of his frame, said: —

"The device on his coat-of-arms might be ROBUR."

Now, reader, if you will look into the Latin dictionary, you will find that the word *Robur* means something more than oak. It means the very hardest kind of oak, and was, therefore, sometimes applied to anything that was eminently tough and enduring. The poet bore his years well, and he confidently expected to outlast the vigorous frame his grandfather transmitted to him. He said in a moment of poetical inspiration: —

"Yes, I feel that I shall only be complete up yonder. Now I stammer what by and by I shall speak. I shall continue my being in sublimating it. I am the tadpole of an archangel!"

Of Joseph Hugo, grandfather of the poet, we know a few things, but they mean much. After the revolution, there was a custom in France of celebrating in a public manner the virtues of men who had lived honorably in private and non-military stations, such as those of farmer and mechanic. We learn from the "History of Nancy" (the birthplace of Joseph Hugo) that, at a festival held there in April, 1797, three years before the birth of the poet, the master carpenter was signally honored by his fellow-citizens. The historian of Nancy, Jean Cayon, says: —

"Among the citizens crowned at the Festival of the Patriarchs, we remark, at that of April 29, 1797, Joseph Hugo, joiner, a very excellent republican, and father of nine children, of whom several were at the frontier [defending their country against the allied invaders]. He is the ancestor of our celebrated Victor Hugo, peer of France."

BARON VON STEIN,

PRIME MINISTER.

Prussia stands to-day the strongest military empire the modern world has seen. This rank among the nations of the earth it directly owes to three rulers: Frederick the Great, Baron von Stein, and Prince Bismarck. Of Frederick and Bismarck the world has heard much; but of Baron von Stein, whom posterity, perhaps, will pronounce the greatest of the three, little is known out of Germany.

He was born in 1757, when Frederick, in the flower of his days, was fighting the first campaign of the Seven Years' War. His family was of great wealth and antiquity, who preserved the simplicity of ancient manners, and had given many valuable servants to the state. Those old noble families of Germany, unlike some of our effeminate people of the present time, rejoiced in an abundance of children. Baron von Stein was the ninth child of his father. After the education usual to young men of his rank, he entered the service of King Frederick, and was appointed to the

Department of Mines, in which he rose rapidly to high rank. He was otherwise employed by the aged Frederick, particularly in efforts to unite the Protestant States of Germany in a league to hold in check the menacing power of Austria.

The old king died in 1786, leaving Prussia three times as strong as he had found her. Baron von Stein seized the opportunity to visit England in company with two of his young friends. For various reasons, England was then much in vogue among the educated classes of the Continent, and consequently these three young noblemen were predisposed to relish and admire the institutions and laws of the country in which they found themselves. At the Prussian court, the writings of no man were so much read as those of Voltaire, and I do not doubt that these three gentlemen had read his Letters upon England, published many years before, in which English freedom and English tolerance of diverse religions were so amusingly exhibited.

In a word, Baron von Stein was delighted with England. He discovered the mighty power which freedom gives to a nation, when that nation is also submissive to just and equal laws. Compared with Prussia, England *was* such a country, and this gifted nobleman noted well the fact, and desired then to transplant some of the institutions of England to his native land. His holiday ended, he returned to Prussia, where he married a lady of his own rank, who brought him a great increase of fortune.

Resuming his public labors, he was advanced from post to post, until, in the year 1804, the king appointed him one of his ministers, placing him at the head of a department somewhat similar to that which we call the Department of the Interior. Napoleon was then advancing rapidly towards his brief and desolating mastery of Europe. Having nothing to do with foreign politics, Baron von Stein bore no part in the series of events which, in 1806, brought Napoleon and all his hosts down upon the little kingdom of Prussia. Stein was only in a position to discern and foretell the coming tempest. Convinced of the fatal tendency of the policy of breaking with Napoleon, but unable to change that policy, he resigned his office and withdrew to his estates. The storm broke upon the kingdom, and in a month Napoleon was master of Prussia. The conqueror levied a contribution equal in our present currency to one hundred and twenty millions of dollars. He divided the kingdom into two nearly equal parts, took one away, and left the other to the Prussian king, with the remark that he would not even have given him so much but for the intercession of his friend, the Emperor of Russia.

Then it was that the King of Prussia, instructed by calamity, turned for advice and assistance to Stein. The baron accepted the post of chief minister, and thus had the opportunity to apply to his prostrate country the reviving magic of freedom and equality.

"What the state has lost in magnitude it must make up in force," said he.

He proposed to the king to reorganize the entire administrative system, and the king assented to his scheme. Many superfluous offices were suppressed, with, of course, due compensation to the holders thereof. Other offices were consolidated, and the service simplified. Every remaining vestige of feudal vassalage was abolished. Land was set free from entail, so that it could be bought and sold like other property. All unjust privileges and exemptions from taxation were done away with, and citizens were made equal before the law. Commissions in the army were given without respect to rank or caste, so that every soldier had a chance to be a field-marshal. He established local town governments, similar to those he had studied in England. He announced the principle that every ablebodied citizen lived under a natural obligation to take part in defending his country against an invader, and should be qualified to do this by taking a turn of service in the army. This last idea, which has now become a part of the Prussian system, is perhaps destined to go round the world. With proper limits and restrictions, it is the true mode of endowing nations with the power of self-defense.

Baron von Stein had come to the ministry with the approval of Napoleon, who approved him because he did not know him. Napoleon Bonaparte was the natural foe of every man in Europe who had a mind of his own. While the baron was in the midst of his reforms, a letter of his was intercepted in which the *régime* of despotism was frankly criticised, much to the disadvantage of the despot. This letter having been published in the newspapers, Napoleon responded by demanding the dismission of the patriotic minister who wrote it. He made this demand with that peculiar, contemptuous insolence which marked all his dealings with prostrate Prussia. In one of Bonaparte's letters to Soult, of 1808, there is an allusion to the Stein affair, which illustrates what I mean.

"You will see in the newspapers," wrote Napoleon, "in what manner they speak of M. Stein's letter. I have demanded that he should be turned out of the ministry; and if that is not done, the King of Prussia shall not have his kingdom again. Besides, I have caused his estates in Westphalia to be sequestered."

The word which I have translated "turned out," is *chassé*, which is employed by the French to express the dishonorable dismission of a household servant. It shows to what a point of degradation Prussia was reduced, that the king was obliged to obey the insolent command of his conqueror. Before leaving the ministry, however, the baron drew up a complete explanation of all his plans for the regeneration of his country, which included a national representation, similar to that which Prussia now enjoys. This paper also reached the vulgar despot of France, who thereupon ordered Stein to leave his country, and confiscated all his effects. The baron took refuge in Austria, where he became the centre and organizer of the whole anti-Napoleon German movement. He took a leading part in forming the secret society, or system of societies, which gradually pervaded all the German States, the object of which was to seize the first opportunity of rising against the common enemy.

When, at last, the Emperor of Russia recovered from his infatuation, and joined the coalition against Bonaparte, Stein went to St. Petersburg, and lent the aid of his administrative ability to direct the resources of that empire against the invader. In 1814, he entered Paris with the allies, and there he opposed those favorable conditions of the treaty of peace which obliged the allies, only one year after, to fight Napoleon at Waterloo. Bismarck, no doubt, had that in his mind when he demanded, fifty years after, the cession of the two provinces which rendered it so easy for a French army to cross the frontier.

Baron von Stein was fifty-eight years of age at the time of the general peace of 1815. But it did not devolve upon him to carry out the system which he had begun. He was fifty years in advance of his country. It was part of his system that there should be but two German powers, — an Austrian and a Prussian confederation, — both governed constitutionally, with a reasonable and safe ingredient of popular representation. The intrigues of interested princes and ministers caused him to be honorably shelved. He was decorated with the order of the Black Eagle, became member of the Privy Council, and had everything the government could bestow except the only thing he wanted, — power to serve his country. He died in 1831, aged seventy-four, leaving to his successor, Bismarck, the task of forming a Prussian confederation, and throwing up a rampart of conquered provinces against the incursions of any future adventurer who may chance to get possession of France.

www.ingramcontent.com/pod-product-compliance
Lightning Source LLC
Chambersburg PA
CBHW030427300426
44112CB00009B/883